Windows XP
explained

Books Available

By the same authors:

BP522   Microsoft Works Suite 2002 explained
BP514   Windows XP explained
BP513   Internet Explorer 6 and Outlook Express 6 explained*
BP512   Microsoft Access 2002 explained
BP511   Microsoft Excel 2002 explained
BP510   Microsoft Word 2002 explained
BP509   Microsoft Office XP explained
BP505   Microsoft Works Suite 2001 explained
BP498   Using Visual Basic
BP493   Windows Me explained*
BP491   Windows 2000 explained*
BP487   Quicken 2000 UK explained*
BP488   Internet Explorer 5 explained*
BP486   Using Linux the easy way*
BP478   Microsoft Works 2000 explained
BP474   Microsoft Access 2000 explained
BP473   Microsoft Excel 2000 explained
BP472   Microsoft Word 2000 explained
BP471   Microsoft Office 2000 explained
BP465   Lotus SmartSuite Millennium explained
BP456   Windows 98 explained*
BP448   Lotus SmartSuite 97 explained
BP433   Your own Web site on the Internet
BP430   MS-Access 97 one step at a time
BP429   MS-Excel 97 explained
BP428   MS-Word 97 explained
BP426   MS-Office 97 explained
BP420   E-mail on the Internet*
BP409   MS Office 95 one step at a time
BP408   Access 95 one step at a time
BP407   Excel 95 explained
BP406   MS Word 95 explained
BP388   Why not personalise your PC
BP341   MS-DOS explained
BP284   Programming in QuickBASIC
BP259   A Concise Introduction to UNIX*
BP258   Learning to Program in C

If you would like to purchase a Companion Disc for any of the listed books by the same authors, apart from the ones marked with an asterisk, containing the file/program listings which appear in them, then fill in the form at the back of the book and send it to Phil Oliver at the stipulated address.

Windows XP explained

by

N. Kantaris
and
P.R.M. Oliver

Bernard Babani (publishing) Ltd
The Grampians
Shepherds Bush Road
London W6 7NF
England

www.babanibooks.com

Please Note

Although every care has been taken with the production of this book to ensure that any projects, designs, modifications and/or programs, etc., contained herewith, operate in a correct and safe manner and also that any components specified are normally available in Great Britain, the Publishers and Author(s) do not accept responsibility in any way for the failure (including fault in design) of any project, design, modification or program to work correctly or to cause damage to any equipment that it may be connected to or used in conjunction with, or in respect of any other damage or injury that may be so caused, nor do the Publishers accept responsibility in any way for the failure to obtain specified components.

Notice is also given that if equipment that is still under warranty is modified in any way or used or connected with home-built equipment then that warranty may be void.

First Published - December 2001
Reprinted - March 2002
Reprinted - May 2002
Reprinted - August 2002
Reprinted - October 2002
Reprinted - December 2002
Reprinted - April 2003

British Library Cataloguing in Publication Data:

A catalogue record for this book is available from the British Library

ISBN 0 85934 514 9

Cover Design by Gregor Arthur
Printed and Bound in Great Britain by Cox & Wyman Ltd, Reading

The Windows Background

Microsoft produced the first version of Windows in 1983 as a graphical extension to its Disc Operating System (MS-DOS). However, it was not a great success because, being DOS based, it was confined to the DOS memory limit of 1 MB of RAM. Mind you, at that time, not many PCs had that much memory!

In 1987, an Intel 386 processor specific version of Windows was brought out that was able to run in multiple 'virtual 8086' mode, but Windows applications were still unable to use any extended memory above the 1 MB. In 1990, however, Windows version 3.0 solved this problem and became a huge success.

Two years later, the much needed update, Windows 3.1, was released to fix most of the program bugs in version 3.0. The horrendous and frequent 'Unrecoverable Application Error' message became a thing of the past (well, almost!). Windows for Workgroups 3.1, followed in October 1992, and started to give the program the power to control small networked groups of computers. This was strengthened in October 1993 with the 3.11 release, which included 32-bit file management and more networking support.

Then, three year later, came Windows 95, a 32-bit operating system in its own right which made full use of the 32-bit features of the then available range of Intel processor chips. Microsoft had also put a lot of effort into this system to make it compatible with almost all existing Windows and MS-DOS based applications. This was obviously necessary, but it meant that parts of Windows 95 were still only 16-bit in operation.

June 1998, saw the launch of Windows 98, the long awaited refined upgrade to Windows 95, which ran faster, crashed less frequently, supported a host of new technologies, such as Digital Video Disc for storing digital video on PCs, improved MMX multimedia, and was year 2000 compliant. In May 1999 Windows 98 Second Edition was released.

In September 2000, Microsoft released Windows Me, as the direct upgrade to Windows 95/98 for the home PC. Windows Me had many improvements incorporated into it, such as added features that made it load faster, run more reliably, and if things went radically wrong through interference by the user, the ability to return to a previous working version of the Operating System. In addition, Windows Me incorporated Wizards that let you set up home networks and gave you the ability to share Internet connections, had improved support for digital cameras, video recorders, and multimedia with the introduction of the Windows Media Player 7. Also, improved features and tools in Internet Explorer 5.5 allowed better Web communication from e-mail to instant messaging to video conferencing.

Running parallel with the desktop Windows development, Microsoft set up the Windows NT development team in 1989. Its mission was to design and build a PC operating system, primarily for the business server community. From the beginning, the priority design objectives of Windows NT were robustness and extensibility, and in October 1991, the first version of Windows NT was shown to the public at a demonstration at COMDEX - the world's largest computer exhibition.

In August 1993 we saw the release of Windows NT 3.1 with 6 million lines of code, followed a year later by Windows NT 3.5 with 9 million lines of code. In June 1995 Windows NT 3.51 was released capable of supporting upcoming Windows 95 programs. Then, in August 1996 Microsoft released Windows NT 4.0 with 16 million lines of code. Since then, much has changed with Windows NT 4.0, as customer requirements evolved to include support for Windows applications, Web services, communications, and much more. These improvements came in the guise of several Service Packs.

In February 2000, Microsoft released Windows 2000 Professional, together with two additional Windows NT compatible versions of the software; Server and Advanced Server. Users of Windows 95/98 could easily upgrade (and many have) to the Windows 2000 Professional version of this Operating System (OS), while users of Windows NT could use one of the other two versions of the OS to upgrade their system according to their requirements.

Finally, in October 2001, Microsoft released Windows XP (XP for eXPerience) in two flavours; the Home edition (less expensive) as the direct upgrade to Windows 98/Me for home users and the Professional edition (more expensive but with additional functionality) for Windows 2000 or business users. Of course, provided you are running Windows 98/Me or Windows 2000, you can upgrade to either version of Windows XP.

At first glance, Windows XP looks slightly different to previous versions of Windows. The changes to the desktop icons, Start menu and the Control Panel are there for all to see, while other concepts are borrowed from Windows Me or Windows 2000. Windows XP has many improvements incorporated into it which fall into several general categories. These are:

- Added features that make Windows XP load faster than any previous version of Windows, run more reliably, and the ability to return to a previous working version of the Operating System (similar to that under Windows Me).

- Improved Wizards (similar to those under Windows Me) let you set up home networks a lot easier and give you the ability to share Internet connections.

- Improved support for digital cameras, video recorders, and multimedia with an improved version of the Windows Media Player (now version 8).

- Improved features and tools in Internet Explorer 6 allow faster performance, and better Web communication from e-mail (using version 6 of Outlook Express) to instant messaging to video conferencing using the MSN Explorer.

- Improved Windows File Protection (similar to that under Windows 2000) which prevents the replacement of protected system files such as .sys, .dll, .ocx, .ttf, .fon, and .exe files, so that installing software does not corrupt the operating system by overwriting shared system files such as dynamic-link libraries (.dll files) and executable files (.exe files).

All these improvements will be introduced and discussed in due course at the appropriate section of the book.

Although we have used Windows XP Professional Edition to write this book, it is equally valid for the Windows XP Home Edition as the Professional Edition offers all the capabilities of the Home Edition plus additional features designed to meet the needs of the business community. These enhancements provide more options for networking computers with added security and simplified management.

Windows XP Professional also includes features for power users, such as enhanced file security, remote access to your computer's desktop and a personal Web server. However, most home PC users will find that Windows XP Home Edition contains all the facilities they will ever need or want. Which version you choose will ultimately be your choice with the price differential being a factor to be taken into account.

About this Book

Windows XP Explained was written to help both the beginner and those moving from older versions of Windows to the Windows XP Professional or Home edition (the latter being a cut-down version of the former). The material in the book is presented on the 'what you need to know first, appears first' basis, although you don't have to start at the beginning and go right through to the end. The more experienced user can start from any section, as they have been designed to be self-contained.

We start this book by discussing what preparations you need to make to your system, depending on your present desktop Windows version, prior to installing Windows XP. For example, you might like to keep your present Windows installation because you would like to first try Windows XP without committing yourself. We will show you how to achieve this with the dual boot system which lets you boot in either Windows XP or your current Windows version. In fact, one of our PCs is configured to start with either Windows XP, Windows Me, or Linux. Of course, to do this you will need a rather large hard disc, but these days this is hardly unusual.

Windows XP comes with a Graphical User Interface (GUI) front end similar to that of previous versions of Windows, and includes built-in accessories such as a text editor, a paint program and many other multimedia, networking, electronic communication, and power saving features, most of which are examined in this book. Getting to grips with Windows XP, as described, will also reduce the learning curve when it comes to using other Windows application packages. For example, once you have installed your printers and learned how to switch between them and print from them, you should never again have any difficulty printing from any Windows program. Also, learning to manipulate text and graphics in WordPad and Paint will lay very strong foundations on which to build expertise when you need to master a full-blown word processor with strong elements of desktop publishing.

The book was written with the busy person in mind. You don't need to read many hundreds of large format pages to find out most of what there is to know about the subject, when fewer pages can get you going quite adequately! It is hoped that with the help of this book, you will be able to get the most out of your computer, when using Windows XP, in terms of efficiency and productivity, and that you will be able to do it in the shortest, most effective and enjoyable way.

An attempt has been made not to use too much 'jargon', but with this subject, some is inevitable, so a fairly detailed glossary of terms is included, which should be used with the text of this book where necessary. Have fun!

About the Authors

Noel Kantaris graduated in Electrical Engineering at Bristol University and after spending three years in the Electronics Industry in London, took up a Tutorship in Physics at the University of Queensland. Research interests in Ionospheric Physics, led to the degrees of M.E. in Electronics and Ph.D. in Physics. On return to the UK, he took up a Post-Doctoral Research Fellowship in Radio Physics at the University of Leicester, and then in 1973 a lecturing position in Engineering at the Camborne School of Mines, Cornwall, (part of Exeter University), where between 1978 and 1997 he was also the CSM Computing Manager. At present he is IT Director of FFC Ltd.

Phil Oliver graduated in Mining Engineering at Camborne School of Mines in 1967 and since then has specialised in most aspects of surface mining technology, with a particular emphasis on computer related techniques. He has worked in Guyana, Canada, several Middle Eastern and Asian countries, South Africa and the United Kingdom, on such diverse projects as: the planning and management of bauxite, iron, gold and coal mines; rock excavation contracting in the UK; international mining equipment sales and international mine consulting. In 1988 he took up a lecturing position at Camborne School of Mines (part of Exeter University) in Surface Mining and Management. He retired from full-time lecturing in 1998, to spend more time writing, consulting and developing Web sites for clients.

Acknowledgements

We would like to thank friends and colleagues, for their helpful tips and suggestions which assisted us in the writing of this book.

Trademarks

HP and LaserJet are registered trademarks of Hewlett Packard Corporation.

IBM is a registered trademark of International Business Machines, Inc.

Intel is a registered trademark of Intel Corporation.

Microsoft, **MS-DOS**, **Windows**, **Windows NT**, and **Windows Me**, **Windows XP**, are either registered trademarks or trademarks of Microsoft Corporation.

PostScript is a registered trademark of Adobe Systems Incorporated.

All other brand and product names used in the book are recognised as trademarks, or registered trademarks, of their respective companies.

Contents

1

Package Overview

Windows XP (Professional or Home edition) is Microsoft's latest desktop Operating System (OS). It is an easier to run and more efficient operating system to install, far more stable, and for business users the Professional edition is less expensive to deploy for large number of networked computers. Microsoft has employed the scripting process, first encountered in Windows 2000, which automates the installation process and makes it a lot easier, particularly for large networks. Ordinary desktop users also benefit as this version of Windows is by far the easiest to install and the most stable to operate under.

Upgrading to Windows XP

Windows XP is a 32-bit Operating System which, just like its predecessors (Windows 95/98/Me/2000), uses a Graphical Interface. However, unlike Windows 95/98/Me, this Graphical Interface does not act as a graphical front end to the Disc Operating System (MS-DOS), but as in Windows 2000 it actually is a replacement of it.

In other words, both Windows 2000 and Windows XP break away from the old MS-DOS dependency of previous versions of desktop Windows - no more MS-DOS prompt, but there is a Command prompt which allows you to run DOS-based programs. So, if you are a Windows user, you could either upgrade to Windows XP, or install Windows XP on a separate partition of your hard disc without losing your previous Windows installation. To achieve the latter, select 'new installation' when installing the OS, as opposed to 'upgrade' which replaces the previous Windows installation on your system.

The upgrade path to Windows XP (Professional or Home editions) is as follows:

	Windows XP Home Edition	Windows XP Professional Edition
Windows 98/Me	✓	✓
Windows NT 4.0	✗	✓
Windows 2000 Prof.	✗	✓

For earlier versions of the above operating systems, you must make a new (clean) installation of Windows XP (Home or Professional edition).

If, however, you are currently using Windows 98/Me/2000, and want to retain your present installation, <u>and</u> you have a second empty partition on your hard disc, then you can make a new (clean) install of Windows XP in the empty partition and adopt the dual-boot procedure. So, some thinking ahead is necessary!

System Preparation

Before you start installing Windows XP you need to prepare your system depending on your requirements.

- If your system is to run under Windows XP only, or Windows XP is to be installed on a separate, bootable, hard disc, then you don't need any preparation; you can skip the rest of this section, but refer to the 'Selecting a File System' section.

- If your system has only one hard disc on which you have one of the above four operating systems installed and you intend to retain it, then you need to consider the following:

    1. If your hard disc is partitioned into, say, a C: and a D: drive, then move all the programs and data you want to retain from drive D: into drive C:, and use

the space on drive D: to install Windows XP provided there is enough space on it. Application programs under Windows 98/Me might have to be uninstalled from drive D:, and reinstalled in drive C:.

2. If your hard disc is not partitioned and you have enough free space at the end of it to install Windows XP, then use the commercial software package PartitionMagic to create a partition for Windows XP on your hard disc. Such a program partitions your hard drive without any loss of data. Alternatively, make a **complete backup** of your hard drive, use the *fdisk* utility to re-partition the drive, then restore your application programs and data as necessary.

3. If you have more than two partitions on your hard drive, none of which is big enough to load Windows XP, then make a **complete backup** of your hard drive, then use PartitionMagic to rearrange and/or delete such partitions to create a sufficiently large partition for Windows XP. Alternatively, use the *fdisk* utility to re-partition the drive into more suitable sizes, then restore your application programs and data as necessary.

Note: Do not upgrade to Windows XP on a compressed drive.

Finally, make sure that your computer can run Windows XP before you start its installation (see next section). If you install Windows XP on a computer without the dual-boot option, and your hardware is unsuitable, you will not be able to return to your previous version of Windows unless you completely reinstall your older version of Windows and all of your programs! Furthermore, if you intend to go for the dual-boot option, make sure you have made a 'boot disc' for the operating system you want to retain - this is extremely important and cannot be overemphasised.

Hardware Requirements

To install Windows XP Home edition according to Microsoft, you will need an IBM-compatible computer with the following recommended specifications:

- 300 MHz or higher Pentium-compatible CPU (233 MHz minimum).

- 128 MB of RAM (64 MB minimum); more memory generally improves the operating system's response.

- 1.5 GB of available hard disc space. (Additional hard disc space is required if you are installing over a network.)

- A SVGA (800x600) or higher resolution video adapter.

- Keyboard, mouse, and CD-ROM or DVD drive.

To search for specific hardware and software or BIOS compatibility, visit Microsoft's Web site at

www.microsoft.com

where you should find the answers to almost all your questions. However, most users with a PC which meets the above specifications can go ahead with the installation in the knowledge that they are unlikely to encounter any hardware problems. In any case, the distribution CD includes options which can scan your system for any hardware/software incomparability, as we shall see shortly.

Information Required Prior to Installation

Before you start installing Windows XP, make sure you have appropriate information to hand. What you need to know, depends on the type of proposed installation. For example:

A. If you are setting up a standalone computer and you plan to connect to the Internet, then you will need to provide the Setup program during installation with your Internet Provider's (IP) address which was assigned to you for your Internet and e-mail accounts.

B. If you are setting up a networked computer then you need to know what type of network you are connected to - peer-to-peer or client/server. For the first one of these you will need to supply 'your workgroup name', while for the second one you will need to provide 'your domain name', 'your domain user name', and 'your domain password'. Such information is best obtained from your Network Administrator.

Finally, make absolutely sure you are not running any memory resident programs such as 'virus protection utilities' during installation. If you do, disable them before you start. This is usually done by double-clicking the program's icon and selecting to 'unload' it. Do not use such programs unless they were specifically written for Windows XP.

Selecting a File System

During Setup, Windows XP gives you the choice of using the Windows NT file system (NTFS) or the File Allocation Table (FAT16 or FAT32) file system. If you intend to retain your Windows 98/Me/2000 installation, and you want to exchange document files between the two systems (in both directions), then choose the FAT16/32 file system, otherwise select NTFS which has the following advantages over FAT16/32.

• Better file security, including the Encrypting File System (EFS) which protects data on your hard drive by encrypting each file with a randomly generated key.

• Better disc compression and better support for very large hard discs without performance degradation.

Finally, from an NTFS partition you can browse, read and write to files on the FAT16/32 partitions, but Windows 98/Me cannot detect the NTFS partition, so it cannot interfere with its settings, and you can profit from the enhanced security of Windows XP. However, the conversion to NTFS is one-way; you will not be able to convert back to FAT16/32. You can decide to switch to NTFS either during Setup or after Windows XP is installed.

Installing Windows XP

To start the installation process, switch on your computer, start Windows, and insert the Windows XP distribution CD into the CD-ROM drive. After a few seconds the Setup program will run automatically from the CD.

If the Setup program does not run, click the **Start** button, shown here, which is adopted by both Windows 98/Me and Windows NT/2000 and select **Run** from the pop-up menu. Next, type E:\setup, where E is the letter that represents your CD-ROM drive, and click the **OK** button.

The Setup program then displays the screen shown in Fig. 1.1 below. At this stage it is a good idea to let Windows XP check your system automatically for any incompatibilities, by first selecting the third option, then choosing the first option on the next displayed screen.

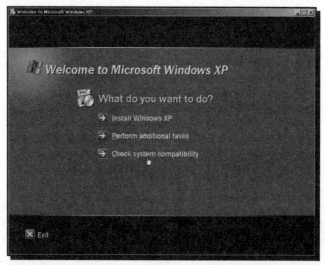

Fig. 1.1 The Microsoft Windows XP Welcome Screen.

A report will be compiled which you can print and act upon accordingly. You can also select the second option in Fig. 1.1 to look at other important information, such as the 'Release notes'. Finally, when you are ready, select the first option in Fig. 1.1 to start the installation process. The first of several Setup Wizard screens is then displayed as shown in Fig. 1.2

Fig. 1.2 The Welcome to Windows Setup Wizard Screen.

It is at this point you have to decide between 'upgrading' your current Windows system to Windows XP, or installing a new copy of it. We selected the latter option because we wanted to retain Windows Me and, at the same time, we had the required hard disc capacity and a separate partition. Hence the choice for a 'New Installation' in the **Installation Type** box on the screen in Fig. 1.2.

If you do not need to keep your current Windows version, and this happens to be Windows NT 4.0 or 2000, or Windows 98/Me, then select the 'Upgrade' option. This option will preserve the settings of all your program applications.

However, if your current operating system is an earlier version of the above four Windows systems, then you must select the 'New Installation' option which will require you to reinstall all your Windows applications from scratch.

Selecting one of the options and clicking the **Next** button displays the License Agreement screen in Fig. 1.3 below.

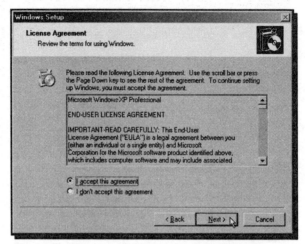

Fig. 1.3 The Windows XP License Agreement Screen.

Clicking the **I accept this agreement** radio button followed by **Next**, displays the next Installation Wizard screen (Fig. 1.4).

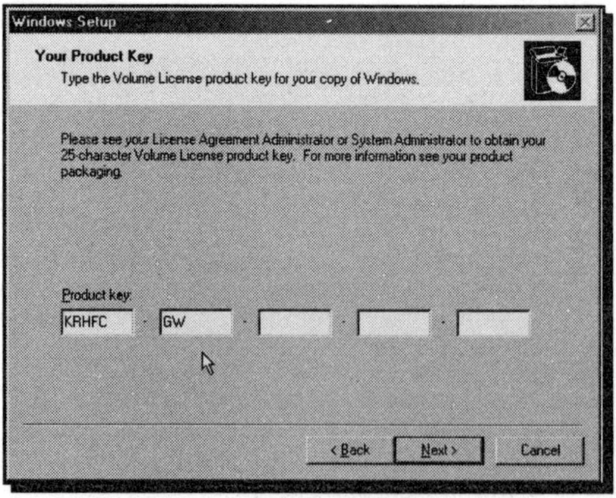

Fig. 1.4 Product Key Screen.

Type in your Product Key, then press **Next** to display the screen in Fig. 1.5 below.

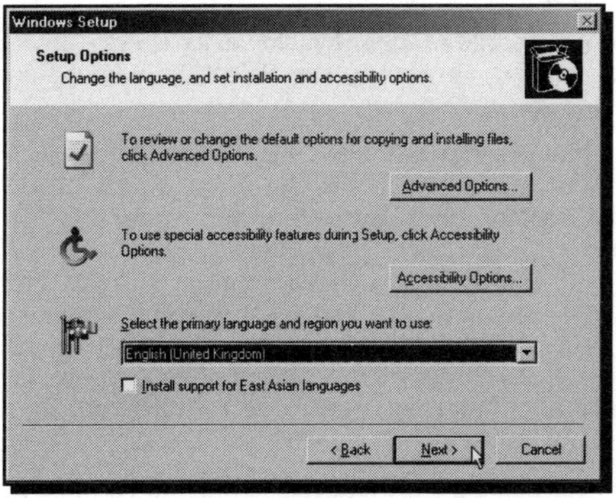

Fig. 1.5 The Regional Settings Screen.

The **Advanced Options** button allows you to specify whether you want to choose the installation partition during Setup by checking an appropriate box in a further dialogue box, as shown in Fig. 1.6 below.

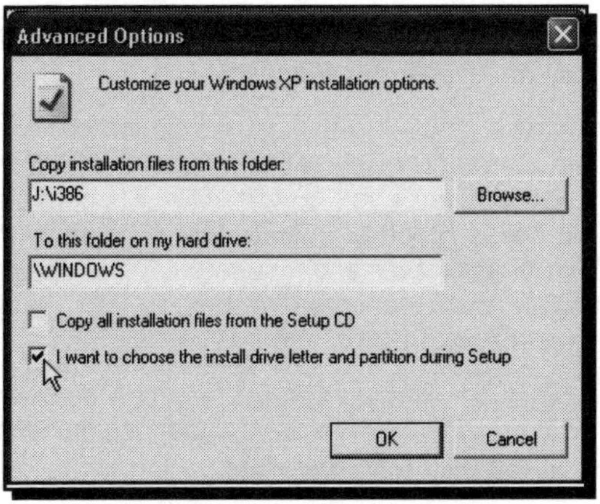

Fig. 1.6 The Advanced Options Screen.

If you don't check this option, as shown in Fig. 1.6, Setup will automatically choose the next empty partition on our primary hard drive to install Windows XP.

The **Accessibility Options** button is for users with impaired sight or hearing. Finally you can Select the primary language and region you want to use.

Having made your selection, return to the Regional Settings screen (Fig. 1.5) and press the **Next** button. The Setup program restarts your computer, and depending on your selection of installation requirements, the Setup program displays a blue screen with all your hard drives and their partitions, if any, detected and listed (if you have chosen this option in the Advanced Options screen - Fig. 1.6). You can now select on which hard drive, or partition of a hard drive, to install Windows XP. The drive must be a bootable drive - not an external hard drive.

Next, you are asked whether to format the selected partition using the NTFS file system, or the FAT32 file system, convert the partition to NTFS, or leave the current file system intact. The choice is yours - see the Selecting a File System section on page 5. Setup then carries out the following tasks:

- Examines the selected hard disc which takes about a minute or so, depending on its size.

- Copies files to the Windows XP installation folder which takes another three minutes.

- Initialises your installation configuration and reboots your computer, displays the Microsoft Windows XP logo screen and asks you to wait while it is configuring itself. This takes another minute or so, before the Setup Wizard takes over and first detects, then installs various devices, such as keyboard, mouse, etc., while display-ing useful information about Windows XP.

- Displays the Regional and Language screen again, so that you can customise previously selected settings to be different for different users.

- Displays the Personal Details screen, asking you to type in your name and organisation (if applicable), followed by the Computer Name and Administrator Password screen in which you can change the suggested computer name and type in an administrator's password (we left this blank).

- Displays the Modem Dialling Information screen, followed by the Date and Time Setting screen with the current date and time already selected. You might need to change the Time Zone, depending on your location - we selected GMT.

- Installs networking components which you might need later. This takes a few more minutes.

- Installs the Start menu items, registers components, saves settings, and removes any temporary files used. These actions take about 30 minutes to complete.

- Reboots your computer and displays a dual-boot screen (if you chose such an installation method), giving you the option to start with Windows XP or Windows. If you select the Windows XP option, Setup displays the Welcome to Microsoft Windows screen accompanied by soothing music! Pressing the **Next** button at the bottom right of the screen displays the Registration screen in which you type your name, address, etc., after which the computer rings Microsoft's number (if Setup has detected a modem) and registers your copy of Windows XP for that particular computer. If Setup does not detect a modem, you must register by telephone.

Windows XP Home Edition is the second Microsoft product to use the Product Activation system; the first one was Office XP. The product key plus a code produced from ten hardware components in your PC, such as processor type, memory size, disc drives, graphics and controller cards, and type of CD/DVD drives is then merged with the code supplied by Microsoft to produce a 'specific to your system' activation code. Any more than four changes to these components requires you to apply to Microsoft for a reactivating code! For new PCs supplied with Windows XP, product activation is tied only to the BIOS.

Next, the Setup program asks you in successive Wizard screens if you would like to:

- Connect to the Internet. Selecting **Yes** displays a further screen with three option: Get on line with MSN; use an existing account with your Internet Service Provider (ISP); or create a new Internet account. We selected to use our existing ISP.

- Receive help setting up your Internet account. If you answer **Yes** you will be connected to the Microsoft Referral Service immediately for an account with MSN! If you select **No**, have your user name, password, and ISP name and phone number ready. Setup then displays the 'Set up your Internet account' screen for you to fill in.

- Register more than one user who might be using the computer in the 'Who will use this Computer?' screen.

Finally Setup displays the Congratulations screen, restarts your computer and displays its starting pastoral screen!

Fig. 1.7 The Windows XP Starting Screen.

Whether you have chosen to connect your computer to the Internet during installation or later (we will show you how to do this in detail later when we discuss e-mail), once connected you can then use the Internet Explorer 6.0 program that comes bundled with the operating system to surf the Net, or the Outlook Express 6.0 program to send and receive e-mail. In addition, Windows XP features a range of tools that make it easier to receive personalised information from Web content providers using push technology via active channels.

Windows XP comes with a number of new features, retaining all 'accessory' programs from Windows 98/Me or Windows NT/2000, such as 'Communications' and 'Entertainment' utilities, 'System' tools, the 'Paint' graphics programs, the word processor 'WordPad' and the text editor 'Notepad'. All these accessories, as well as the 'Windows Explorer' which helps you to view local, network, intranet and Internet data simultaneously, will be discussed in some detail. Of course, Windows XP caters for many new technological developments, some of which will be discussed, while others such as its full-blown networking capability and the remote access administration associated with the Professional version of the package, are beyond the scope of this book.

Finally, one of the strengths of Windows XP lies in its ability to manage all other programs that run on your computer, whether these programs were specifically written for the Windows environment or the DOS environment. Windows allows easy communication between such programs, as well as other computers which might be connected to a network, but to what extent depends on the type of hardware at your disposal.

In general, this version of Windows is far more stable, polished and professional than its predecessors. For the most part, however, Windows XP has not changed that much, only in its outward appearance. Once these are mastered, it should help cut the learning curve for users upgrading from Windows 98/Me or Windows NT 4.0/2000.

Following the completion of the Windows Installation, you are prompted to start a Windows XP Tour by clicking an icon at the extreme bottom-right of the screen. If you don't do this there and then, you can activate it later from the **Start** menu.

Taking the Windows XP Tour

You can activate the Windows XP Tour at any time by
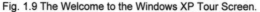 left-clicking the **Start** button, shown here, to be
found at the bottom-left of the Windows screen.
This opens the new look and feel **Start** menu
shown in Fig. 1.8 below.

Fig. 1.8 The Cascade Start Menu.

On this menu, click the **Tour Windows XP** option to start the tour. On the first Windows XP Tour screen, shown in Fig. 1.9 below, you have the option of either running the tour in animated format that features text, animation, music, and voice narration, or in non-animated format that features text and images only. Do spend some time going through this tour; you will learn a lot.

Fig. 1.9 The Welcome to the Windows XP Tour Screen.

2

Starting Windows XP

Once Windows XP has been installed, switching on your PC automatically loads the operating system (or displays the dual-boot option, if you have another Operating System on your hard disc).

The Windows Desktop

Below we show the Windows XP working screen, called the 'Desktop', with one item on the bottom right of it identified as 'Recycle Bin'. In addition, the 'My Documents' item has been clicked with the left mouse button to open its window.

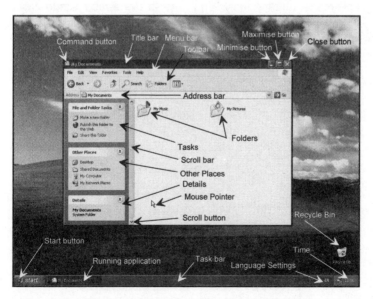

Fig. 2.1 Windows XP Desktop with Running Application.

Parts of a Window

It is worth spending some time looking at the various parts that make up the Windows screen - we use the word 'Windows' to refer to the whole environment, while the word 'windows' refers to application or document windows. Application windows contain running applications, while document windows appear with applications that can open more than one document, but share the application window's menu. Each application, and some documents you choose to work with, open and use separate windows to run in. Although every window has some common elements, not all windows use all of these elements.

An application window is easily opened by either double-clicking its icon on the Desktop, or clicking its name on one of the cascaded menus resulting from clicking the **Start** button followed by the **All Programs** button. When a program is running, an icon is placed on the Taskbar, which allows you to switch between running programs by simply left-clicking them on the Taskbar.

Although multiple application or document windows can be displayed simultaneously, only one is the active window and displays on the top of any other non-active windows. Title bars of non-active windows appear with a lighter shade than that of the active one, as shown below.

Fig. 2.2 Simultaneous Display of Running Applications.

The typical window is subdivided into several areas which have the following functions:

Area	*Function*
Command button	Clicking on the program icon (see upper-left corner of the My Documents window in Fig. 2.1), displays the pull-down Control menu which can be used to control the program window. It includes commands for restoring, moving, sizing, minimising, maximising, and closing the window.
Title bar	The bar at the top of a window which displays the application name and the name of the current document.
Minimise button	The button you point to and click to store an application as an icon on the Taskbar. Clicking on such an icon will restore the window.
Maximise button	The button you point to and click to fill the screen with the active window. When that happens, the Maximise button changes to a Restore button which can be used to restore the window to its former size.
Close button	The extreme top right button that you click to close a window.
Menu bar	The bar below the Title bar which allows you to choose from several menu options.

Clicking on a menu item displays the pull-down menu associated with that item. The options listed in the Menu bar depend on the specific application.

Toolbar

A bar of icons that you click to carry out some common actions.

Address bar

Shows the location of the current folder, or the URL of the new page to go to next.

Scroll bars

The bars on the extreme right and bottom of each window (or pane within a window) that contain a scroll box. Clicking on these bars allows you to see parts of a document that might not be visible in that size window.

Scroll buttons

The arrowheads at each end of the scroll bars which you click to scroll the window contents up and down one line, or left and right one item at a time.

Mouse pointer

The arrow which appears when the pointer is placed over menus, scroll bars, buttons, and folder lists.

Tasks

These change according to the function of the activated application. For example, if you activate My Computer, the Tasks refer to the System; you can view system information, add or remove programs, or change a setting. If you activate My Documents, the Tasks refer to files and folders; you can make a new folder, publish this folder to the Web, or share this folder with other users.

Other Places | The list shown under this heading also changes according to the function of the activated application. For example, if you activate My Computer, the list refers to activities related to it, such as My Network Places, My Documents, Shared Documents, and Control Panel. If you activate My Documents, the list refers to activities related to it, such as Desktop, Shared Documents My Computer, and My Network Places.

Details | Gives details of the displayed Task.

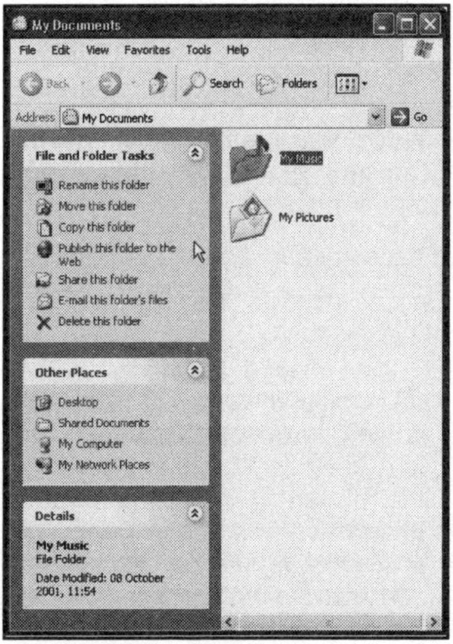

Fig. 2.3 Activity Related Tasks.

Fig. 2.3 shows activity related Tasks. Here we have selected a folder and, as you can see, the Tasks and Other Places lists change to reflect the current activity. For example, you can rename, move, delete, etc., a folder. This allows you to reach easily and quickly related activities that in previous versions of Windows you had to dig deep in menus and sub-menus to find.

The Mouse Pointers

In Windows, as with all other graphical based programs, using a mouse makes many operations both easier and more fun to carry out.

Windows has many different mouse pointers, with the most common illustrated below, which it uses for its various functions. When a program is initially started up probably the first you will see is the hourglass, which turns into an upward pointing hollow arrow. Some of the other shapes, as shown below, depend on the type of work you are doing at the time.

 The hourglass which displays when you are waiting while performing a function.

The arrow which appears when the pointer is placed over menus, scrolling bars, and buttons.

The I-beam which appears in normal text areas of the screen.

 The large 4-headed arrow which appears after choosing the **Control, Move/Size** command(s) for moving or sizing windows.

The double arrows which appear when over the border of a window, used to drag the side and alter the size of the window.

The Help hand which appears in the help windows, and is used to access 'hypertext' type links.

Windows applications, such as word processors, spreadsheets and databases, can have additional mouse pointers which facilitate the execution of selected commands, such as highlighting text, defining areas for the appearance of charts, etc.

The Menu Bar Options

Each window's menu bar option has associated with it a pull-down sub-menu. To activate the menu of a window, either press the <Alt> key, which causes the underlining of one letter per menu option and activates (turns to a button) the first option of the menu (in this case **File**). Next, use the right and left arrow keys to activate the other options in the menu, or use the mouse to point to an option. Pressing either the <Enter> key, or the left mouse button, reveals the pull-down sub-menu of the activated option.

The sub-menu of the **View** option of the My Computer window, is shown in Fig. 2.4 below.

Fig. 2.4 Menu Bar Options.

Menu options can also be activated directly by pressing the <Alt> key, followed by the under-lined letter of the required menu option. Thus pressing **Alt+V**, opens the pull-down sub-menu of **View**. You can use the up and down arrow keys to move the highlighted bar up and down a sub-menu, or the right and left arrow keys to move along the options in the menu bar. Pressing the <Enter> key selects the highlighted option or executes the highlighted command. Pressing the <Esc> key once, closes the pull-down sub-menu, while pressing the <Esc> key for a second time closes the menu system.

Items on the pull-down sub-menu which are marked with an arrow to their right, as shown here, open up additional options when selected, as shown on the My Computer screen dump of Fig. 2.4.

The items on the menu bar of a specific application might be different from the ones shown here. However, almost all Windows XP system applications offer the following options:

File   Produces a pull-down menu of mainly file related tasks, which allow you, amongst other options, to **rename**, **move**, **copy**, **publish on the Web**, **e-mail**, **print**, or **close** a file or folder.

Edit   Gives access to the most common editing tasks which can be applied on selected items, such as **cut**, **copy** and **paste**, **copy** or **move** such items to a folder, or **select all** files or folders.

View   Gives you complete control over what you see on your screen. For example, selecting the **toolbars**, **status bar**, or **Explorer bar** options checks these options and allows their display (selecting them once more removes the check mark and toggles them off). Allows you to display files as **thumbnails**, by their **titles**, **icons**, as **lists** or display their **details**, **arrange icons** in various ways and control what detail is displayed.

Favorites   Allows you to **add** and **organise** useful URL addresses, customise **links**, or access various pre-set **media** addresses on the Internet.

Tools   Allows you to **map** or **disconnect** network drives, and set **folder options**.

Help   Activates the **help and support centre**, or opens a window and displays basic system information.

Some applications display a '?' button on the right end of their title bar, as shown here. Clicking this button changes the mouse pointer from its usual inclined arrow shape to the 'What's this?' shape. Pointing with this to an object in the window and clicking, opens a Help topic.

Shortcut Menus

To see a shortcut menu containing the most common commands applicable to an item, point with your mouse at the item and click the right mouse button. For example, right-clicking the Recycle Bin icon on the desktop, reveals the options in Fig. 2.5.

Fig. 2.5 Shortcut Menu for the Recycle Bin.

In this case we have the option to **Open** the Recycle Bin which has the same effect as double-clicking its icon, **Explore** its contents, **Empty** it of any files or folders held in it, **Create Shortcut** icon on the desktop, or see its **Properties**.

Right-clicking the desktop itself, displays the shortcut shown in Fig. 2.6. From this menu you can select how to **Arrange Icons** on your desktop, or create a **New** folder or a shortcut icon on the desktop, for your favourite word processor maybe.

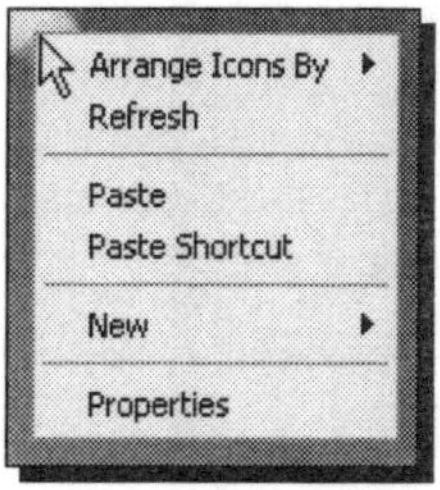

Fig. 2.6 Shortcut Menu for the Desktop.

It might be worth your while to right-click a Windows application icon on your desktop, such as that of a word processor, if one was installed on your computer, to find out what the difference is between this shortcut menu and that of the Recycle Bin. For example, you will find that the My Documents icon has an additional option to delete it might exist, while the Recycle Bin icon does not offer such an option. You will also find out that with a desktop application icon there might be an option to rename the icon, while there is no such option with the Recycle Bin.

Note: Having activated a shortcut menu, you can close it without taking any further action by simply pressing the <Esc> key, or clicking the mouse somewhere else.

Dialogue Boxes

Three periods after a sub-menu option or command, means that a dialogue box will open when the option or command is selected. A dialogue box is used for the insertion of additional information, such as the name of a file.

To see a dialogue box, click **Start** then the My Computer menu option, select **Tools** on the menu bar of the displayed window and **Folder Options** from its sub-menu. This opens the Folder Options dialogue box shown in Fig. 2.7 below with its General tab selected.

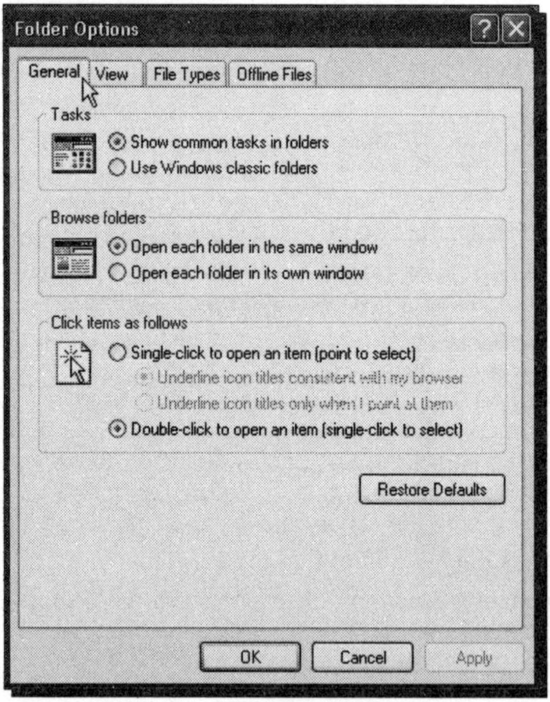

Fig. 2.7 The Folder Options Dialogue Box.

When a dialogue box opens, the <Tab> key can be used to move the dotted rectangle (known as the focus) from one field to another (<Shift+Tab> moves the focus backwards).

Alternatively you can move directly to a desired field by holding the <Alt> key down and pressing the underlined letter in the field name. With the mouse, you simply point and click the left mouse button at the desired field.

Some dialogue boxes (such as the one shown in Fig. 2.7) contain List boxes which show a column of available choices. If there are more choices than can be seen in the area provided, use the scroll bars to reveal them. Such dialogue boxes may contain Check boxes which offer a list of features you can switch on or off. Selected options show a tick in the box against the option name. Another type of dialogue box option is the Option button (sometimes called Radio button) with a list of mutually exclusive items. The default choice is marked with a black dot against its name, while unavailable options are dimmed.

Another type of List box may display a column of document files. To select a single file from such a List box, either double-click the file, or use the arrow keys to highlight the file and press <Enter>. Again, if there are more files than can be seen in the area provided, use the scroll bars to reveal them.

Other dialogue boxes may contain groups of options within a field. In such cases, you can use the arrow keys to move from one option to another. Having selected an option or typed in information in a text box, you must press a command button, such as the **OK**, **Cancel** or **Apply** button (unavailable options or command buttons are dimmed), or choose from additional options. To select the **OK** button with the mouse, simply point and left-click, while with the keyboard, you must first press the <Tab> key until the focus moves to the required button, and then press the <Enter> key.

To cancel a dialogue box, either press the **Cancel** button, or the <Esc> key enough times to close the dialogue box and then the menu system.

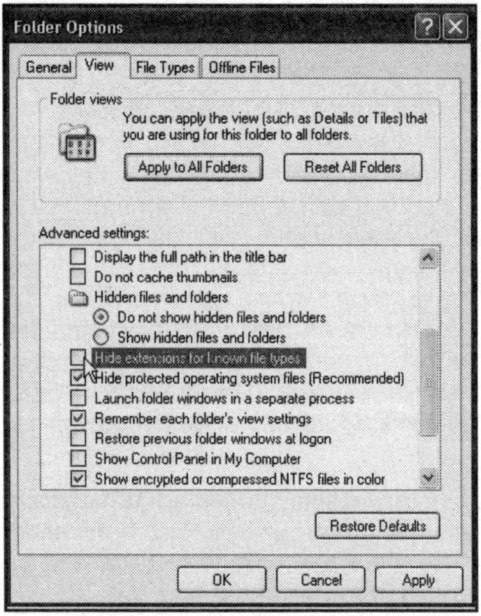

Fig. 2.8 Making Visible the Extensions of Known File Types.

Note: At this stage it might be a good time to change the default settings under the **View** tab of Fig. 2.7 by unchecking the **Hide extensions for known file types** option, as shown in Fig. 2.8.

Doing so could alert you to rogue and potentially lethal e-mail attachments (see the E-mail and Outlook Express chapter).

Taskbar Buttons

At the bottom of the Desktop screen is the Taskbar. It contains the **Start** button which, as we have seen, can be used to quickly start a program. Later on we will discuss how we can search for a file, and how to get Help.

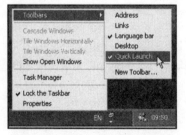

Fig. 2.9 Quick Launch Activation.

Before we go any further, right click an empty part of the Taskbar, point to the **Toolbars** option which displays the sub-menu, shown on the right in Fig. 2.9, and left-click the **Quick Launch** entry. This displays three icons next to the **Start** button; left-clicking one of these, launches its application (see next page for details).

When you open a program, or a window, a button for it is placed on the Taskbar, as shown in Fig. 2.10 below.

start   My Computer   My Documents

Fig. 2.10 The Windows Taskbar.

You can left-click your mouse on this button to make this the active program, or window, which displays in a darker shade of blue on the Taskbar. So, now you can always see what windows you have open, which is the active one, and quickly switch between them. As more buttons are placed on the Taskbar their size shrinks slightly, but up to a point. After that common entries are grouped together with a number indicating the number of open windows. To see details relating to a grouped button, left-click it to open a list of components, as shown in Fig. 2.11. Try it!

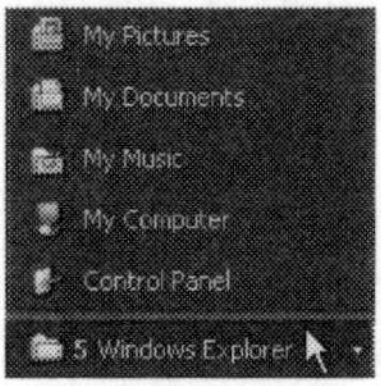

My Pictures
My Documents
My Music
My Computer
Control Panel
5 Windows Explorer

Fig. 2.11 Grouped Taskbar Entries.

Another interesting Taskbar menu option is **Properties** (Fig. 2.9). This allows you to change the Taskbar and **Start** menu options.

If you have activated the Quick Launch option, there will be three buttons displaying next to the **Start** button. These, in order of appearance, have the following functions:

Launch the Internet Explorer Browser.

Show Desktop.

Launch Windows Media Player

Fig. 2.12 Date and Time Properties Dialogue Box.

The Taskbar also shows the current time to the far right, the Windows Messenger, the Options, the Restore and the Language icons. Moving the mouse pointer over the clock will display the date. Double-clicking the clock, opens the Date/Time Properties box, shown in Fig. 2.12, so that you can make changes, if necessary.

The Start Cascade Menu

Left-clicking the **Start** button at the bottom left corner of the Windows screen, displays the two-column **Start** menu. The left column provides shortcuts to Internet Explorer, Outlook Express and the six applications that are used most often.

On the top of the right-hand column there are shortcuts to such folders as My Documents, My Pictures, My Music and My Computer, while on the bottom of the column there are shortcuts to Control Panel, Printers and Faxes, Help and Support and Search facility.

Clicking or hovering over the **All Programs** button, displays the first column of the cascade menu where all Windows applications are to be found. In the screen dump in Fig. 2.13 below we show the System Tools options which are part of the Windows Accessories.

Fig. 2.13 The Start Cascade Menu.

At the top of the **Start** menu the name of the current user is displayed with a picture against it. Left-clicking this picture opens the User Accounts screen shown in Fig. 2.14.

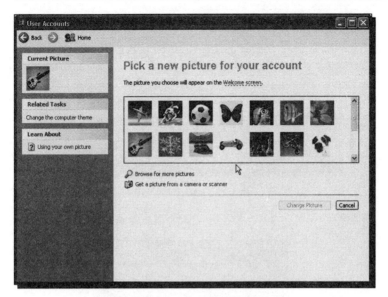

Fig. 2.14 The User Accounts Dialogue Box.

From here you can choose a different picture for the current user either from the ones supplied or from one of your own. You can also change the Computer's theme, desktop, screen savers, etc. Most of these facilities will be discussed later on.

As we mentioned earlier, new to Windows XP is the ability of the first of its two-column menu to adapt to the way you use your computer - an adaptation of what was first introduced with Windows Me. It keeps track of what features and programs you use the most and adds them to the list on the left column. For example, if you use the **Command Prompt** by selecting it from the Accessories sub-menu, next time you click the **Start** button you will see this application pinned to the bottom of the first column of the **Start** menu. This saves time as you don't have to scroll through menu lists to find the application you want to use.

To remove an application from the first column of the **Start** menu, right-click it and select **Remove from this List**. This removes the name of the application from the list, not the application itself from your hard disc. Try it.

Exiting Windows XP

To exit Windows, click the **Start** button and select the **Turn Off Computer** option, as shown in Fig. 2.15.

Fig. 2.15 The Lower Part of the START Menu.

This opens an additional box, shown in Fig. 2.16 below.

Fig. 2.16 The Turn Off Computer Box.

From here you can either put your computer in a **Stand by** mode, **Turn Off** the computer, or **Restart** it. The **Stand by** mode is used to save power by turning off your monitor and/or hard disc after a specified time interval (we will discuss this in detail later on in the book). Selecting the **Turn Off** option, exits all the open programs, carries out any file saves you require and then tells you when it is safe to switch off your computer. The **Restart** option is used if you want to clear the memory settings and restart Windows XP, or if you have a dual boot system the other operating system.

Note: Unlike previous versions of Windows where this was the only way that you should end a session, with Window XP you can just switch off your computer - the **Turn Off** the computer procedure will then be carried out automatically.

3

The Windows Environment

Windows allows the display of multiple applications or multiple documents of a single application. Each of these Windows applications or documents displays on the screen in its own window, which can be full screen size or part screen size.

Manipulating Windows

To use any Windows program effectively, you will need to be able to manipulate a series of windows, to select which one is to be active, to move them, or change their size, so that you can see all the relevant parts of each one. What follows is a short discussion on how to manipulate windows.

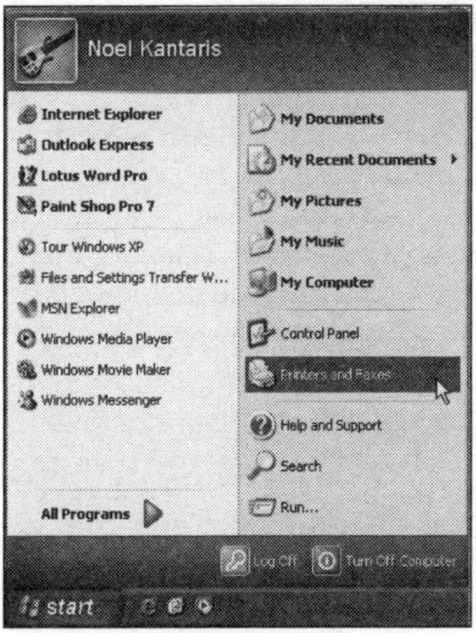

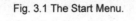

To help with the illustration of the various points to be discussed, we will create three windows. First click the **Start** button to display the Start menu, then click the **Printers and Faxes** option. Repeat this process two more times, but click the **Control Panel** option on the second time, followed by the **My Computer** option on the third time. What you should see on your screen is shown in Fig. 3.2 on the next page. Don't worry about what these

Fig. 3.1 The Start Menu.

applications do; we will explain later.

All we are concerned with at the moment is to open three windows on the screen with each window containing a different application. If the contents of these windows do not look exactly like ours, i.e., containing large icons, again don't worry as it is not important. Our settings under the **View** command on each window was **Tiles**. These viewing options will be explained later.

Fig. 3.2 Three Opened Application Windows on Screen.

If you followed the order we suggested for opening these application windows, then the active window (the last one to be opened) will display on top of the others, as shown in Fig. 3.2.

Changing the Active Window

To select the active window amongst those displayed on the screen, point to it and click the left mouse button, or, if the one you want to activate is not visible, click its icon on the Taskbar.

It is a good idea to practise what we are describing here. Do not be afraid if you make mistakes - the more mistakes you make the more you will learn!

Moving Windows and Dialogue Boxes

When you have multiple windows or dialogue boxes on the screen, you might want to move a particular one to a different part of the screen. This can be achieved with either the mouse or the keyboard, but not if the window occupies the full screen, for obvious reasons.

Fig. 3.3 Moving a Window with the Mouse.

To move a window, or a dialogue box, with the mouse, point to the title bar, as shown in Fig. 3.3, and drag it (press the left button and keep it pressed while moving the mouse) until the window is where you want it to be on the screen, then release the mouse button.

To move a window with the keyboard, press <Alt+Spacebar>

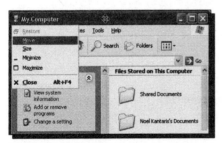

Fig. 3.4 Moving a Window with the Keyboard.

to open the Application Control menu, shown in Fig. 3.4 (or <Alt+-> to open the Document Control menu), then press **M** to select **Move,** which causes a four-headed arrow to appear in the title bar, also shown in Fig. 3.4 (this is a composite screen dump which shows the action to be taken and its effect). Next, use the arrow keys to move the window to the required place and press <Enter> to fix it there.

Sizing a Window

You can change the size of a window with either the mouse or the keyboard. With the mouse, move the window so that the side you want to change is visible, then move the mouse pointer to the edge of the window or corner so that it changes to a two-headed arrow, then drag the two-headed arrow in the direction you want that side or corner to move.

To size a window with the keyboard, press either <Alt+Spacebar> to open the Application Control menu (or <Alt+-> to open the Document Control menu), then press **S** to select **Size** which causes the four-headed arrow to appear. Next, press the arrow key that corresponds to the edge you want to move, or if a corner, press the two arrow keys (one after the other) corresponding to the particular corner, which causes the pointer to change to a two-headed arrow. Having pressed the appropriate arrow key in the direction you want that side or corner to move, continue to do so until the window is the size you require, then press <Enter> to fix it to that size.

Minimising and Maximising Windows

Windows can be minimised into Taskbar icons to temporarily

free desktop space. This can be done either by using the mouse to click the 'Minimise' button (the negative sign in the upper-right corner of the window), shown in Fig. 3.5 or by pressing <Alt+Spacebar> or <Alt+-> to reveal the Application Control

Fig. 3.5 Minimising a Window.

menu or the Document Control menu, and selecting **n** for **Mi<u>n</u>imise**.

To maximise a window so that it fills the entire screen, either click on the 'maximise' button (the rectangle in the upper-right corner of the window), or press <Alt+Spacebar> or

<Alt+-> to display the Application Control menu or the Document Control menu, and select **x** for Ma**x**imise.

An application which has been minimised or maximised can be returned to its original size and position on the screen by either clicking on its Taskbar icon to expand it to a window, or clicking on the 'Restore' button in the upper-right corner of the maximised window, to reduce it to its former size. With the keyboard, press <Alt+Spacebar>, then select **R** for **R**estore from the Control menu.

Closing a Window

A document window can be closed at any time to save screen space and memory. To do this, either click the X Close button (on the upper-right corner of the window), or double-click on the Control menu button (the icon in the upper-left corner of the window title bar). With the keyboard, press <Alt+–> and select **C** for **C**lose from the window Control menu.

If you try to close a window of an application document, such as that of a word processor, in which you have made changes since the last time you saved it, you will get a warning in the form of a dialogue box asking confirmation prior to closing it. This safeguards against loss of information.

Windows Display Arrangement

In Windows and most Windows application programs, you can display multiple windows in both tiled and cascaded (overlapping) forms - the choice being a matter of balance between personal preference and the type of work you are doing at the time. If you want to organise these automatically, right-click on an empty part of the Taskbar which opens the menu shown in Fig. 3.6.

Fig. 3.6 The Taskbar Shortcut Menu.

Below we show two forms of windows display; the **Cascade Windows** option and the **Tile Windows Vertically** option.

Fig. 3.7 Windows Displayed in Cascade Form.

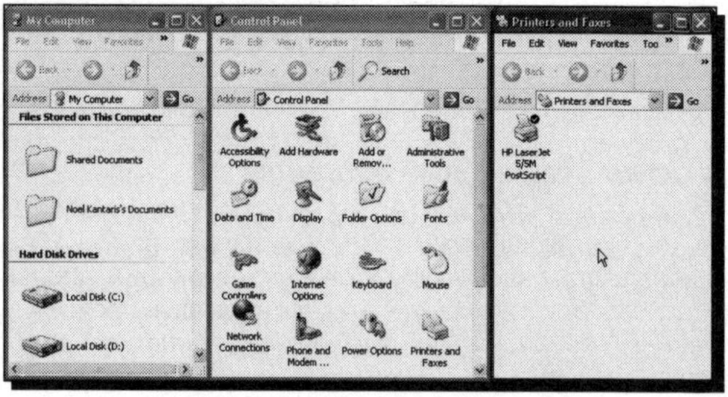

Fig. 3.8 Windows Displayed in Vertical Tile Form.

As we have discussed earlier, the size of these windows can be changed, hence you might have to alter their size to display exactly what is displayed in Fig. 3.7 and Fig. 3.8.

The Windows Control Panel

The Control Panel provides a quick and easy way to change the hardware and software settings of your system. To access it, click the **Start** button, then click the **Control Panel** entry on the displayed menu to open the Control Panel window shown in Fig. 3.9 below.

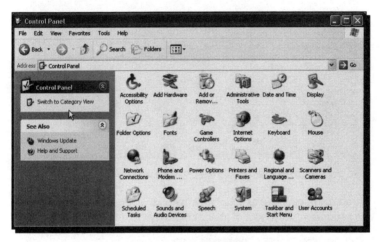

Fig. 3.9 The Control Panel Window.

Double-clicking at the Control Panel icons allows you to add new hardware, add or remove programs, change the display type and its resolution, change the printer fonts, and change the keyboard repeat rate. Further, you can change the settings of your mouse, install and configure your printer(s), specify regional settings, such as the formatting of numbers and dates, and access a variety of system administrative tools. If your system is connected to the outside world or supports multimedia, then you can also configure it appropriately.

All of these features control the environment in which the Windows application programs operate and you should become familiar with them.

New to Windows XP is the ability to group the various Control Panel options by category. Left-clicking the entry

Switch to Category View on the left panel (pointed to) provides the display shown in Fig. 3.10 below.

Fig. 3.10 The Control Panel Window in Category View.

Which view you choose to work with is a matter of preference. We suspect that those of you new to Windows might prefer the

Fig. 3.11 Appearance and Themes Screen.

Category view as it appears to be less daunting. However, each option within this view displays an additional screen in which you are asked to **Pick a task** or **Pick a Control Panel icon**, as shown in Fig. 3.11.

Those of you who have used Windows before will be more familiar with the Classic view of Fig. 3.8, which is also our preference.

Changing your Display

If your VDU (visual display unit or screen) is capable of higher resolution than the required 800 by 600 pixels (picture elements) by Windows XP, you might like to increase its resolution to, say, 1024 by 768 pixels, or higher. This will allow you to see a larger number of icons on a screen when a given application is activated. To do this, follow the steps below.

- Click the **Start** button, then the **Control Panel** button.

- In the Control Panel window (Classic view), double-click the **Display** icon shown here.

- In the Display Properties dialogue box, click the Settings tab.

The last dialogue box is shown in Fig. 3.12 below with the settings changed appropriately. For the new settings to take effect, click the **Apply** button followed by the **OK** button.

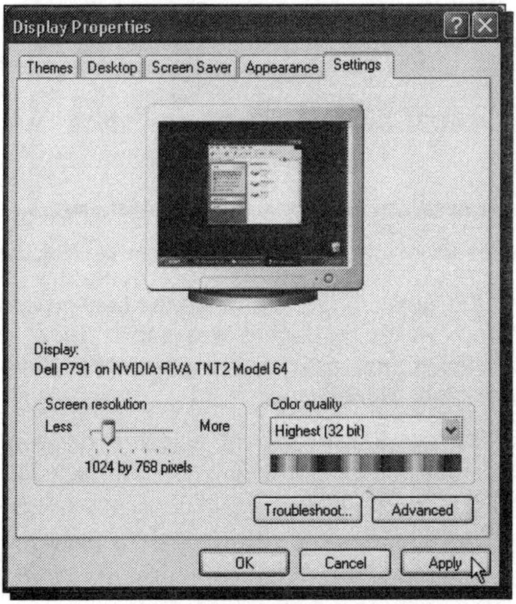

Fig. 3.12 The Settings Screen of the Display Properties Dialogue Box.

While the Display Properties dialogue box is open, you might like to explore the other available settings. For example:

- Click the Themes tab to change the looks of your active windows. Selecting the Windows Classic view presents you with a display more akin to that of previous versions of Windows, as shown in Fig. 3.13 below.

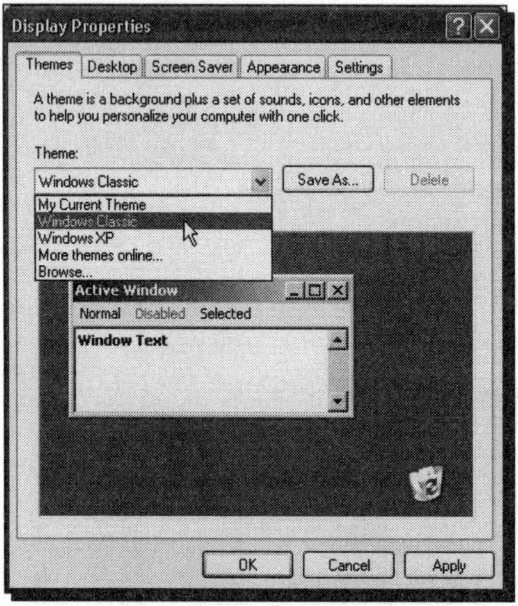

Fig. 3.13 The Themes Screen of the Display Properties Dialogue Box.

- Click the Desktop tab to change the background of your desktop, which by default was set to 'Bliss'. The first four background options are quite interesting, or you could select 'None'.

- The Screen Savers tab to select a different screen saver - you will be able to preview your selection before making a final choice.

- Click the Appearance tab to select a different look for your windows and buttons, apply a different colour scheme and select a different font size.

The Start Menu Appearance

If you have upgraded from a previous version of Windows, you might like to know that you can change the appearance of the **Start** menu to a more familiar look. You do this through the Taskbar and Start Menu Properties dialogue box which, however, will be discussed in greater detail in Chapter 6.

To change the **Start** menu appearance, right-click at an

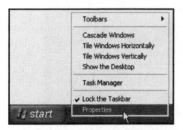

empty part of the Taskbar and select the **Properties** option on the displayed quick menu, as shown in Fig. 3.14.

This opens the Taskbar and Start Menu Properties dialogue box shown in Fig. 3.15 with its Start Menu tab selected. Click the Classic Start menu option followed by the **OK** button to see the old style **Start** menu, as shown in Fig. 3.16 below.

Fig. 3.14 The Taskbar Shortcut Menu.

Fig. 3.15 The Start Menu Properties.

Nevertheless, we find the new style **Start** menu quite appealing, so even though we have been using Windows for years, we will continue using the new look.

Fig. 3.16 The Old Style Start Menu.

Installing a Fax Printer

Windows XP includes its own Fax printer driver. To install it click the **Start** button, then click the **Control Panel** button and double-click the **Printers and Faxes** icon shown here.

In the displayed dialogue box click the Install a local fax printer option in the Printer Tasks box as shown in Fig. 3.17 below.

Fig. 3.17 The Printers and Faxes Dialogue box.

This starts the Instal Fax Wizard which might ask you to insert the Windows XP distribution CD in the CD-ROM drive so that required files could be copied. Once that is done and you supply the information you want to be included in your faxes, a Fax printer is installed in your Printers and Faxes folder - folders will be discussed in detail in the next chapter.

All the printers installed on your system are available to you from within any of the word-processing applications you might have on your computer so that you can either print a document to your local printer, to a shared printer (if you are connected to a network) or the fax printer (if you are connected to a phone line). Controlling your printers will be discussed in some detail in Chapter 6, while the Fax utility will be discussed in Chapter 9.

Additional Plug and Play printers are automatically detected at installation time or during the boot-up process. You will be prompted for the necessary driver files if they are not already in the Windows folder. Such printer drivers are normally supplied with all new Plug and Play printers. For other situations click the Add Printer option in the Printer Tasks box for a Wizard to step you through the printer installation process.

The choice of installing an additional printer driver could be dependent on whether such a printer was connected to your system but was not of the Plug and Play variety, or the printer was available to you at, say, your office on a shared basis. This latter option would allow the preparation of documents incorporating fonts and styles not available on your local printer, to be saved with your file and printed later on a printer which supports such enhancements. This is also discussed in Chapter 6.

The Common User Interface

The front end of Windows XP remains similar (or can be made to look identical) to previous versions of Windows, with the user interface resembling that of the Internet Explorer which is bundled with it. You must have noticed by now that the My Computer, My Documents, Recycle Bin, Control Panel, and Printers and Faxes folder windows, to mention but a few, have a toolbar with browser-style forwards and backwards arrows. The Printers and Faxes window is shown in Fig. 3.18 below fully extended so that all the toolbar icons are visible.

Fig. 3.18 The Toolbar of the Common Windows User Interface.

Note that to see the display exactly as it appears in Fig. 3.18, you need to click the down arrow against the Views button on the toolbar and select the **Icons** option from the drop-down menu, as shown. Try the different display options available to you and see which one you prefer. For the display in Fig. 3.19, we chose the **Details** option. Highlighting an item,

Fig. 3.19 The Details View Option.

in whichever display option you operate, gives you information about that item.

If you have upgraded from a previous Windows version, you might find it preferable to use the **Tools, Folder Options** command and select the **Use Windows classic folders** option under **Tasks** in the General tab sheet.

Additional information can be obtained from the Properties dialogue box, shown in Fig. 3.20. First select printer, then use the **File, Properties** command.

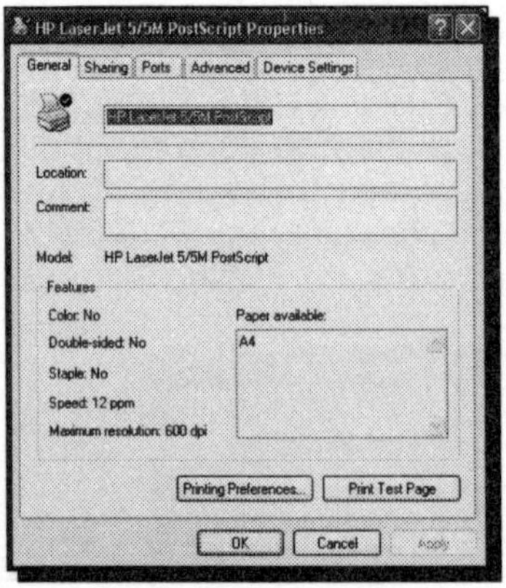

As you can see, the Properties dialogue box for the selected item gives you quite a bit of information relating to it. For example, the little tick against the printer name tells you that this is the default printer. You can also find out whether it can be shared and to which computer port it is connected by clicking the appropriate tab. Additional tab sheets give more advanced information.

Fig. 3.20 The Properties Dialogue Box.

Similar Properties dialogue boxes can be accessed for a drive or a program/document file displayed in My Computer. Do try it for yourself.

Returning to the common user interface toolbar, apart from the default buttons appearing on it, there are several others which can be added to invoke extra facilities. To do this, use the **View, Toolbars, Customize** command to display the screen shown in Fig. 3.21.

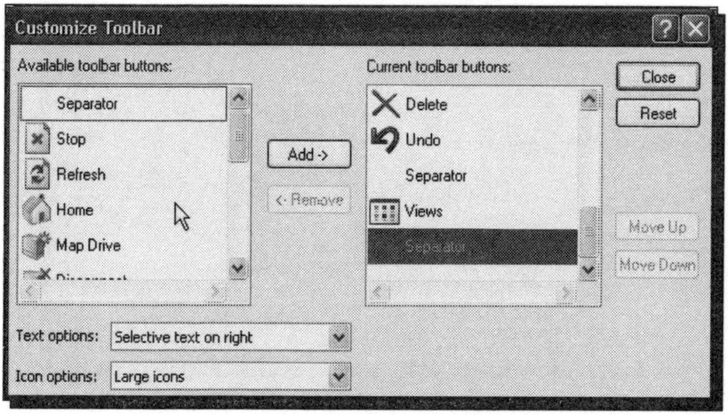

Fig. 3.21 The Customize Toolbar Dialogue Box.

To place an additional button on to the Toolbar, select it in the left pane, and press the **Add** button. Its place on the Toolbar depends on the position of the focus in the right pane. Try adding the 'Home' button to the Toolbar at a position to the left of the 'Search' button.

One interesting aspect of this common user interface is, that no matter which application you used to add the extra button to its Toolbar, the same button will appear on the Toolbar of all other program applications that use the same common user interface. Furthermore, if this was the 'Home' button, clicking it on any of these program applications, will cause the application to attempt to connect you to the Internet, provided your system is geared up to it, and will jump to a Web site without you having to load up a browser. The default Web site is that of Microsoft's MSN, as shown in Fig. 3.22 on the next page.

Fig. 3.22 The Default Home Web Site.

If you are connected to the Internet, it is worth examining this facility. If not, you can always use this facility off-line and give it an address pointing to your own Home page on your hard disc, as shown below. How to design this, is another story!

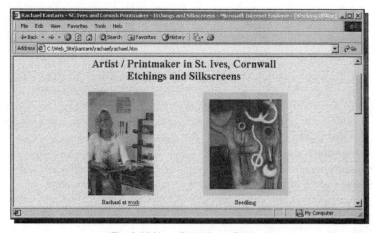

Fig. 3.23 Your Own Home Page.

Using the Help System

To obtain help in Windows XP, click the **Start** button, then click the **Help and Support** menu option which opens the main Help window, shown in Fig. 3.24 below.

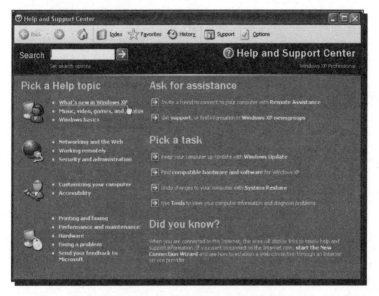

Fig. 3.24 The Windows XP Help and Support Centre.

The **Pick a Help topic** option give you off-line help on various listed topics, while the **Ask for assistance** topics require connection to the Internet, as do the first two options under **Pick a task**. It might be worth your while spending some time here investigating the various options available to you. If you are new to Windows, you might like to have a look at the 'What's new in Windows XP' option.

With all options you get a 'Search' facility, and with all but the 'start a New Connection Wizard' under the **Did you know?** option you are presented with an extraordinary number of hypertext links to various topics. Clicking such a hypertext link, can open up a further list of hypertext links until you home onto the specific subject you are searching for.

The Search facility gives you access to a very powerful individual word search of the Help system, as shown in Fig. 3.25 below. For example, if you wanted to know something about e-mail, type the word *e-mail* in the Search box and click the 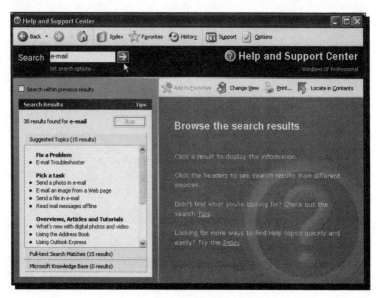 button to have Windows display everything there is to know about e-mail.

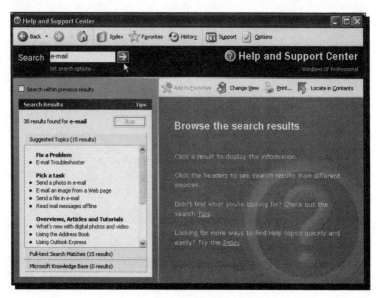

Fig. 3.25 Using the Help Search Facility.

The last item under each Search screen's **Browse the search results** statement is always the **Index** link. Clicking this link, opens up a Help index facility and typing the first few letters of a word in its input box homes onto the available topics in the list. Selecting one and clicking the **Display** button opens its help page on that item. Try it.

4

Discs, Folders and Files

Windows XP, being an operating system, controls the use of your system's disc drives and allows for the manipulation of the data stored on them. To do this, you have the choice between two utilities; Windows Explorer, or My Computer.

Windows Explorer

To use Windows Explorer you might need to be logged on as an administrator in order to perform certain tasks. To open the program, click **Start**, **All Programs**, **Accessories**, then click the **Windows Explorer** icon.

Windows Explorer displays the hierarchical structure of discs, folders (the old directories) and files on your computer, as

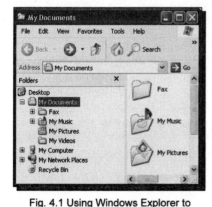

Fig. 4.1 Using Windows Explorer to Look at My Documents Folders.

shown in Fig. 4.1. It also shows any network drives that might have been mapped to drive letters on your computer. In Windows Explorer almost everything is done graphically, by clicking and dragging icons between windows, folders and the desktop itself.

Apart from being able to use Windows Explorer as the administrator and manipulate other users' folders, everything else can be done in a similar manner using My Computer which now is capable of delivering more facilities than before.

My Computer

In Windows XP you can work with files using My Computer in two different ways; in the hierarchical structure form that Windows Explorer uses, or by using commands in the Tasks pane. Both these methods will be discussed, starting with the hierarchical structure, while the other will be discussed later.

 As we have seen, earlier in the book, left-clicking the My Computer icon on the **Start** menu, gives you immediate visual access to all the disc drives in your computer, as well as the My Documents folder. The My Computer window opens with the last settings you selected, a Web browser type toolbar, and each time you double-click an icon its contents are shown in the same window.

To make the program function in a similar visual manner to Windows Explorer, click the **Folders** icon on its Toolbar. To see all the folders held on your computer's drive, click the appropriate disc icon that holds Windows XP (in our case this is Local Disc E:, yours could be different).

Note: If you select to open the WINDOWS folder that holds Windows XP system files, the message 'This folder contains files that keep your system working properly ...' appears in the right pane of the displayed window. Left-clicking the **View the entire contents of this folder** link allows you to have a look (Fig. 4.2). But, as the warning tells you, do not move, delete, or in any way change the content of these folders or files - just look.

![Screenshot of the WINDOWS folder contents in My Computer]

Fig. 4.2 The Contents of the WINDOWS Folder.

Note the **Back** icon on the toolbar has been activated. Pressing this icon returns you to the previous display and in doing so, activates the **Forward** icon on the toolbar. This simulates the way a Web browser works.

Folders are graphical devices, as shown here, similar to directories in that they can contain files, other folders and also icons. To examine this, locate the Program Files folder on your drive (ours is found immediately above the WINDOWS folder) and click it to display the following:

Fig. 4.3 The Contents of the Program Files Folder.

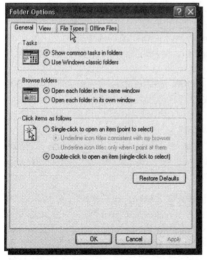

Fig. 4.4 The Folder Options Dialogue Box.

Icon settings are easy to change, not only from the **Views** button on the toolbar, but also from the **View** menu. However, to control general settings, view options and edit the files you view, use the **Tools**, **Folder Options** menu command, which opens the Folder Options dialogue box shown in Fig. 4.4.

To see what program associations are valid on your system, click the File Types tab. This opens the dialogue box shown in Fig. 4.5 on the next page.

If you work your way down the list of **Registered file types** you can see the association details in the lower half of the box. Our example shows that a file with the .AU extension is a sound file.

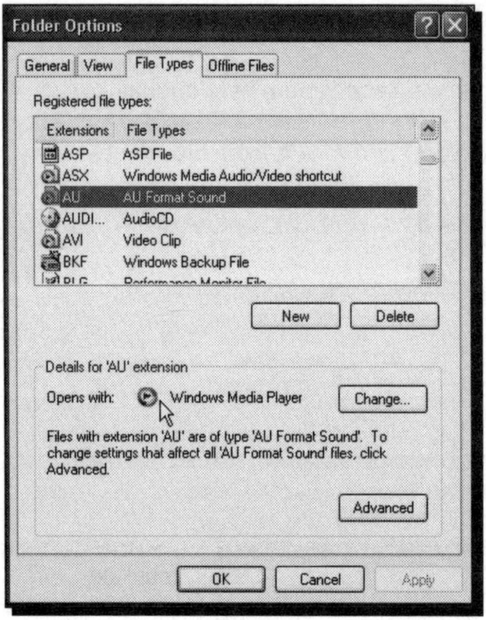

Fig. 4.5 Program File Associations.

From this box you can add new associations by clicking the **New** button, delete them with the **Delete** button and change them with the **Change** button. Without getting too involved at this stage, it is worth spending a few minutes just browsing through the list. It will help you to recognise the icons. These extensions are used by Windows XP to associate files with the application that created them.

Any file displayed within the My Computer window, whether with its extension showing or not, can be opened by double-clicking its icon. If it is a program file, the program will run. If it is a document, it will be opened in a running version of its application program.

Creating a New Folder

Before you start manipulating any files, create a new folder to hold copies of some existing files. It should then be safe to 'play around' with them.

To create a new folder:

* Open in succession by double-clicking, the Program Files folder, then the Messenger. Next, left-click the **File** menu command and hold the mouse pointer over **New**, which opens the cascade menu shown in Fig. 4.6.

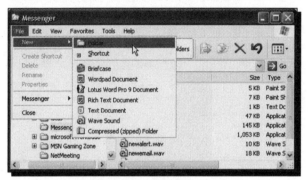

Fig. 4.6 Creating a New Folder.

* Clicking the **Folder** option places a 'New Folder' inside the currently active window, as shown in Fig. 4.7, with its name highlighted ready for you to type a different name.

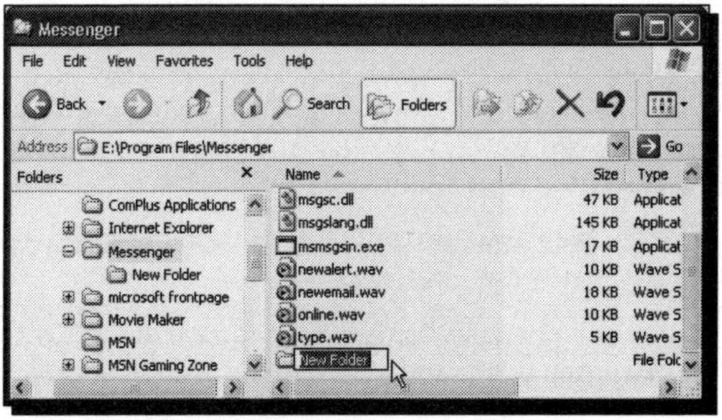

Fig. 4.7 A New Folder Added Inside the Active Window.

- Next, type **Test Folder** into the name slot and click at an empty area of the window. It's as easy as that to create and name a folder. At any time in the future you can rename it by clicking its existing name and typing in the new one. This works for files too.

Selecting Folders and Files

What we demonstrate below with files could also be done with folders, or a mixture of folders and files within any folder. Before selecting such items you would like to copy, arrange the new Test Folder next to the other icons in the Messenger folder (viewed as icons) as shown in Fig. 4.8.

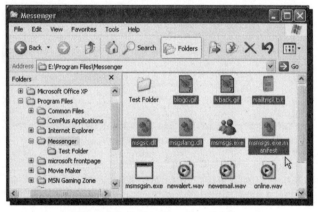

Fig. 4.8 Selecting Items in a Folder.

To select several objects, or icons, you have three options:

- If they form a rectangle, as above, left-click one corner, then with the <Shift> key depressed, click the opposite corner.

- To select random objects hold the <Ctrl> key down and left-click them, one by one.

- To select all the items in a window use the **Edit**, **Select All** menu command, or the keyboard shortcut <Ctrl+A>.

To cancel a selection, click in an empty area of the window.

Copying Folders and Files

There are several ways to copy selected items from one window into a target folder.

- *Using the menu bar icon:* If the destination folder is on a different drive or in a folder which is not displayed in the current window, then select the object you want to copy and left-click the **Copy To** menu bar icon pointed to below. This opens the Browse For Folder dialogue box for you to locate the required destination.

- *Using the menu:* Select the objects you want to copy, then use the **Edit, Copy** command from the menu bar. Double-click the folder into which you want to insert a copy of the selected objects, and use the **Edit, Paste** command.

- *Using the keyboard:* Select the objects to copy and press the <Ctrl+C> keyboard shortcut. Double-click the destination folder and press <Ctrl+V> to paste the objects there.

- *Using the mouse:* Press and hold down the <Ctrl> key, then drag the selected objects to the destination folder.

Use one of the above methods to copy the files selected in Fig. 4.8 into the Test Folder. Then double-clicking the Test Folder should reveal its contents, as shown in Fig. 4.9.

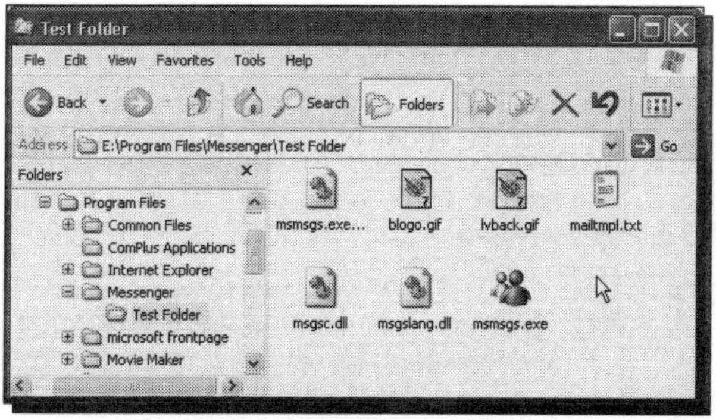

Fig 4.9 The Contents of the Test Folder.

Moving Folders and Files

When you **copy** a folder or file to somewhere else, the original version of the folder or file is not altered or removed, but when you **move** a folder or file to a new location, the original is actually deleted. As with the copy operation there are several ways to move selected folders or files.

- *Using the menu bar icon:* If the destination folder is on a different drive or in a folder which is not displayed in the current window, then select the object you want to move and left-click the **Move To** menu bar icon (the one to the left of the **Copy To** icon pointed to in Fig. 4.9). This opens the Browse For Folder dialogue box for you to locate the required destination.

- *Using the menu:* Choose the **Edit**, **Cut** command from the source window, then use the **Edit**, **Paste** command from the destination window menu bar.

- *Using the keyboard:* Select the items to move and press the <Ctrl+X> keyboard shortcut. Then select the destination window and press <Ctrl+V> to paste them there.

- *Using the mouse:* Drag the selected items to the destination folder. This will move files between windows, or folders, **of the same drive** (see note below).

Note: It is possible to use the drag and drop technique to copy or move objects between different drives. However, dragging can be a little confusing until you get used to it. To drag-copy objects to a folder or window of *another disc drive*, you don't have to hold down the <Ctrl> key. This is the same action as drag-moving objects between folders of the *same* drive. Therefore, take special care or you will end up moving objects instead of copying them.

 One easy way of telling what action a drag operation will result in, is to look for a + sign on the drag pointer. This indicates that a copy action will take place, as shown here, where the Test Folder is about to be copied to the D: drive.

Perhaps a safer way of copying or moving objects with the mouse is to drag them with the *right* mouse button depressed to the desired destination. Releasing the mouse button produces a menu which gives you a choice between **Copy Here** and **Move Here**. Clicking one of these, completes the required task.

Renaming Folders and Files

Before you rename folders or files, copy a folder into your Test Folder. Anything done to it in the Test Folder should not have any effect on the rest of your system.

To rename a folder or file, first click on it to select it, then click the existing name below the icon. This will place a rectangle around the name and put you into edit mode. Type a new name and click somewhere else, or press <Enter>, to finish the task. Try renaming the Test Folder to Practice Folder.

File Properties

If you want to know more about a particular file, first select it, then either use the **File, Properties** menu command, or

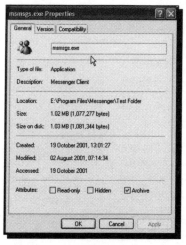

right-click the filename and select **Properties** from the drop-down menu to open the Properties dialogue box. Here, the full properties of the file are listed, including its name, type, location, size, the date when it was created, last modified, etc. You can also change the file's attributes, by making it, say, **Read-only**, to prevent accidental changes to its contents. The Properties dialogue box of some types of files has an extra tab which allows you to preview, or even play, their contents.

Fig. 4.10 The Properties Dialogue Box.

Creating Shortcuts

With Windows XP, just as with previous versions of Windows, you can put a shortcut to any program, document, or printer on your desktop or in any folder. Shortcuts are quick ways to get to the items you use often; they save you having to dig deep into your system files to access them.

One program we seem to use a lot to process our system text files is the Notepad (we will discuss its use later), so we will step through the process of placing a shortcut to it onto the desktop.

You must first find the actual program. An easy way is to use the **Start, Search** command which opens the Search Dialogue box, the left panel of which is shown in Fig. 4.11. Next, click the All Folders and Files link and specify the drive you want to search and the item you are searching for (the E: drive in our case, or whichever drive Windows is installed on your PC), as shown in Fig. 4.12.

Fig. 4.11 Specifying Type of Search.

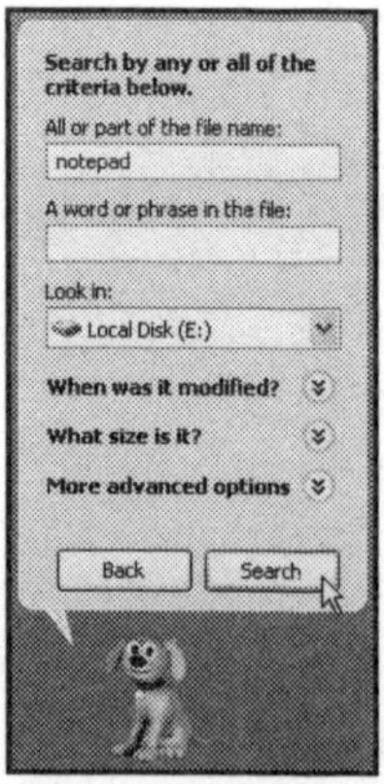

Soon enough the NOTEPAD.EXE file is found in the Windows XP folder. Select it, right-click it and drag it onto the desktop. Releasing the right mouse button displays the shortcut menu shown in Fig. 4.13 below.

Fig. 4.13 The Placement Shortcut Menu.

Click the **Create Shortcuts Here** option to place the new shortcut icon on the desktop, as shown in Fig. 4.14 on the next page.

Fig. 4.12 Specifying the Item and Drive for a Search.

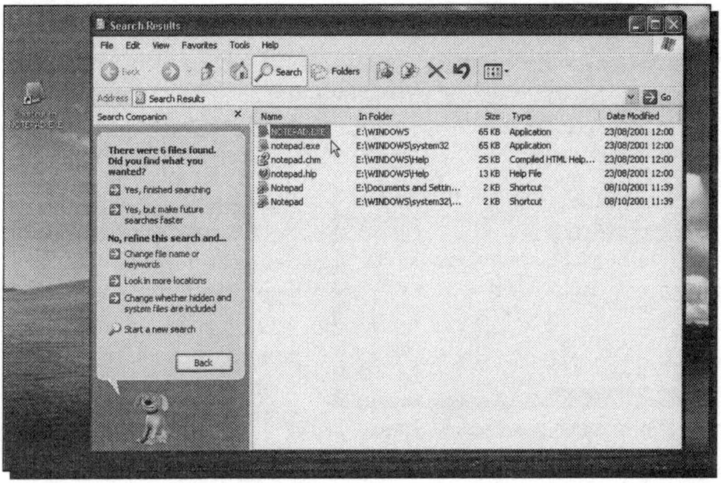

Fig. 4.14 Placing Notepad on the Desktop.

Note that the icon has a right pointer arrow on it. This is how you can tell that an icon is a shortcut, not the actual file. If you find the icon name a little lengthy, you can rename it, using the same procedure as described earlier for renaming files.

If your desktop does not let you place the icons where you want them, you need to change its settings. Right-click on the desktop, click the **Arrange Icons By** option on the shortcut menu and click **Auto Arrange** to remove the tick mark alongside it (Fig. 4.15).

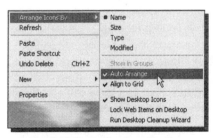

Fig. 4.15 Controlling Icon Position.

You should now be able to arrange your desktop icons in any way you wish, by simply dragging them around the desktop - though you might have to remove the tick mark against the **Align to Grid** option of the desktop shortcut menu for complete freedom in positioning the icons.

Sending Folders and Files

A very useful feature of Windows is the ability to quickly send files and folders to specific destinations.

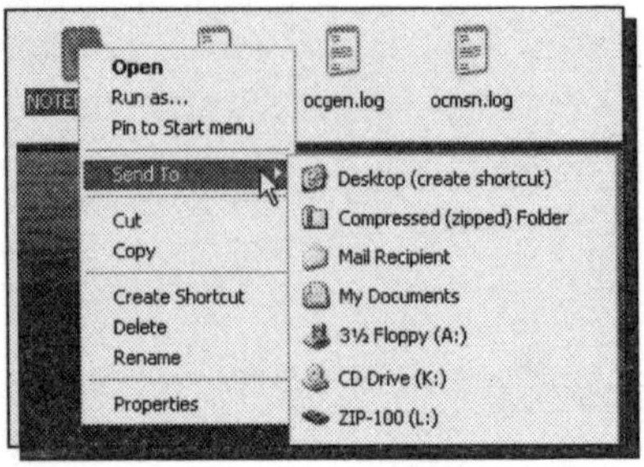

Fig. 4.16 Sending Folders and Files.

Right-clicking selected folders, or files, will open the menu shown in Fig. 4.16. Selecting the **Send To** option opens the list of available destinations. In your case these are bound to be different, for example, the last two options might not be available to you.

Selecting the **3½ Floppy (A)** option will copy any selected folders and files to a removable disc in the (A:) drive, as shown by the very decorative animated window that appears while the process is being carried out.

Fig. 4.17 Copying Folders and Files.

It is easy to add more locations to the **Send To** menu, as it is controlled by the contents of the SendTo folder, which is itself in the Windows folder. However, the SendTo folder is hidden by default, so if you use the **Start, Search** command, you may not find it. To make it visible, start My Computer, then use the **Tools, Folder Options** command, click the View tab and finally click the **Show hidden files and folders** option.

To add a destination to the **Send To** menu do the following:

- Click the Documents and Settings folder on the drive where Windows XP is installed.
- Double-click the folder of a specific user.
- Double-click the SendTo folder.

- Use the **File, New, Shortcut** command.

- Follow the instructions on your screen.

It is useful to be able to send text files straight to the Notepad so that you can see, and maybe edit, their contents. To add Notepad to the **Send To** menu, you don't have to go through the above procedure because you already have a shortcut to it on your desktop. Instead, copy this shortcut icon from your desktop to the **SendTo** window, as shown in Fig. 4.18.

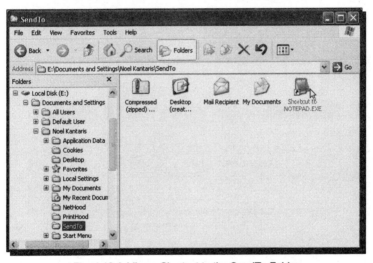

Fig. 4.18 Adding a Shortcut to the SendTo Folder.

When you next open the Send To menu it should have the extra item as shown here in Fig. 4.19. As you can see, we have renamed the shortcut to simply 'Notepad'. We did this by using My Computer, opening the SendTo folder right-clicking the file and selecting the **Rename** command from the shortcut menu.

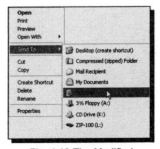

Fig. 4.19 The Modified
Send To Menu.

Deleting Folders and Files

The operations described here must only be carried out on the folders or files held in the Test Folder (or Practice Folder if you have renamed it), unless you really want to delete specific items. To experiment, copy all the files in the Messenger folder into the Test Folder first (see page 55).

- To delete or remove files, first highlight them, and then either press the <Del> key on the keyboard, or press the **Delete** button on the toolbar, shown here, or use the **File**, **Delete** command from the window menu bar.

Either method opens the confirmation box shown in Fig. 4.20 which gives you the chance to abort the operation by selecting **No**.

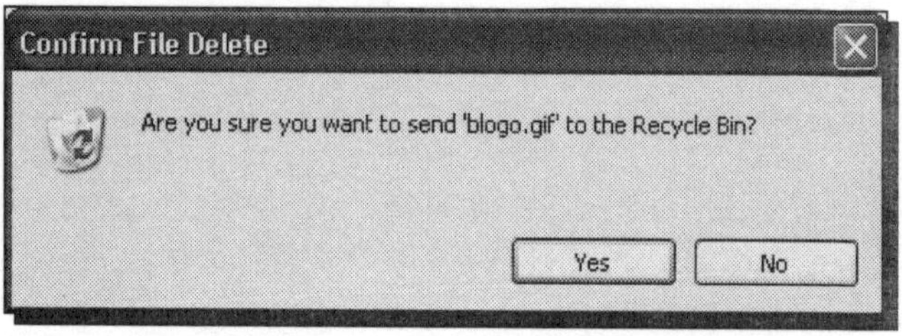

Fig. 4.20 The Delete File Warning Dialogue Box.

To delete folders, follow the same procedure as for files. A similar dialogue box to the one in Fig 4.20 will be displayed. The only difference is that the word 'File' is replaced by the word 'Folder'. To carry on with the deletion in either case, select **Yes**.

Now is the time to first delete two files from our Test Folder (any files will do), then delete the folder itself. Do carry out this suggestion as we need to demonstrate what happens to deleted items when we discuss the Recycle Bin.

Handling Folders from the Tasks Pane

Up to now in this chapter we have used only one of the two ways of manipulating folders and files; the treelike structure in My Computer. Windows XP has a second method of dealing with these topics by using the Tasks panel. To see this facility, use the **Start**, **My Documents** command to display the screen shown in Fig. 4.21.

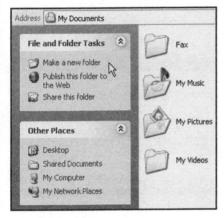

Fig. 4.21 The My Documents Folder.

Note that when no folder is selected, Windows displays the **Make a New Folder** option in the Tasks panel, as shown in Fig. 4.21. The same options are displayed in the Tasks panel when you are using My Computer to examine a specific disc drive, or a specific folder in that drive.

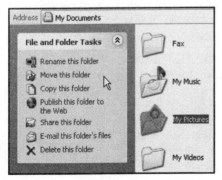

Fig. 4.22 The My Documents Folder.

If you now click a folder to select it, the contents of the Tasks panel change to give you access to the other files and folder commands, as shown in Fig. 4.22. We suggest you create a new folder in the My Documents folder, then copy a few files from your Pictures folder into it so that you can get some practice.

Which method you choose when manipulating your folders and files is a matter of personal preference. Try them both.

The Recycle Bin

As you can see from the message boxes on the previous page, by default all files or folders deleted from a hard disc, are actually placed in a holding folder named the Recycle Bin.

If you open the Recycle Bin, by double-clicking its **Desktop** icon, shown here, you will see that it is just a special folder. It lists all the files, folders, icons and shortcuts that have been deleted from fixed drives since it was last emptied, as shown in Fig. 4.23.

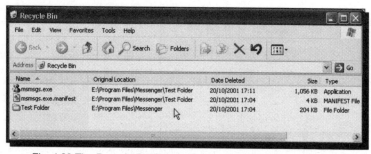

Fig. 4.23 The Recycle Bin Folder Showing Deleted Files and Folder.

Note that Windows keeps a record of the original locations of the deleted files, so that it can restore them if necessary. To see the display as it appears in fig. 4.21, use the **View** command and select the **Details** option.

To restore or delete specific files or folders from the Recycle Bin, first select them then use the **File** menu command to open  the drop-down sub-menu shown in Fig. 4.24. Choosing **Restore** will restore a selected file within the folder it was originally in, even if you have deleted that folder; check it out for yourself by restoring one of the files you deleted earlier from the Test Folder. Choosing **Delete**, removes the selected items from the Recycle Bin. To save disc space, every now and then, open the Recycle Bin and delete unwanted files or folders.

Fig. 4.24 The File Sub-menu.

Formatting Discs

We assume, here, that your hard disc has already been formatted according to your manufacturer's instructions when setting up your system. New floppy discs, if not already pre-formatted, must be formatted before they can be used by your computer's operating system. A floppy disc that has been formatted in one type of computer, can only be used in another computer if they are compatible and use the same operating system.

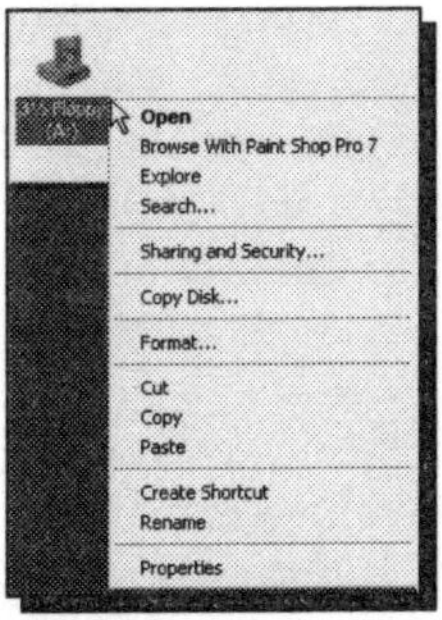

To format a floppy disc, put it into the correct disc drive, open My Computer right-click on the icon for the drive. In our case, this would be the (A:) drive, as shown in Fig. 4.25. From the displayed drop-down menu, select the **Format** option, which opens the dialogue box shown in Fig. 4.26. It only remains now to choose options in this box and press **Start** to carry out the formatting.

Fig. 4.25 The A: Drive Shortcut Menu.

If you want to name your disc, so that the system will recognise it by that name (in the My Computer windows, for example), enter the name in the **Volume label** text box. Choosing **Quick Format** in the **Format options** section, deletes the File Allocation Table of a previously formatted disc - you cannot use this option on a new disc.

Formatting will destroy any files on the disc, so take care. If you have not created an MS-DOS start-up disc for your system already, you can do so now from this dialogue box.

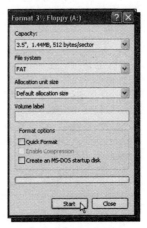

Fig. 4.26 The Format Dialogue Box.

Copying Discs

Copying whole floppy discs is quite straightforward with Windows XP. It is best carried out from the menu opened when you right-click the disc drive icon from within My Computer. Put the disc to copy into the drive and select **Copy Disk** from the menu.

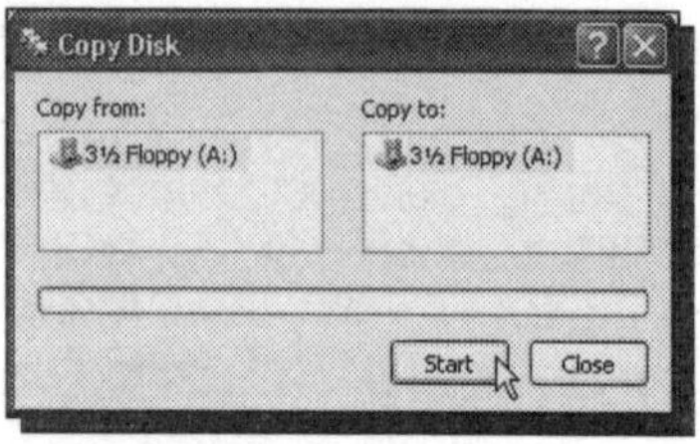

Fig. 4.27 The Copy Disk Dialogue Box.

A box, similar to that shown in Fig. 4.27, will open with your floppy disc drives listed. In our case, only one drive type shows on each side. If you have more, select the drive to **Copy from** and that to **Copy to**, but the discs must be of the same type. You can't carry out this operation between different capacity discs. When ready, click the **Start** button. You will be told when to insert the destination disc, but be warned, any files already on this disc will be lost.

Other Features in My Computer

It is perhaps worth looking at some other features in My Computer which greatly enhance its functionality. These are to be found mainly in the **View, Explorer Bar** menu options, as shown in Fig. 4.28, and include:

Fig. 4.28 The Explorer Bar Options.

- **Search** - click this to display the **Search** facility in the left pane of My Computer window which is identical in functionality to the **Start, Search** command.

- *Favorites* - click this to display a list of favourite links in the left pane of My Computer window. It allows you to add and organise useful URL addresses, or access various pre-set media addresses on the Internet.

- *Media* - click this to be connected to the Internet (provided you have this facility) and display the Web site WindowsMedia.com in the left pane of My Computer, as shown in Fig. 4.29. In this window click the Media Options down arrow at the bottom of the screen to select which media you want to connect to. For example, selecting **Radio Guide** displays a full screen in the right pane of My Computer window, as shown in Fig. 4.30. If you are not connected to the Internet, you can work off-line with files in My Music or My

Fig. 4.29 The Media Window.

Videos folder. More about this when we discuss the Media Player latter on.

Fig. 4.30 The WindowsMedia.com Web Site.

- Selecting one of the radio stations, connects you to it and opens up a separate Internet Explorer window to display a visual accompaniment to the music. For example, selecting Classic FM displays the screen shown in Fig. 4.31.

Fig. 4.31 An Internet Explorer Screen of Classic FM.

- ***History*** - Click this to display the **History** facility in the left pane of My Computer window. It allows you to see which 'pages' (includes files and folders on your system, other computers connected to your system or sites on the Internet) were visited recently, as shown in Fig. 4.32.

Fig. 4.32 The History Pane.

- ***Folders*** -   Click this to display a hierarchical 'system tree' on the left panel of My Computer window showing all the resources of your computer, as well as those of a network you might be connected to. In your case, the display in Fig. 4.33 will obviously have different contents from ours, as your system is bound to be structured differently.

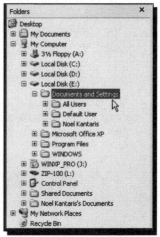

Fig. 4.33 The System Tree.

The system tree lists Objects which are marked with a plus sign (+), and contain sub-folders. Clicking a (+) sign, opens it up to reveal the sub-folders beneath. When sub-folders are displayed, the (+) sign changes to a minus sign (–), indicating that the parent folder can be collapsed. This is shown in the example above, where the Documents and Settings folder in the E: drive is expanded.

The right-hand, or contents, pane is automatically displayed when you select a folder from the tree. As with most Windows XP system windows, you can change the format of the information shown in the contents pane by using the **View** commands from the menu bar, or clicking the Views button on the toolbar. All the powerful right-click and properties features described previously are supported in My Computer.

Using the Picture and Fax Viewer

New to Windows XP is the Picture and Fax Viewer. You can use it to view, rotate, and perform basic tasks with image documents, including fax documents, without opening an image editing program. Images can be viewed as thumbnails or in a filmstrip and fax documents can be annotated.

In Fig. 4.34 below, we demonstrate some of these features by displaying our Pictures folder in My Computer as thumbnails. The other available viewing facilities are seen in the **View** menu which is also open.

Fig. 4.34 A Pictures Folder Displayed in Thumbnail View.

Icons can be arranged by name, size, type, etc., from the **View** menu, or can be previewed, rotated, set as desktop background, or opened in a variety of imaging programs, from a shortcut (right-click) menu, as shown in Fig. 4.35.

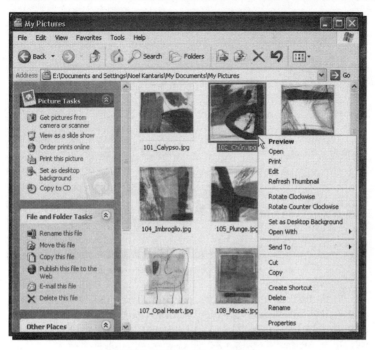

Fig. 4.35 A Picture's Shortcut Menu.

You can also use the Pictures Tasks menu to view pictures as a slide show, copy selected pictures to a CD, or get pictures from a scanner (to be discussed later) or digital camera and save them in a folder on you computer's hard disc.

To see your pictures in another interesting display, use the **View**, **Filmstrip** command. To get the full benefit of this view, you need to increase the size of the displayed window to at least ¾ of the size of your screen. The result should look similar to that in Fig. 4.36 on the next page.

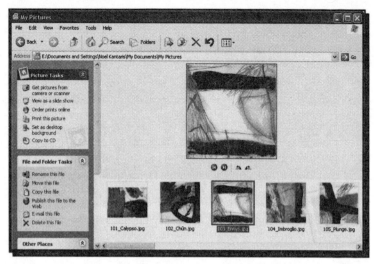

Fig. 4.36 Pictures Displayed in Filmstrip View.

As each picture is selected, an enlarged view of it displays above the filmstrip. The four buttons below the enlarged view can be used to navigate to the previous or the next image, and to rotate the selected picture clockwise or anticlockwise.

Compressing Folders and Files

Compressing folders and files allows you to greatly increase the storage capacity of your discs with no extra hardware cost. To activate the option, select the drive or folder in which you want to create a compressed folder, then use the **File, New** menu command, and select the **Compressed (zipped) Folder** option from the drop-down menu shown in Fig. 4.37.

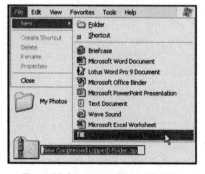

Fig. 4.37 Creating a Zipped Folder.

In the screen dump of Fig. 4.37 we show both the action required to create a compressed folder and the result of that action. The created folder has the extension **.zip** and you must retain this when renaming it. We called our folder **Books.zip**.

We then opened a second copy of My Computer and located the word processor file of the current chapter of this book with all its screen dumps and dragged it into the newly renamed folder, as shown in Fig. 4.38.

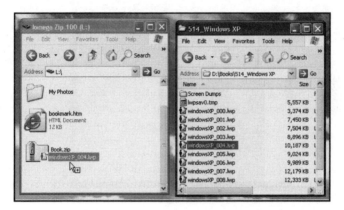

Fig. 4.38 Dragging a File into a Compressed Folder.

Releasing the mouse button displayed momentarily the box in Fig. 4.39.

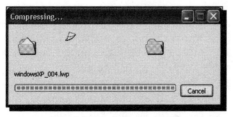

Fig. 4.39 Compressing a File.

You can send other files and folders into the compressed folder by dragging them onto it. Selected files are then compressed one at time before they are moved into the folder, while the contents of the dragged folders are also compressed.

To find out the size of the file before and after compression, double-click the compressed folder, right-click the file and select **Properties** from the drop-down menu to display the box in Fig. 4.40.

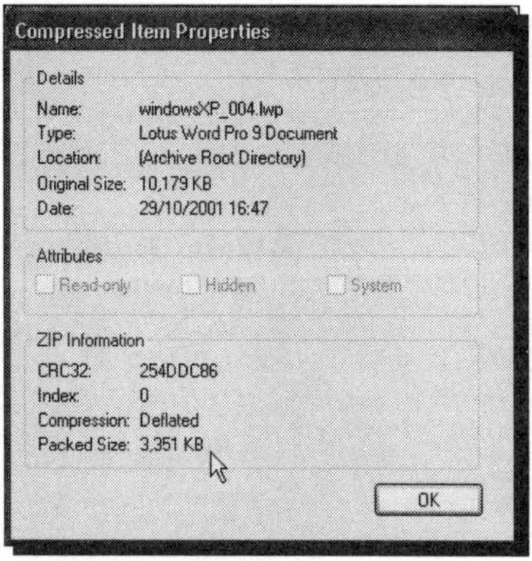

Fig. 4.40 Compressed File Properties.

Note that the original file size is displayed as 10.18 MB, while its packed size as 3.35 MB. This is quite a large compression ratio and worth while exploiting.

You can open files and programs in a compressed folder by double-clicking them. If a program requires **.dll** or data files to run, then those files must first be extracted. To extract a file or folder from a compressed folder, simply drag it to its new location. To extract all files and folders within a compressed folder, right-click the folder and select **Extract All**. In the Extract Wizard you can specify where you want these files and folders to be extracted to. When you extract a file or folder it leaves a copy of it in the compressed folder. To remove files and folders from a compressed folder you must delete them.

5

Controlling Information

When you are using Windows XP or one of its applications, you will invariably come across a **Readme.txt** file which contains last minute information not available in printed form in the User Guides. Vendors create such text files which can be read by either the WordPad or the Notepad accessories. What follows will show you how to read such files, print them, or copy them onto the Clipboard, so that you can transfer the information into another package.

Microsoft's WordPad

WordPad supports mainly text document formats, plus Word (.doc) documents, but has no pagination features. It is a useful accessory for writing and reading simple documents or memos.

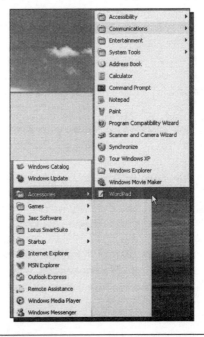

To access WordPad, click the **Start** button and select **All Programs**, **Accessories**, and click the **WordPad** icon, shown here, on the cascade menu as shown in Fig. 5.1 to the right.

Fig. 5.1 Accessing the Text Editor WordPad.

The WordPad Window

Opening the WordPad accessory, displays an application window similar to the one in Fig. 5.2 below.

The top line of the WordPad window is the 'Title' bar which contains the name of the document, and if this bar is dragged with the mouse the window can be moved around the screen. Also, just like any other window, its size can be changed by dragging any of its four sides in the required direction.

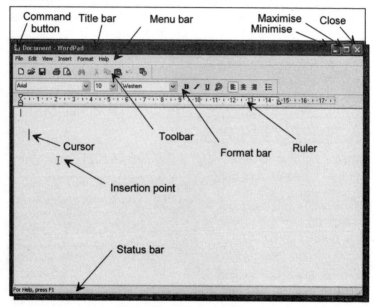

Fig. 5.2 The WordPad Window.

The second line of the window displays the 'Menu' bar which allows access to the following sub menus:

File   Edit   View   Insert   Format   Help

As described in Chapter 2 - 'Starting Windows XP' - the sub-menus are accessed either with your mouse, or by pressing the <Alt> key which underlines one letter per menu option.

The Toolbar

As with most Windows applications, the Toolbar contains a set of icon buttons that you click to carry out some of the more common menu functions. The actions of each icon are outlined below.

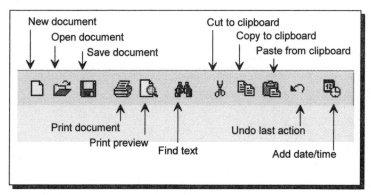

Fig. 5.3 The WordPad Toolbar.

The Format Bar

WordPad has an extra bar of icons that are used to more easily control the format of text in a document.

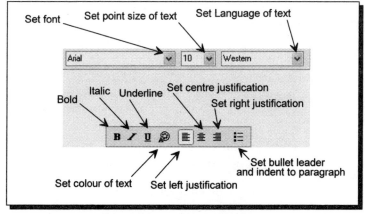

Fig. 5.4 The WordPad Format Bar.

Opening a WordPad Document

In order to illustrate this section, either type in a short letter, or if you have the Windows XP CD, place it in the CD Drive and left-click the Open button on WordPad's Toolbar, shown here, which displays the following dialogue box.

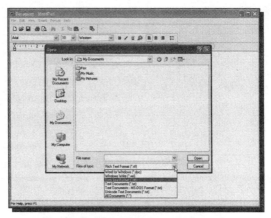

Fig. 5.5 The WordPad Open Dialogue Box.

You can use this Open box to open documents that might have been created by different applications, as shown on the drop-down list against **Files of type**, or documents that are kept in different locations. For example, you can open a document which might be on your computer's hard disc, or on a network drive that you have a connection to. To locate other drives, simply click the Up One Level button pointed to in Fig. 5.6.

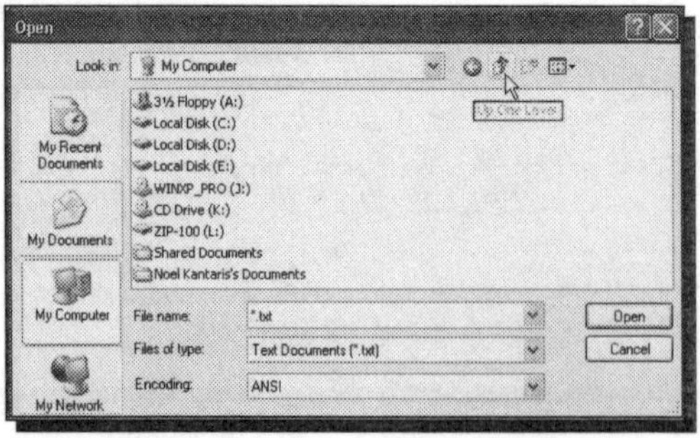

Fig. 5.6 Moving Up One Level in the Open List.

Having selected a drive, you can then select the folder within which your document was saved, select its filename and click the **Open** button on the dialogue box. For our example, first choose the CD-ROM drive (if not already selected), then the DOCs folder, then choose 'All Documents' (*.*) in the **Files of type** box to reveal the **READ1ST.TXT** file, as shown below.

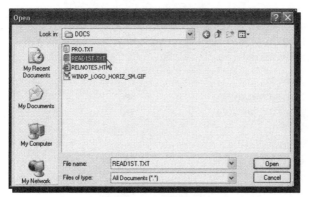

Fig. 5.7 Selecting the READ1ST.TXT File.

Select this file and click the **Open** button to display:

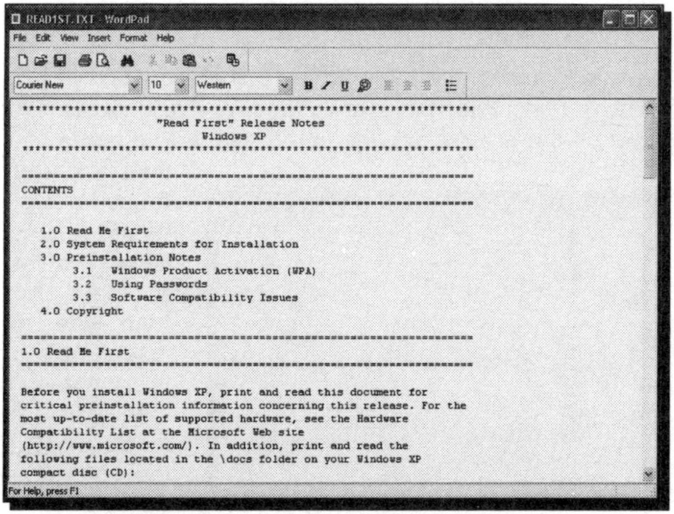

Fig. 5.8 The READ1ST Text File Opened in WordPad.

WordPad can read (and write) six types of file formats; Word for Windows (.doc) files, Windows Write (.wri) files, Rich Text Format (.rtf) files, Text Document (.txt - both ANSI and ASCII formats), Text Document - MS-DOS Format (.txt) files, and Unicode Text Document (.txt) files.

Moving Around a WordPad Document

You can move the cursor around a document with the mouse, the normal direction keys, and with key combinations, the most useful of which are listed below.

To move	*Press*
Left one character	⇐
Right one character	⇒
Up one line	⇑
Down one line	⇓
To beginning of line	Home
To end of line	End
Up one window	Page Up
Down one window	Page Down
To beginning of file	Ctrl+Home
To end of file	Ctrl+End

Saving to a File

To save a document, click the Save Toolbar icon, shown here, or use the **File, Save** command. A dialogue box appears on the screen with the cursor in the **File name** field box waiting for you to type a name. You can select a drive or a folder, other than the one displayed, by clicking the 'Up One Level' icon on the Toolbar - the one we are pointing to.

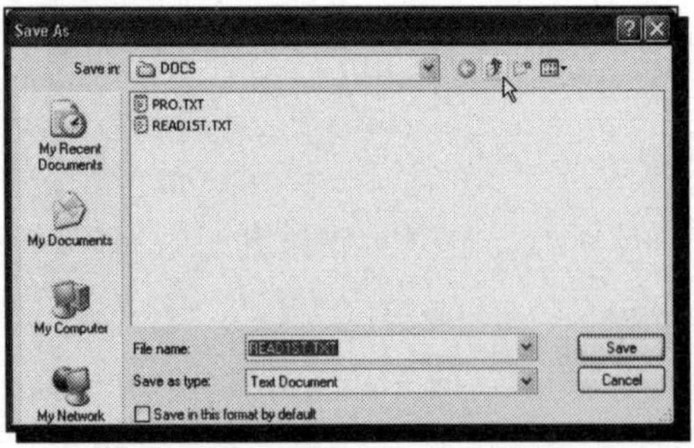

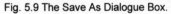

Fig. 5.9 The Save As Dialogue Box.

There are five formatting choices in the **Save as type** box when you first save a WordPad document:

(i) Word for Windows (.doc) which can then be read by Microsoft Word, (ii) Rich Text Format (.rtf) which retains most of its text enhancements and can be imported into many other applications, (iii) Text Document which is a Windows ANSI file to be used if your document is a program or you intend to transmit it to someone, (iv) Text - MS-DOS format which is an unformatted ASCII file, and (v) Unicode Text Format which is another type of text file.

To save your document in the future with a different name use the **File**, **Save As** menu command.

Document Editing

For small deletions, such as letters or words, the easiest way is to use the <Delete> or <BkSp> keys. With the <Delete> key, position the cursor on the first letter you want to remove and press <Delete>; the letter is deleted and the following text moves one space to the left. With the <BkSp> key, position the cursor immediately to the right of the character to be deleted and press <BkSp>; the cursor moves one space to the left pulling the rest of the line with it and overwriting the character to be deleted. Note that the difference between the two is that with <Delete> the cursor does not move at all.

Text editing is usually carried out in the insert mode. Any characters typed will be inserted at the cursor location and the following text will be pushed to the right, and down. Pressing the <Insert> key will change to Overstrike mode, which causes entered text to overwrite any existing text at the cursor.

When larger scale editing is needed, use the **Cut**, **Copy** and **Paste** operations; the text to be altered must be 'selected' before these operations can be carried out. These functions are then available when the **Edit** sub-menu is activated, or Toolbar icons are used.

Selecting Text

The procedure in WordPad, as in all Windows applications, is that before any operation such as formatting or editing can be carried out on text, you first select the text to be altered. Selected text is highlighted on the screen. This can be carried out in several ways:

a. **Using the keyboard**; position the cursor on the first character to be selected, hold down the <Shift> key while using the direction keys to highlight the required text, then release the <Shift> key. Navigational key combinations can also be used with the <Shift> key to highlight blocks of text.

b. **With the mouse**; click the left mouse button at the beginning of the block and drag the cursor across the block so that the desired text is highlighted, then release the mouse button. To select a word, double-click in the word, to select a larger block, place the cursor at the beginning of the block, and with the <Shift> key depressed, move the mouse pointer to the end of the desired block, and click the left mouse button.

Using the 'selection area' and a mouse; place the mouse pointer in the left margin area of the WordPad window where it changes to a right slanting arrow, and click the left mouse button once to select the current line, twice to select the current paragraph, or three times to select the whole document.

Try out all these methods and find out the one you are most comfortable with.

Copying Blocks of Text

Once text has been selected it can be copied to another location in your present document, to another WordPad document, or to another Windows application. As with most of the editing and formatting operations there are many ways of doing this.

The first is by using the **Edit, Copy** command sequence from the menu, or clicking the Copy Toolbar icon, moving the cursor to the start of where you want the copied text, and using the **Edit, Paste** command, or clicking the Paste icon. Another method uses the quick key combinations, <Ctrl+C> to copy and <Ctrl+V> to paste.

To copy the same text again to another location in the document, move the cursor to the new location and paste it there with either of the above methods.

Drag and Drop - Maybe the easiest way to copy selected text, or an object such as a graphic, is to drag it with the left mouse button and the <Ctrl> key both depressed and to release the mouse button when the vertical line that follows the pointer is at the required destination.

As you get used to Windows application packages you will be able to decide which of these methods is best for you.

Moving Blocks of Text

Selected text can also be moved, in which case it is deleted in its original location. Use the **Edit**, **Cut**, command, or the <Ctrl+X> keyboard shortcut, or click the Cut icon, move the cursor to the required new location and then use the **Edit**, **Paste** command, <Ctrl+V>, or click the Paste icon. The moved text will be placed at the cursor location and will force any existing text to make room for it. This operation can be cancelled by simply pressing <Esc>.

Drag and Drop - Selected text, or an object such as a graphic, can be moved by dragging it with the left mouse button depressed and releasing the button when the vertical line that follows the mouse pointer is at the required destination.

Deleting Blocks of Text

When text is deleted it is removed from the document. With WordPad any selected text can be deleted with the **Edit**, **Cut** command, or by simply pressing the <Delete> key. However, using **Edit**, **Cut** (or <Ctrl+X>) places the text on the Windows clipboard and allows you to use the **Edit**, **Paste** (or <Ctrl+V>) command, while using the <Delete> key does not.

The Undo Command

As text is lost with the delete command you should use it with

caution, but if you do make a mistake all is not lost as long as you act immediately. The **Edit**, **Undo** command (or <Ctrl+Z>), or clicking the Undo Toolbar button, reverses your most recent action, so you need

to use it before carrying out any further operations.

Finding and Changing Text

WordPad allows you to search for specified text, or character combinations. In the 'Find' mode it will highlight each occurrence in turn so that you can carry out some action on it. In the 'Replace' mode you specify what replacement is to be carried out.

For example, in a long memo you may decide to replace every occurrence of the word 'program' with the word 'programme'. To do this, first go to the beginning of the document, as searches operate in a forward direction, then choose the **Edit**, **Replace** menu command to open a dialogue box, like the one shown in Fig. 5.10.

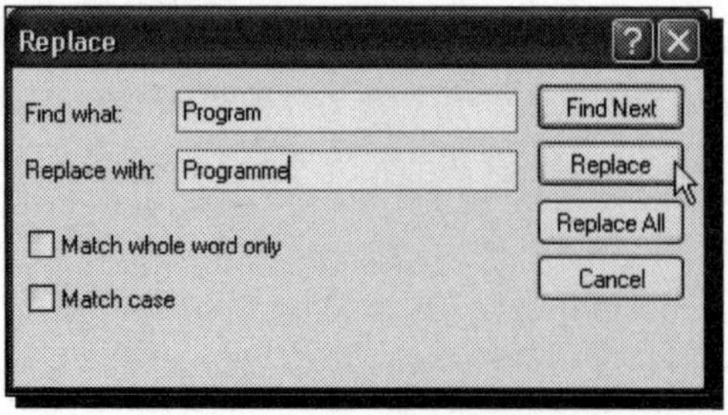

Fig. 5.10 The Replace Dialogue Box.

You type what you want to search for in the **Find what** box. You can then specify whether you want to **Match whole word only**, and whether to **Match case**, (upper or lower case) by check-marking the appropriate boxes. Type the replacement word in the **Replace with** box, and then make a selection from one of the four buttons provided. Selecting **Replace** requires you to manually confirm each replacement, whilst selecting **Replace All** will replace all occurrences of the word automatically.

Formatting your Work

When working with text files you cannot format your documents, but in Microsoft Word, or RTF modes, you can. Such formatting can involve the appearance of individual characters or words, and the indentation, addition of bullet leaders and the alignment of paragraphs. These functions are carried out in WordPad from the **Format** menu options or from the Format bar. To activate the latter, use the **View** command and click the **Format Bar** option, as shown in Fig. 5.11.

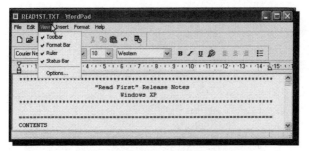

Fig. 5.11 Activating the Formatting Bar.

As an example of some of the formatting options, we have carried out a few changes to the **READ1ST.TXT** document opened earlier. First, we used the **Save As** command to save the document as an RTF type file on our hard drive, say within a Docs folder we created on our drive containing Windows XP, so that we could carry out certain formatting commands (such as justification) which are not available to a TXT type file.

We then removed the dotted line above and below the title and all spaces before each of the two title lines. Then we highlighted the two title lines, and changed their point size to 16, then emboldened them and centre justified them by clicking appropriate format bar options.

The date was then added below the title by clicking the Date/Time icon on the Toolbar and choosing the date

format required. The two paragraphs with preceding asterisks under section 1.0 were then selected and the Bullet icon clicked on the Format bar. This indented the paragraphs and gave them bullet leaders.

Finally, the whole document was selected and its font changed from Courier New to Arial by choosing the font type from the drop-down list shown In Fig. 5.12. To get the formatted document shown in Fig. 5.13, we found

Fig. 5.12 The Font List.

it necessary to remove hard returns at the end of each line so word wrap could display correctly.

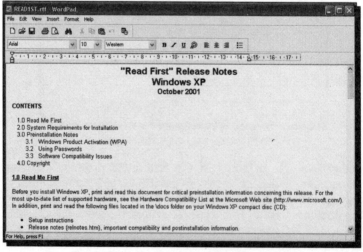

Fig. 5.13 The Display of a Formatted Document.

The Ruler

The ruler is activated/deactivated by using the **View**, **Ruler** command. The Ruler displays at the top of the text area of the WordPad window (see Fig. 5.13), and lets you set and see Tab points for your text, or visually change the left and right margins, (the empty space to the left and right of the text area) of your document.

Setting your own tabs is easy by clicking within the ruler where you want to set the tab. Tabs can be moved within the ruler by dragging them with the mouse to a new position, or removed by simply dragging them off the ruler. Default tab settings do not show on the ruler, but custom tabs do.

Printing Documents

As long as your printer has been properly installed and configured (see Chapter 6), you should have no problems printing your document from the WordPad application.

Setting up your Page

Before attempting to print, make sure that WordPad is set to the same page size as the paper you plan to use. To do this, use the **File**, **Page Setup** menu command to open the dialogue box shown in Fig. 5.14. From here you can control the paper **Size** and **Source**, the size of all the **Margins** around the edge of the sheet, and the **Orientation** of the paper. The **Printer** button lets you select between different printers, including network printers (if you are connected to any), and set their properties.

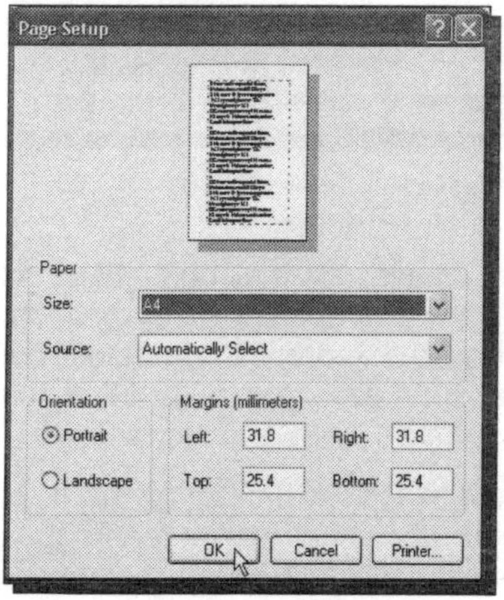

Fig. 5.14 The Page Setup Screen.

Print Preview

Before actually committing yourself and printing your document to paper, it is always best to look at a Preview on the screen. This can save both your paper and printer toner or cartridge bills.

To preview the current document and settings, either click the Print Preview icon on the Toolbar, or use the **File, Print Preview** menu command to display the following screen.

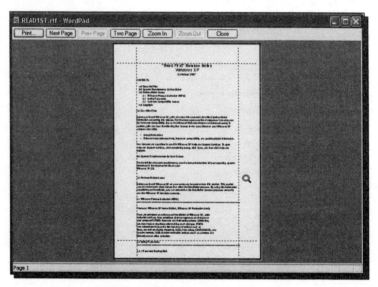

Fig. 5.15 The Print Preview Screen.

The preview screen, shown above, is the only place in WordPad that you can actually see your document's pagination, and then you have no control over it! A dreadful omission, but perhaps intentional, to make sure everyone buys Microsoft Word instead!

To zoom in on the document, just click the pointer on it, or use the **Zoom In** button. If your document has several pages you can select a **Two Page** view of it. When you are happy your document is perfect, press the **Print** button.

Using the Clipboard

In Windows XP (just as in Windows 2000, but unlike Windows 98/Me), you do not have direct access to the Clipboard, which is a temporary storage location for information you want to cut or copy, but you can nevertheless use it.

We have already used the Clipboard when using the **Cut** and **Paste** features found in WordPad, and in most other Windows programs. Apart from cutting, copying and pasting operations in Windows applications, you can also use the Clipboard to copy the contents of an application's window, or to copy Windows graphics images, so that you can transfer such information to other applications. There are two ways of copying information:

- Press the <Print Screen> key to copy onto the Clipboard the contents of a whole Windows screen, even if that screen is a DOS application.

- Press the <Alt+Print Screen> key combination to copy onto the Clipboard the contents of the current open window, or dialogue box.

To illustrate these techniques follow the step-by-step instructions given below.

To Copy a Full Windows Screen:

- Close all running applications and start My Computer.

- Move the My Computer displayed window next to the Recycle Bin but without obscuring its icon on the desktop.

- Press the <Print Screen> key, then activate WordPad and click the New icon on the Toolbar to open a blank page and finally click the Paste Toolbar icon. What now appears on the WordPad screen, or something like it, is shown in Fig. 5.16 on the next page.

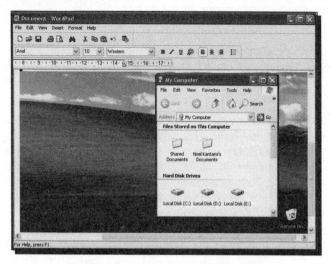

Fig. 5.16 The Contents of the Clipboard.

To Copy the Contents of a Current Open Window:

- Close all running applications and start My Computer.

- Press the <Alt+Print Screen> key, then activate WordPad and click the New icon on the Toolbar to open a blank page, then click the Paste Toolbar icon. What is displayed now is the current window only.

To copy a DOS screen:

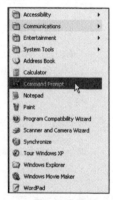

- Close all running applications, click the **Start** button and select **All Programs**, **Accessories** and click the Command Prompt option on the cascade menu shown in Fig. 5.17.

- Start your DOS application, then continue as above.

DOS applications can run in a window or in full screen. You can switch from one to the other by pressing <Alt+Enter>.

Fig. 5.17 The Accessories Menu.

The Windows Paint Program

Paint is a 32-bit Windows application, first introduced with
Windows 95 and improved in subsequent versions of
Windows. You can use Paint to create, view and edit,
simple or complicated graphics.

Paint is an OLE (Object Linking and Embedding) program, and
allows the creation of OLE object information that can be
embedded or linked into other documents, as we shall see at
the end of the chapter. It can read and write a number of file
formats, namely, bitmap (.bmp) files (monochrome, and 16,
256 & 24-bit colour), File Interchange Format (.jpg & .jpeg)
files, and Graphics Interchange Format (.gif) files.

Starting Paint

To start Paint, click the **Start** button and select **All Programs**,
Accessories from the cascade menu, then click the **Paint**
entry. In Fig. 5.18, we show the **Water lilies.jpg** file to be found
in My Pictures folder which itself is in My Documents folder.

Fig. 5.18 The Paint Opening Window.

The window is divided into a 'drawing' area (the default size of which depends on your video display), surrounded by the Menu bar at the top, the Palette at the bottom, the Options area at the middle-left side, with the Toolbox above it.

The Paint Toolbox

The drawing area is where you create your drawings with the help of various tools from the Toolbox. Note that the pencil tool is always selected when you start Paint, and that the function of a Toolbox icon is flagged when you move the mouse pointer over it.

To select a tool, simply point to it and click. Several of them have extra functions you can also select in the Options area. Some tools can work with either of the current foreground or background colours - dragging the tool with the left mouse button uses the foreground colour and with the right one the background colour.

More detail of the Toolbox functions is listed below.

Tool	*Function*
Free Form select	Used to cut out an irregular-shaped area of a picture, with either an opaque or transparent background, which can then be dragged to another part of the drawing, or manipulated using the **Edit** menu commands.
Rectangle select	Used to cut out a rectangular-shaped area of a picture, with either an opaque or transparent background, which can then be dragged to another part of the drawing, or manipulated using the **Edit** menu commands.

Eraser

Used to change the selected foreground colours under the eraser icon to a background colour, or automatically change every occurrence of one colour in the drawing area to another.

Colour fill

Used to fill in any closed shape or area with the current foreground or background colour.

Pick colour

Used to set the foreground or background colour to that at the pointer.

Magnifier

Used to zoom the image to different magnifications. Choose from 1x, 2x, 6x or 8x magnification in the options area.

Pencil

Used to draw freehand lines in either the foreground or background colour.

Brush

Used to draw freehand lines with a selection of tools and line thickness shown in the options area.

Airbrush

Used to produce one of three available circular sprays in the foreground or background colours.

Text

Used to add text of different fonts, sizes and attributes in the current foreground colour, with either an opaque or transparent background.

Line

Used to draw straight lines between two points in the current foreground or background colours and drawing width.

Curve

Used to draw curved lines in the current colours and drawing width.

Rectangle

Used to draw hollow and filled rectangles or squares (<Shift> key depressed), in the current colours and drawing width.

Polygon

Used to draw hollow and filled triangles and other polygon shapes, in the current colours and drawing width.

Ellipse

Used to draw hollow and filled ellipses or circles (<Shift> key depressed), in the current colours and drawing width.

Rounded Rectangle

Used to draw hollow and filled rectangles or squares (<Shift> key depressed), with rounded corners, in the current colours and drawing width.

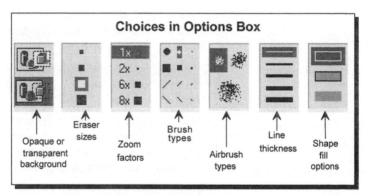

Fig. 5.19 Choices Available in the Options Area of the Toolbox.

Preparing for a Drawing

Before you start drawing, you may need to set the size of the image you want. To do this, use the **Image**, **Attributes** menu command to open the dialogue box shown in Fig. 5.20.

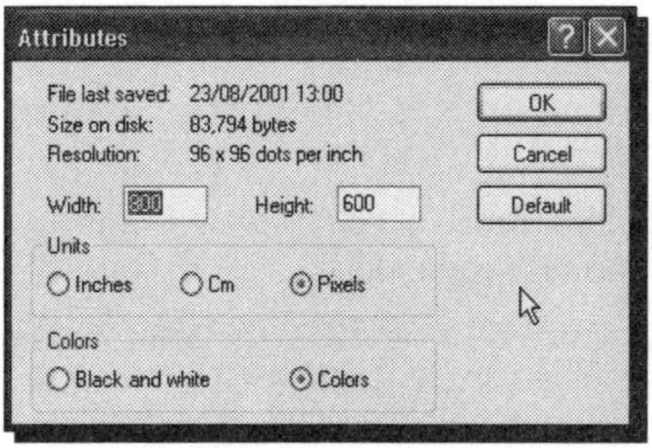

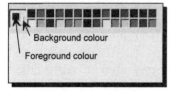

The default **Width** and **Height** settings for a new image are given in **Pixels**. If you need a specific image size when it is printed to paper, you can work in **Inches** or **Cm**. Lastly in this box, you can set whether to work in colour or in black and

Fig. 5.20 The Attributes Dialogue Box.

white. Clicking the **Default** button will make your new settings the default for any new working sessions.

Selecting Working Colours

The current background and foreground colour settings are always shown in the two squares to the left of the palette, as shown in Fig. 5.21.

To select a new background colour, point to the colour in the Palette and click the right mouse button. If you now select the **File**, **New** command, Paint will open a new document with the selected background

Fig. 5.21 The Paint Palette.

colour. Alternatively you could 'flood' the existing background by selecting the Colour fill icon and right-clicking it on the background of the drawing area.

To select a different foreground colour to be used with any of the drawing tools in the Toolbox, left-click the colour in the Palette.

Entering Text in a Drawing

If you intend to enter text within a drawing, carry out the following steps:

- Select the foreground colour for the text.

- Select the **Text** tool from the Toolbox.

- Select opaque or transparent from the options box.

- Click the pointer on the working area to open the text box, drag it to the correct size and type the text.

- Open the Fonts toolbar, if not already opened, with the **View**, **Text Toolbar** menu command.

- Select the font, point size or other style you want to use from the Fonts toolbar , as shown in Fig. 5.22.

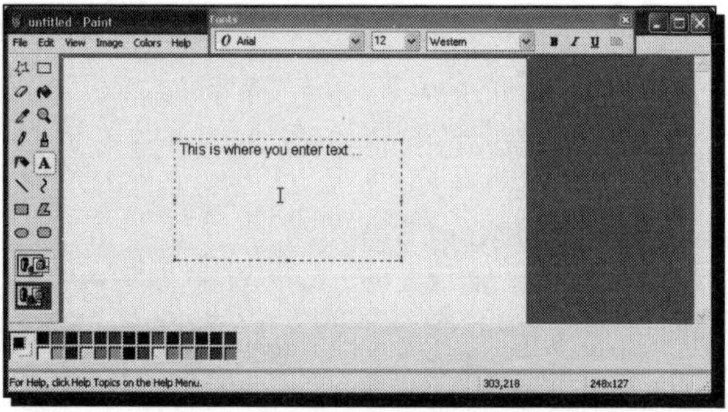

Fig. 5.22 Inserting Text in a Drawing Area.

- When you are happy with the text, click outside the text box to 'fix' it in the drawing and close the toolbar.

While the Fonts toolbar is open you can change any of its options, or use the palette, and see the entered text change straight away.

In the future, as long as the **Text Toolbar** option is ticked in the **View** menu, the Fonts toolbar will open whenever you start to enter text.

Using the Paint Tools

Most of the other tools in Paint's Toolbox are quite easy and straightforward to use. To select a tool, point to it and click the left mouse button which depresses its icon in the Toolbox. To use them, you move the pointer to a suitable position within the drawing area and drag the tool around to accomplish the required task.

With most of the Toolbox options, dragging with the left mouse button uses the active foreground colour, and with the right button the active background colour. Releasing the mouse button stops the action being performed. If you make a mistake, you can select the **Edit, Undo** command from the menu bar up to three times, to cancel the last three actions you carried out.

To complete this discussion, we need to describe how to use the 'Curve' and 'Polygon' tools, which differ slightly from the rest. For example:

To draw a curve, first click the Curve toolbar icon, choose a line thickness in the options box, left-click the pointer in the required starting position within the drawing area, then press the left mouse button to anchor the beginning of the curve and move the mouse to the required end of the eventual curve and release it. A 'flexible' line in the current foreground colour will be produced between the two points. Next, click the mouse buttons away from the line and drag it around the window, which causes the line to curve as you move the pointer. When you are happy with the produced curvature, release the mouse button.

To draw a polygon, place the Polygon pointer in the required starting point in the drawing area, left-click and drag the mouse to the required end of the first side of the polygon and release it. A line in the foreground colour is produced between the two points. Next, continue adding sides to the polygon in this way until you complete it, at which point you should double-click the mouse button.

Embedding a Graphic into WordPad

Embedding a graphic into WordPad is similar to copying, but with the important advantage that you can actually edit an embedded object from within WordPad.

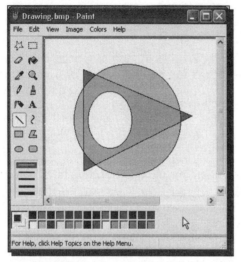

Fig. 5.23 Creating a Graphic in Paint.

To embed a Paint image, first create it in Paint (we created the object shown in Fig. 5.23 in order to illustrate the process), then save it as a bitmap file. Next, start WordPad, open the letter or memo you want to embed a graphic into (or just use an empty document), place the cursor where you want to embed it, and press the <Enter> key twice to make some room for it.

Now from the WordPad menu bar, use the **Insert, Object** command which displays the Insert Object dialogue box shown in Fig. 5.24. Click the **Create from File** radio button, **Browse** to locate your bitmap drawing, and press **OK** to place the selected graphic into the WordPad document, as shown in Fig. 5.25 on the next page.

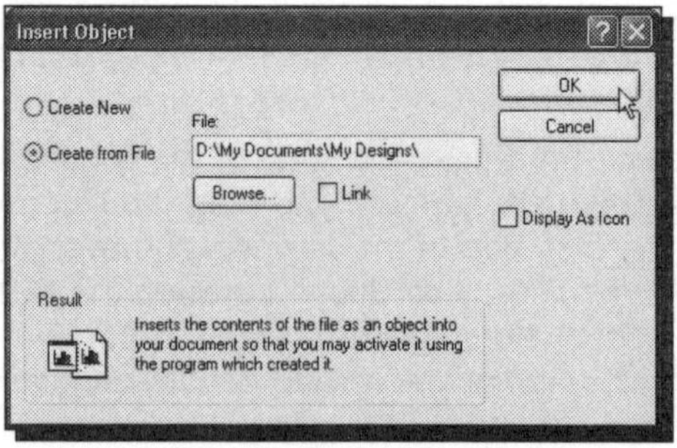

Fig. 5.24 The Insert Object Dialogue Box.

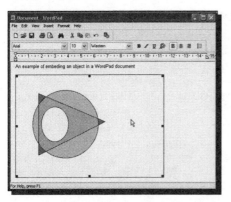

Fig. 5.25 An Embedded Graphic in WordPad.

What has happened here is that the graphic has been embedded in the WordPad document. If you double-click it, the WordPad window will change to a Paint window. You can then edit the image without leaving WordPad, and clicking outside the image will bring WordPad's features back.

The **Display As Icon** option in the Insert Object dialogue box (Fig. 5.24), embeds an icon in the destination document. Not much help in our example, but useful for embedding speech or movie clips in a document. Double-clicking the icon would then play the sound, or movie.

Linking a Graphic into WordPad

Linking, the other main OLE feature, links files dynamically so that information held in one file is automatically updated when the information in the other file changes.

To link our graphic to WordPad, select the **Link** option in the Insert Object dialogue box of Fig. 5.24, before clicking the **OK** button. When you double-click a linked image, its file is opened into a separate Paint window. Any changes made are saved in this file as well as being reflected in the document.

These are very clever features that can save a lot of time with full Windows applications. What we have covered here should be a good grounding for the future. You must try these features for yourself, the time will be well spent.

Getting Pictures from a Scanner or Camera

If your Scanner or digital Camera are Plug and Play, Windows XP will detect them (if connected to your PC) and will start the

Scanner and Camera Wizard. If your camera is not Plug and Play, or you are using a scanner, right-click the camera or scanner from which you want to get pictures, then click the appropriate option for that device. In Fig. 5.26 we show the shortcut menu for our scanner.

Fig. 5.26 The Scanner Shortcut Menu.

 Another way of starting the Scanner and Camera Installation Wizard is to click **Start**, **Control Panel**, then double-click the **Scanner and Cameras** icon.

If your scanner or camera are not Plug and Play, follow the instructions that came with that device. It is possible, however, that you might need to get the latest driver for your device which is compatible with Windows XP or Windows 2000.

Many Windows imaging applications can use a scanner or camera to import a picture directly into the application for

further image manipulation. One such application is Paint and we will use it to demonstrate how to get a picture from a scanner.

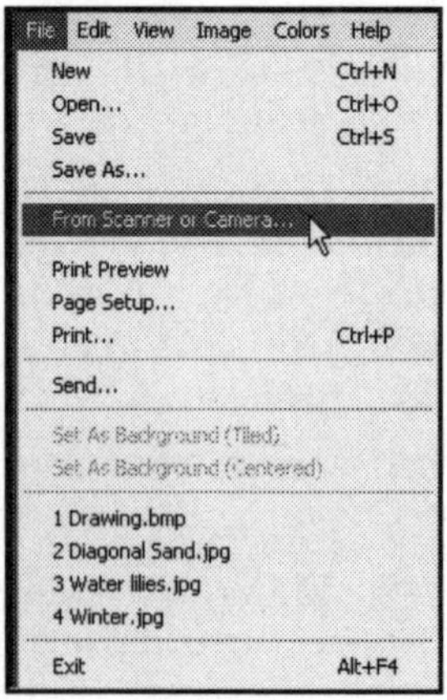

To begin the process, start Paint, place the picture you want to scan on your scanner's glass plate, then use the **File**, **From Scanner or Camera** command, as shown in Fig. 5.27. This opens the dialogue box in Fig. 5.28 shown on the next page. As you can see, in this instance we have three scanning choices; colour, grey-scale, or black and white.

Fig. 5.27 Using Paint to Scan a Picture.

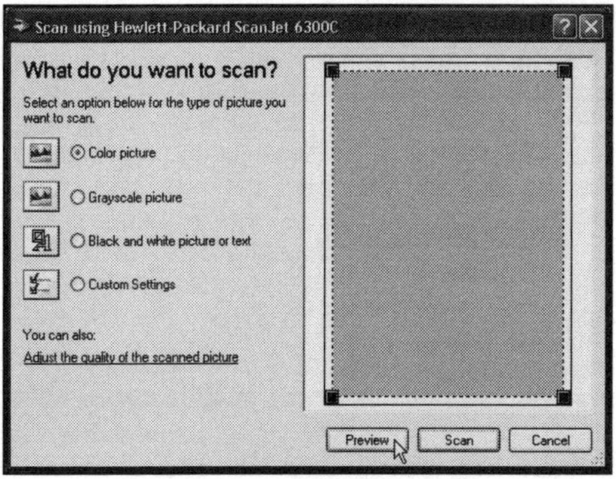

Fig. 5.28 The Scanner Dialogue Box.

Fig. 5.29 A Scanned
Picture in Paint.

Clicking the **Preview** button will activate the scanner and a preview of the object will appear on the right side of the Scanner dialogue box. Clicking the **Scan** button, starts the scanning process and the image is imported into Paint, as shown in Fig. 5.29 - it looks better in colour!

You can now use your editing skills in Paint to completely change the Picture to something you would rather have in place of the original. Good luck!

The Notepad

Notepad is a text editor which can be used to write short notes, or create and edit script files. The program, which supports different fonts and their modifications (bold, underline, italic) is usually used to read text files (with the extension **.txt** of less than 64 KB) supplied by different vendors, or to make short text notes. You read such files by double-clicking their filename - trying to read larger files than 64 KB causes WordPad to be activated instead.

To see Notepad in operation, click its entry in the **Accessories** group of **All Programs** in the **Start** menu. When Notepad is activated, use the **File, Open** command and look in the System32 folder within the WINDOWS folder of the drive it was installed on, probably (C:). Double-clicking the file **eula.txt**, displays:

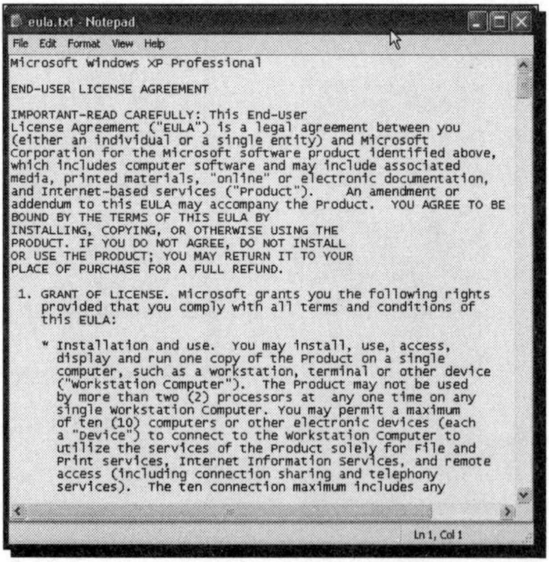

Fig. 5.26 The Task Scheduler Text File.

It is worth reading this file, particularly if you would like to know what licence rights Microsoft has granted you for the use of Windows XP.

Notepad's Edit Features

Although Notepad is not as powerful as WordPad, it has some interesting features, such as the ability to turn on word wrap which causes words that will not fit within its page margins to be placed on the next line automatically. You can turn word wrap on by selecting the **Format**, **Word Wrap** menu command. Another Notepad feature is the **Select All** option from the **Edit** menu which allows you to highlight a whole document at a stroke in order to, say, copy it onto the Clipboard.

To change the font of a selected text, use the **Format**, **Font** command to display the Font dialogue box shown in Fig. 5.27:

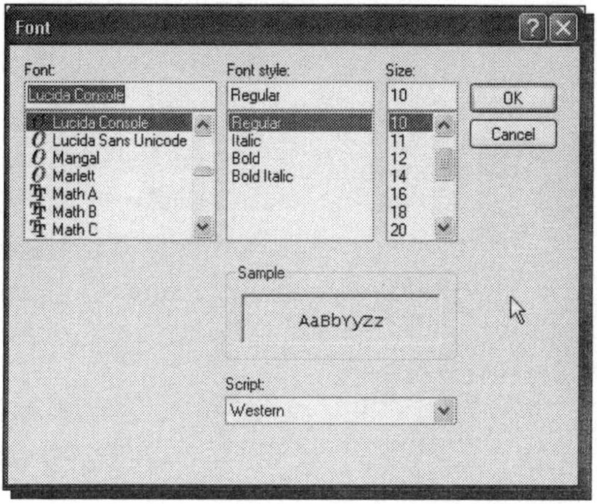

Fig. 5.27 Notepad's Font Dialogue Box.

From here you can also change the **Font style** and font **Size**. However, any changes you make here are reflected in the whole document, as well as all other documents you open using Notepad. In other words, you are configuring Notepad to the font, font style and font size you would like to use when reading or writing text files, rather than applying these changes to individual documents or parts within these documents.

Notepad supports the usual edit features which are useful when working with files, such as cut, copy, paste, and delete, all of which are options of the **Edit** menu. You can even use Notepad to search and find text, by selecting the **Edit**, **Find** command. Once the text is found, pressing the **F3** function key finds the next occurrence. You can also control the **Direction** of the search and use the **Match case** facility.

As you can see, Notepad is a simple text editor and nothing more. If you want more formatting capabilities, use WordPad, or your own word processor.

6

Controlling your System

Controlling Printers

When you upgraded to Windows XP your printers should have been installed automatically. If not, you would have been stepped through the Add Printer Wizard, described later.

Nearly 1,000 different printers are supported by Windows XP so, hopefully, you shouldn't have too much trouble getting yours to work. The printer and printing functions are included in a single Printers and Faxes folder, which you can open by clicking its entry,  shown to the left, in the Start menu. Our Printers and Faxes folder, shown in Fig. 6.1, has several printers available for use, and a list of **Printer Tasks**. Items in this list provide an easy way of adding new printers, configuring existing ones, and managing all your print jobs.

Fig. 6.1 The Printers Folder.

Windows XP, just like Windows 95/98/Me and Windows NT/2000, supports the following printer set-up methods:

- Plug and Play printers are automatically detected at installation time, or during the boot-up process. You will be prompted for the necessary driver files if they are not already in the Windows directory, these should be supplied with a new Plug-and-Play printer.

- Point and Print printing enables you to quickly connect to, and use, printers shared on some other networked PCs.

- For other situations, the Add Printer Wizard steps you through the printer installation process, whether the new printer is connected to your PC, or on a network.

Installing an additional printer (not connected to your system, but available to you, say, at work) allows you to use the additional fonts available to this printer (we will discuss fonts shortly). Below we will step through the procedure of installing such a printer to your system.

To start installation, click the **Add a Printer** entry in the **Printer Tasks** list of the Printers and Faxes window, shown in Fig. 6.1. This opens the Add Printers Wizard, which makes the installation procedure very easy indeed. As with all Wizards, you progress from screen to screen by clicking the **Next** button. In the second Wizard screen, shown in Fig. 6.2, click the **Local printer attached to this computer** option.

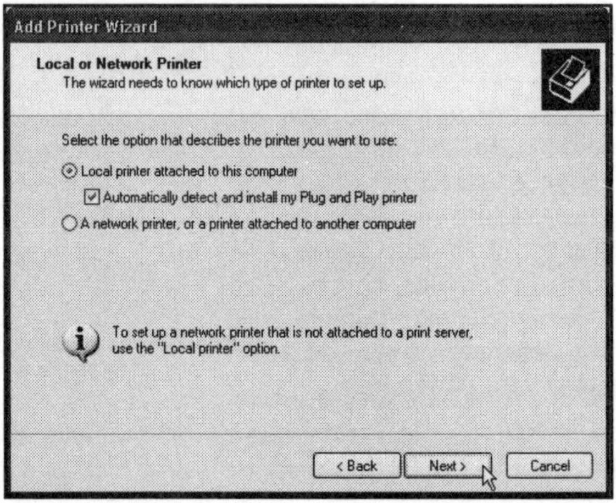

Fig. 6.2 The Second Screen of the Add Printer Wizard.

The first time you activate the Add Printer Wizard, and after pressing the **Next** button on the screen of Fig. 6.2, the Wizard scans your computer for installed plug and play printers and updates its built-in database. If it doesn't find one, it assumes that you want to install a printer manually and asks you to click **Next** to proceed.

On the next Wizard screen choose FILE: as the port you want
to use with the printer and select it from the displayed extensive
list, as shown in Fig. 6.3.

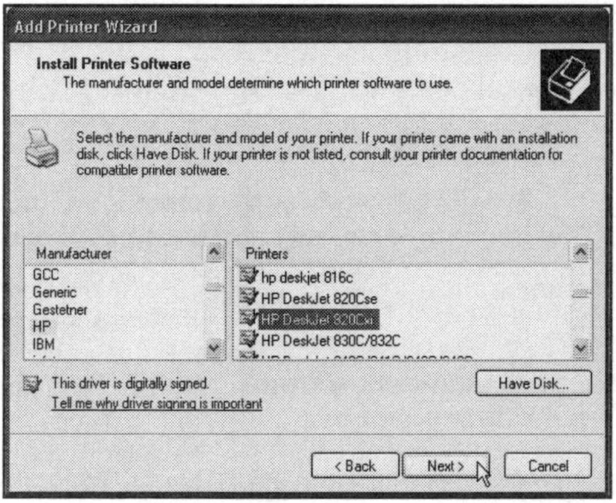

Fig. 6.3 Using the Wizard to Manually Select a Printer.

If your printer is not on the list, then either use the disc provided
by the manufacturer of your printer, or go to the Internet for an
update on the list of printers.

Documents prepared with this printer selection, can then be
printed to file on a 3½" floppy disc, and later printed out on the
selected printer (even if it is not connected to your computer
and does not itself have access to the particular application you
are using). Later you can copy that file to the selected printer
from its attached PC by issuing the simple command

```
COPY A:\Filename LPT1: /B
```

The /B switch in this command tells the printer to expect a
binary file (with embedded printer codes).

Note that the PC which is connected to the additional printer
does not even have to operate under Windows for you to print
your work, as the command is given at the Command prompt.
If the PC does operate under Windows XP, you will need to use
the **Start**, **All Programs**, **Accessories**, **Command Prompt**
command, then issue the COPY command.

Configuring your Printer

All configuration for a printer is consolidated onto a tabbed

property sheet that is accessed from its icon in the Printers and Faxes folder. Right-clicking a printer icon opens the object menu, shown in Fig. 6.4, which gives control of the printer's operation.

Fig. 6.4 The Object Menu.

As a newly installed printer is automatically set as the default printer, you might want to change this by selecting the printer connected to your PC and clicking the **Set as Default Printer** option on the object menu. If you click the **Properties** option, the window shown in Fig. 6.5 opens and lets you control all the

printer's parameters, such as the printer port (or network path), paper and graphics options, built-in fonts, and other device options specific to the printer model. All these settings are fairly self explanatory and as they depend on your printer type, we will let you work them out for yourself.

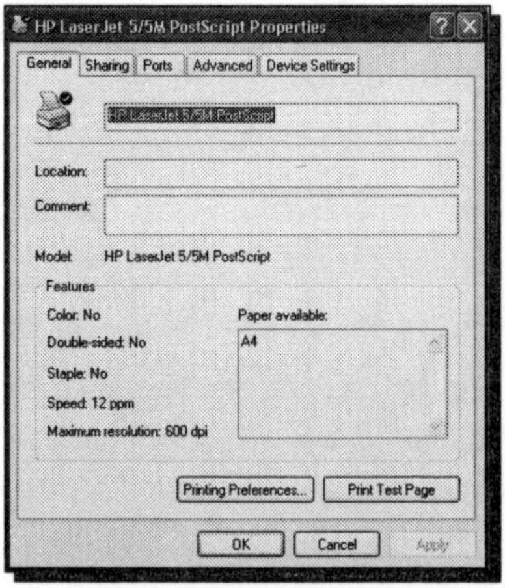

Once you have installed and configured your printers in Windows they are then available for all your application

Fig. 6.5 The Printer Properties Window.

programs to use. The correct printer is selected usually in one of the application's **File** menu options.

Managing Print Jobs

If you want to find out what exactly is happening while a document or documents are being sent to your printer, double-click the printer icon, to open its window.

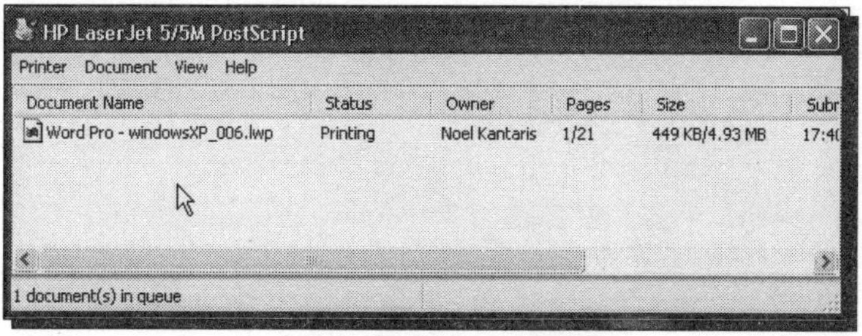

Fig. 6.6 The Print Queue Window.

As shown in Fig. 6.6, this displays detailed information about the contents of any work actually being printed, or of print jobs that are waiting in the queue. This includes the name of the document, its status and 'owner', when it was added to the print queue, the printing progress and when printing was started.

You can control the printing operation from the **Printer** and **Document** menu options of the Print Queue window, from the object menu, or from the **Printer Tasks** list. Selecting **Printer, Pause Printing** will stop the operation until you make the same selection again; it is a toggle menu option. The **Cancel All Documents** option will remove all, or selected, print jobs from the print queue.

Controlling Fonts

Windows XP uses a Font Manager program to control the installed fonts on your system. You can use the Font Manager to install new fonts, view examples of existing fonts, and delete fonts.

To open the Font Manager, click the **Start** button then click the **Control Panel** menu option to reveal the Control Panel window, as shown in Fig. 6.7 on the next page.

Fig. 6.7 The Control Panel Window.

Next, double-click the Fonts icon to display the Fonts window, shown in Fig. 6.8. To control what you see on the Fonts window, click **View** to display the drop-down menu, shown in Fig. 6.9. We have chosen **Status Bar**, **List** and **Hide Variations**.

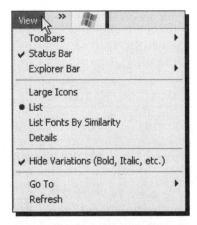

Fig. 6.8 The Fonts Window.

Fig. 6.9 The View Sub-menu.

To see an example of one of the listed fonts, double-click its icon in the Fonts window (Fig. 6.8). Below we show the Arial (TrueType) font in four different sizes.

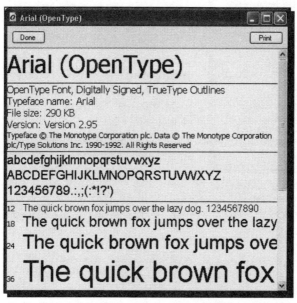

Fig. 6.10 Font Size Sample Window for a Selected Font.

You might find it interesting to know, that the Symbol font contains an abundance of Greek letters, while the Webdings and Wingdings Fonts contain special graphic objects, as shown in Fig. 6.11 below.

Fig. 6.11 Webdings (top) and Wingdings (bottom) Fonts.

We will explain shortly how such characters can be inserted into a document.

Fig. 6.12 Installing
New Fonts.

New fonts can be installed by selecting the **File, Install New Font** menu command in the Fonts window, as shown in Fig. 6.12. This opens the Add Fonts dialogue box in which you have to specify the disc, folder and file in which the font you want to install resides.

Unwanted fonts can be removed by first highlighting them in the Fonts window, then using the **File, Delete** command. A warning box, shown in Fig. 6.13, is displayed.

Windows Fonts Folder

⚠ Are you sure you want to delete these fonts?

| Yes | No |

Fig. 6.13 The Warning Box.

Some Font Basics: Font sizes are measured in 'points' (a point being, approximately 1/72 of an inch), which determine the height of a character. There is another unit of character measurement called the 'pitch' which is the number of characters that can fit horizontally in one inch.

The spacing of a font is either 'fixed' (mono spaced) or 'proportional'. With fixed spacing, each character takes up exactly the same space, while proportionally spaced characters take up different spacing (an 'i' or a 't' take up less space than a 'u' or a 'w'). Thus the length of proportionally spaced text can vary depending on which letters it contains. However, numerals take up the same amount of space whether they have been specified as fixed or proportional.

Windows XP makes available several 'TrueType' fonts which can be used by Windows applications, such as word processors. TrueType are outline fonts that are rendered from line and curve commands. These types of fonts are scalable to any point size, can be rotated, and look exactly the same on the screen as they do when printed.

Controlling Characters

A useful feature in Windows is the Character Map, shown open in Fig. 6.14 below. This should be found in the **All Programs, Accessories, System Tools** menu.

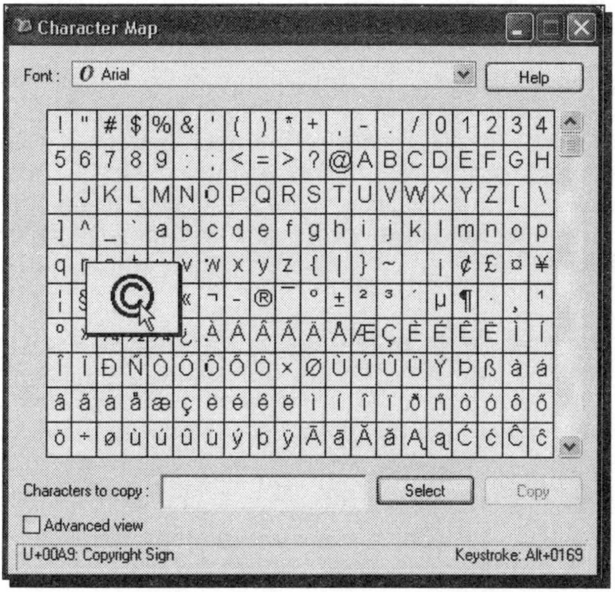

Fig. 6.14 Selecting a Character from the Character Map Utility.

You use this facility from an application, such as a word processor, when you need a special character, such as the 'copyright' sign © above, to be included in your document.

To copy a special character, not found on your keyboard, into your document, open the Character Map, select the **Font**, and click the character to enlarge it, as shown above, click the **Select** button, which places it in the **Characters to copy** box. When you have all the characters you want in this box, clicking the **Copy** button will copy them to the clipboard. Now, return to your application, make sure the insertion point is in the correct position and paste the characters there.

Adding Hardware to your System

Prior to Windows 95, it was difficult to add new hardware to your PC, particularly if you did not understand how a PC works. Since then, all Windows versions automate this process by including a set of software standards for controlling suitably designed hardware devices.

Plug-and-Play: Windows 95 was the first PC operating system to support what is known as Plug-and-Play compatible devices. Adding such hardware devices to your system is extremely easy, as Windows takes charge and automatically controls all its settings so that it fits in with the rest of the system. So, when you buy new hardware, make sure that it is Plug-and-Play compatible.

Add New Hardware Wizard: If you are not lucky and your new hardware is not Plug-and-Play compatible all is not lost, as there is a very powerful Wizard to step you through the process of installing new hardware. Fit the new hardware before you run the Wizard, as it is just possible that Windows will recognise the change and be able to carry out the configuration itself.

If the new hardware is not recognised, start the Wizard (Fig. 6.15) by double-clicking the Add New Hardware icon in the

 Control Panel, and follow the instructions.

The Wizard searches your system for anything new, which takes a few seconds to complete. Eventually you should be given a list of any new hardware additions that are recognised.

Fig. 6.15 The Add New Hardware Wizard.

Adding Software to your PC

Installing Windows applications is very easy with Windows XP.

Place the first disc, or the CD, with the software on it in its drive, double-click the **Add or Remove Programs** icon in the Control Panel and click the **Add New Programs** option button on the left of the displayed dialogue box, shown here in Fig. 6.16. The disc drives will be searched and you will be asked to confirm what you want installed.

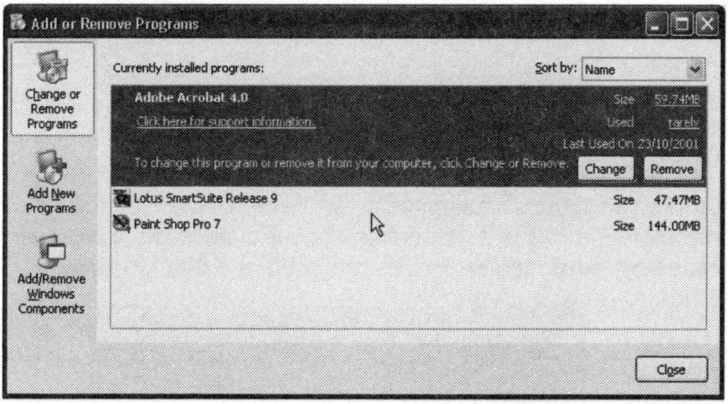

Add or Remove Programs

Fig. 6.16 The Add or Remove Programs Dialogue Box.

The **Change or Remove Programs** option icon only works for programs on your system that were specially written for Windows and are listed in the dialogue box (Fig. 6.16). Using this option removes all trace of the selected program from your hard disc. However, with earlier Windows programs, you will be left with the usual application set-up files on your system.

Adding/Removing Windows' Features

The **Add/Remove Windows Components** option icon in Fig. 6.16, allows you to install or remove specific Windows components at any time. To install or remove such features, open the dialogue box, shown in Fig. 6.17, highlight the group that you think will contain them and click the **Details** button.

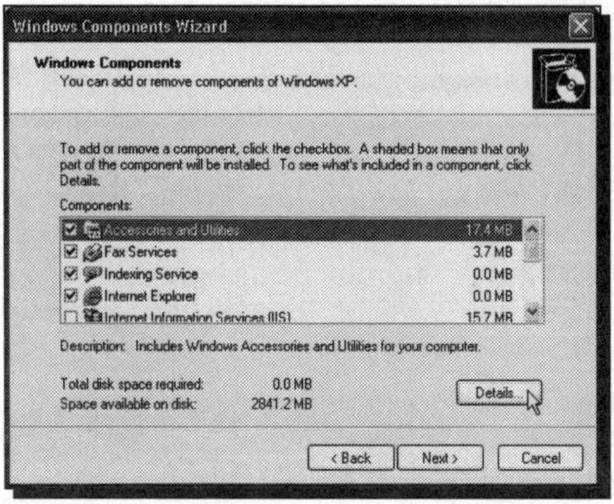

Fig. 6.17 The Windows Components Wizard.

This will examine your system and will list the components of the chosen group, shown in Fig. 6.18 below. Clicking the box to the left of an item name will install the selected component, while any items with their ticks removed, will be uninstalled.

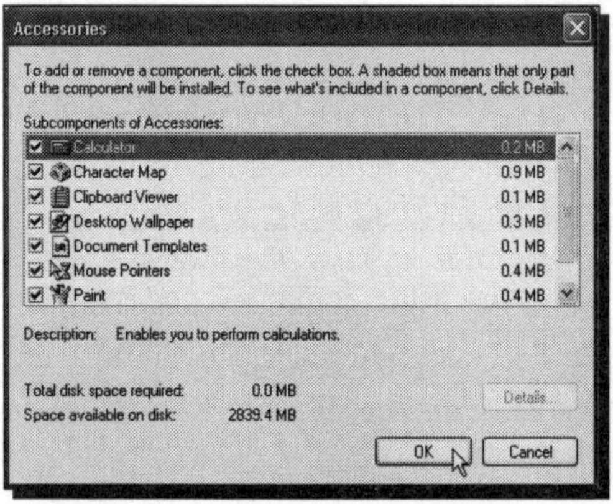

Fig. 6.18 The Accessories Dialogue Box.

You will need to have the original Windows XP CD available, and when you have made the selections you want, keep clicking **OK** to carry out the required changes. It is easy to use up too much hard disc space with Windows XP features, so keep your eye on the **Total disk space required** entry.

Checking your Regional Settings

Most Windows application programs use Windows settings to determine how they display and handle, time, date, language, numbers, and currency. It is important that you ensure your system was correctly set up during the installation process.

Use the **Start**, **Control Panel** option, then double-click the **Regional and Language Options** icon, shown here, to open the tabbed dialogue box shown in Fig. 6.19 below.

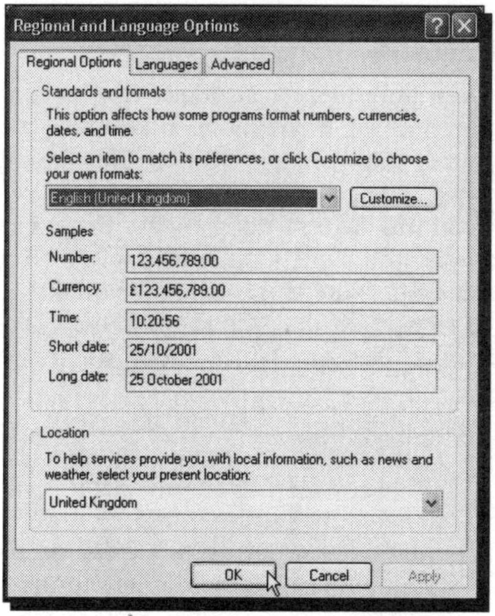

Make sure the various entries are correct. If not, change them by clicking the down arrow to the right of an entry to display a drop-down list and select the most appropriate country and language in the tabbed pages of the dialogue box.

If, in the future, you start getting '$' signs, instead of '£' signs, or commas in numbers where you would expect periods, check your regional settings

Fig. 6.19 The Regional Settings Properties Box.

and click the **Customize** button to change the way currency, time, and date display. You will have to click the **Apply** button before any changes become effective.

To change the actual time and date of your computer's clock, double-click the clock displayed at the bottom right corner of the Windows screen.

Changing the Taskbar Menus

The Taskbar menu system, as we saw in an earlier chapter, is set up originally when Windows XP is installed, the **Start** menu being standard, except for the limited addition of the most often used programs to the lower left column of the menu which, however, change with usage. The **All Programs** cascade menus are based on Windows set-up and on any previous Windows programs you had on your computer. Once you are a little familiar with Windows, we are sure you will want to tailor these menus to your own preferences.

Adding to the Start Menu

It is very easy to add extra programs or Windows applications to the top left-hand column of the **Start** menu where they will always be available for use with a single click of the mouse. This can be useful, as this menu opens with one click of the **Start** button without having to search deep in the Programs cascade menus to find what you want. One such application is the Character Map which you might want to use sporadically, but can't be bothered to remember that it is to be found in the **All Programs**, **Accessories**, **System Tools** folder, as shown in Fig. 6.20.

Fig. 6.20 The Location of Character Map.

To do this, you can simply drag the program icon with the right mouse button depressed onto the precise position you want it to appear on the top-left column of the **Start** menu, as shown in Fig. 6.21 on the next page. When you drag a single icon like this, the drag pointer changes as you move round the screen, to indicate what will happen if you release the mouse button at that location. As shown in Fig. 6.21, the pointer is over the top left column of the **Start** menu and the black line and open arrow with the 'plus' sign

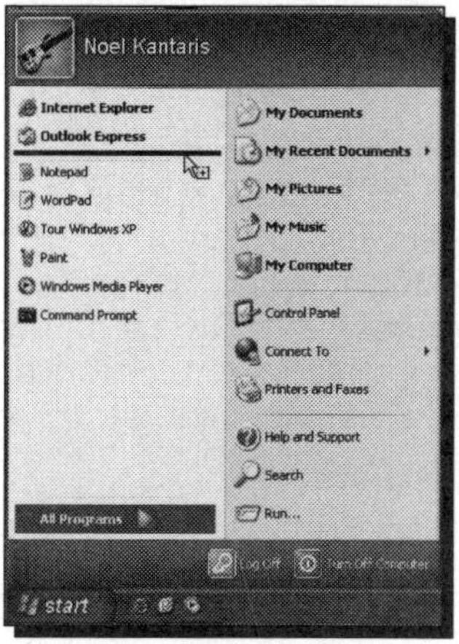

Fig. 6.21 Adding an Entry to the Start Menu.

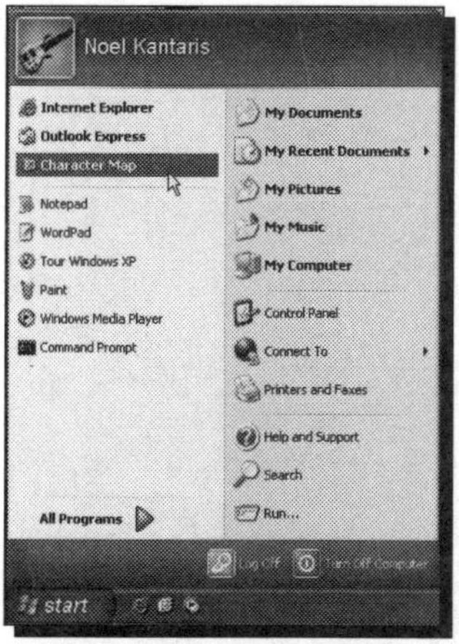

Fig. 6.22 An Added Entry in the Start Menu.

in its bottom right corner shows the position at which the dragged entry will be added. Over some desktop features, including the right-hand column of the **Start** menu, the arrow changes to a 'No entry' sign⊘. Releasing the mouse button at the point indicated in Fig. 6.21 adds the required extra entry to the Start menu, as shown in Fig. 6.22

You can rename the added entry with a more appropriate name by right-clicking the entry and selecting **Rename** from the displayed shortcut menu. If you change your mind, you can remove an entry by right-clicking it and selecting **Remove from This List**.

Within reason, you can add a few more extra items to the **Start** menu, but if this exceeds seven entries, then there is a corresponding decrease in the number of automatic entries at the bottom of the same column. Apart from the Character Map, we have also added our favourite word processing and graphics programs to the list.

Moving Files and Settings

If you are running Windows XP on a new computer and you want to move your data files and personal settings from your old computer to the new one, without having to go through the same configuration you did with your old computer, then you need to use The Files and Settings Transfer Wizard.

The Wizard can help you move easily and quickly your personal display properties, Taskbar and Folder options, and Internet browser and mail settings from your old computer and place them on the new one. Other folders and files that are also moved are My Documents, My Pictures, and Favorites. The transfer can be carried out either by a direct cable connection between the two computers, via a floppy drive or other removable media, or a network drive.

To start the process, you will need to run the **Files and Settings Transfer Wizard** on both your old and new machine. To do this on your old machine, place the Windows XP distribution CD in its CD-ROM drive and on the first intallation screen click the **Perform additional tasks** option to open the screen in Fig. 6.23.

Fig. 6.23 Selecting the Transfer Files and Setting Option
from the Windows XP Distribution CD.

On that screen, click the **Transfer files and settings** option to start the Wizard on your old machine.

To open the Files and Settings Transfer Wizard on your new machine, use the **Start**, **All Programs**, **Accessories**, **System Tools** command, then click the **Files and Settings Transfer Wizard** option. This opens the first screen of the Wizard, as shown in Fig. 6.24.

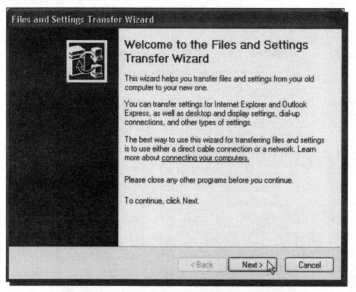

Fig. 6.24 The Files and Settings Transfer Wizard.

In subsequent Wizard screens, on both machines, you are told:

• To state whether this is your new or old computer.

• To state which media you want to use for the creation of a Wizard disc which will contain all your relevant files and settings.

• To specify which files and folders you want to transfer. Don't go overboard with your selection here as it could take a very long time to accomplish the task.

• To go to the new computer with the newly created disc start the Wizard and complete the transfer.

The Games Folder

We will not spend long on this topic, but many people only seem to have a PC to use it for playing games, but maybe not the ones provided with Windows! If that is the case and your games folder was within the My Documents folder, you could use the File and Settings Wizard to transfer them to your new computer. Alternatively, you could reinstall them which might be the best choice.

Our version of Windows XP placed the eleven games shown below in the Games folder of the **All Programs** menu.

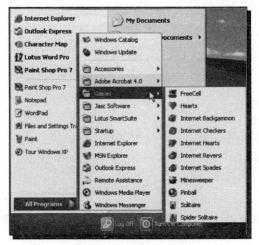

Fig. 6.25 The Games Folder.

Of these, five games require you to connect to the Internet to find opponents of different skill levels, while the other six can be played without additional expense. Classic Hearts can be played over a network against real opponents or against opponents supplied by the computer. FreeCell is a patience based game, while Classic Solitaire, Minesweeper, Spider Solitaire are designed to help with mouse skills. Pinball is a 3D arcade type game with impressive sounds that tests your reactions.

All of these games come with quite good Help sections and we will leave it to you to explore these games at your leisure!

7

E-mail with Outlook Express

To be able to communicate electronically with the rest of the world, many users will need to connect their PC through a modem to an active phone line. This is a device that converts data so that it can be transmitted over the telephone system. Installing such a modem is quite easy with Windows XP.

Modem Properties

Before using your modem, check to ensure it is correctly configured. To do this, double-click the **Phone and Modem Options** icon in the Control Panel. Windows will open the relevant dialogue box which we show on the left in Fig. 7.1 with its Modems tab selected. Click the **Properties** button, then select the Diagnostics tab and click the **Query Modem** button. If it displays the word 'success' your modem is working fine.

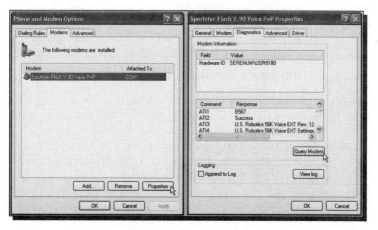

Fig. 7.1 Performing a Diagnostic Test on your Modem.

Microsoft Outlook Express

Windows XP comes with the very powerful mail and news facility, Outlook Express 6, built into it, which makes it very easy for you to send and receive e-mail messages. The program should already have been added to your PC by **Setup** (an entry being placed on the **Start** menu left column. To start the program, left-click the menu option, shown here which displays the screen shown in Fig. 7.2 below.

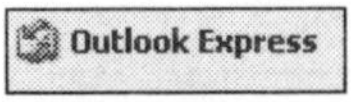

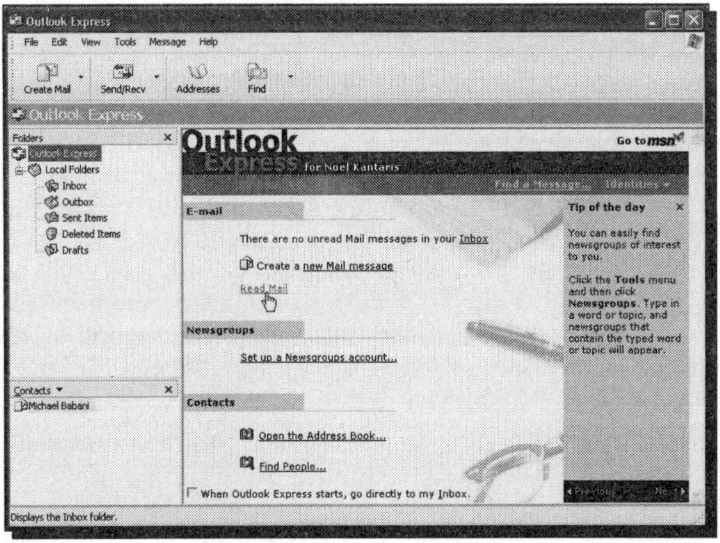

Fig. 7.2 The Outlook Express Opening Screen.

Obviously, to send and receive electronic mail over a modem, you must make an arrangement with a commercial server. There are quite a few around now, and most have Internet options. Try and find one that is free or can provide you with a reduced rate for local telephone calls, to minimise your phone bills. Once you have registered with such a service, you will be provided with all the necessary information to enter in the Internet Connection Wizard, so that you can fully exploit all the available facilities.

Connecting to your Server

To tell Outlook Express how to connect to your server's facilities, you must complete your personal e-mail connection details in the Internet Connection Wizard shown in Fig. 7.3, which opens when you first attempt to use the Read Mail facility pointed to in Fig. 7.2.

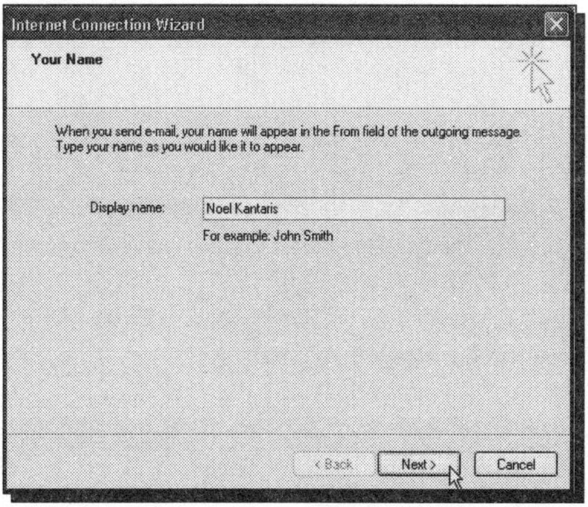

Fig. 7.3 The First Internet Connection Wizard Screen.

If the Wizard does not open, or if you want to change your connection details, use the **Tools**, **Accounts** menu command, select the mail tab and click the **Add** button and select **Mail**.

In the first screen of the Wizard, type your name in the text box, shown above, and click the **Next** button to display the second screen, shown in Fig. 7.4 on the next page. Enter your e-mail address in the text box, if you have not organised one yet you could always sign up for free e-mail with Hotmail (see the extreme right column of the screen dump in Fig. 3.22 on page 46). Hotmail is a free browser-based e-mail service owned by Microsoft.

In the third Wizard screen enter your e-mail server details, as shown for us in Fig. 7.5. To complete some of the details here you may need to ask your Internet Service Provider (ISP), or system administrator, for help.

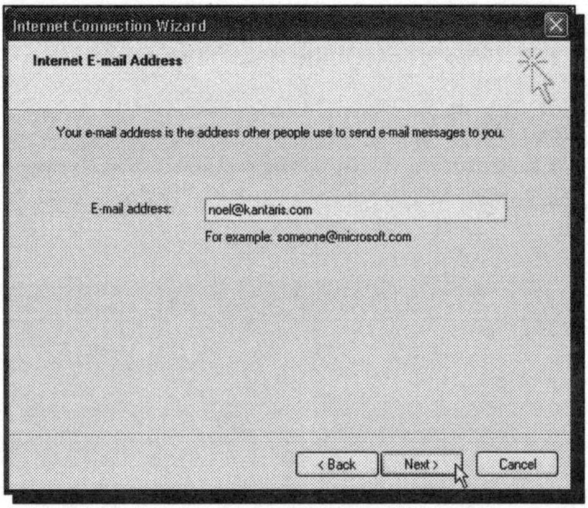

Fig. 7.4 The Second Internet Connection Wizard Screen.

The details shown below will obviously only work for the writer, so please don't try them!

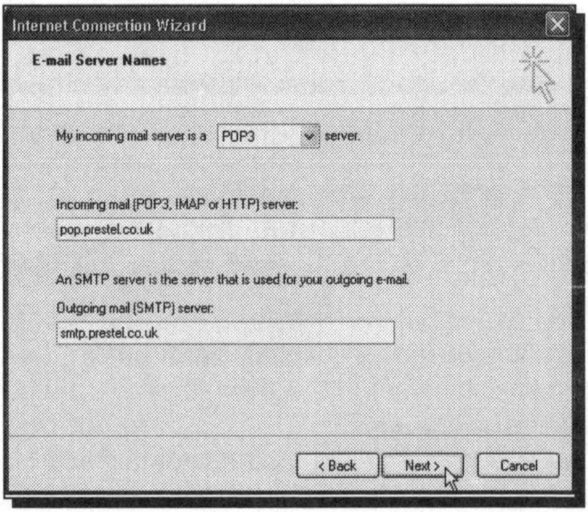

Fig. 7.5 The Third Internet Connection Wizard Screen.

The next Wizard screen asks for your user name and password. Both these would have been given to you by your ISP. Type these in, as shown for us in Fig. 7.6, and click the **Next** button.

If you select the **Remember password** option in this box, you will not have to enter these details every time you log on. **BUT** it may not be wise to do this if your PC is in a busy office - for security reasons.

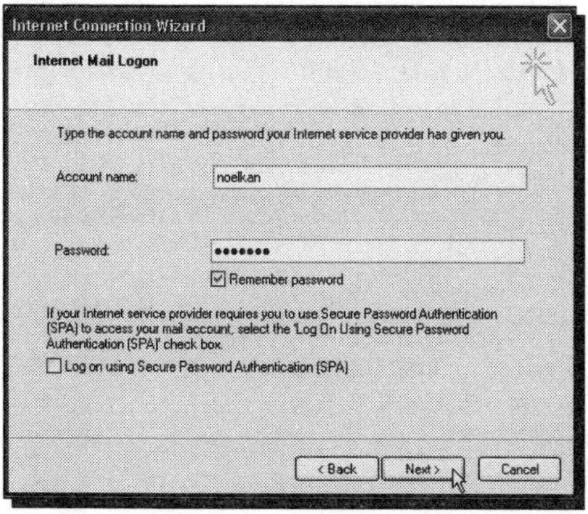

Fig. 7.6 The Fourth Internet Connection Wizard Screen.

This leads to the final Wizard screen informing you of your success, which completes the procedure, so press **Finish** to return you to the Internet Accounts dialogue box, with your new account set up as shown below for us.

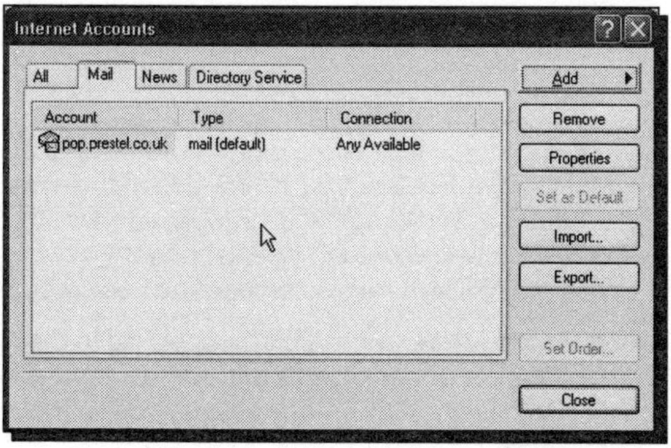

Fig. 7.7 The Internet Accounts Dialogue Box.

In the future, selecting the account in this box and clicking the **Properties** button will give you access to the settings sheets (to check, or change, your details).

Once your connection is established, you can click the Read Mail coloured link, or the **Inbox** entry in the Folder List on the left side of the Outlook Express opening window. Both of these actions open the Inbox, which when opened for the first time, will probably contain a message from Microsoft, like that shown in Fig. 7.8 below.

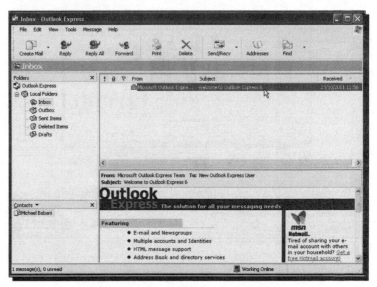

Fig. 7.8 The Inbox Outlook Express Screen.

This shows the default Outlook Express Main window layout, which consists of a Folders List to the left with a Contacts list (from the Address Book) below it, a Message List to the right and a Preview Pane below that. The list under Folders contains all the active mail folders, news servers and newsgroups.

Clicking on one of these displays its contents in the Message List, and clicking on a message opens a Preview of it below for you to see. Double-clicking on a message opens the message in its own window.

A Trial Run

To check your mail, click the Send/Recv Toolbar icon which will connect you to the Internet and download any new messages from your mailbox to your hard disc. You can then read and process your mail at your leisure without necessarily still being connected to the Internet.

Before explaining in more detail the main features of Outlook Express we will step through the procedure of sending a very simple e-mail message. The best way to test out any unfamiliar e-mail features is to send a test message to your own e-mail address. This saves wasting somebody else's time, and the message can be very quickly checked to see the results. To start, click the New Mail icon to open the New Message window, shown in Fig. 7.9 below.

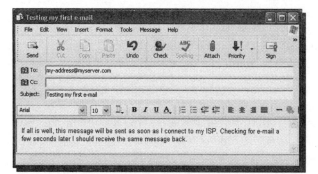

Fig. 7.9 Creating a New E-mail.

Type your own e-mail address in the **To:** field, and a title for the message in the **Subject:** field. The text in this subject field will form a header for the message when it is received, so it helps to show in a few words what the message is about. Type your message and when you are happy with it, click the Send Toolbar icon shown here.

By default, your message is stored in an Outbox folder, and pressing the Send/Recv Toolbar icon will connect to the Internet and then send it, hopefully straight into your mailbox. When Outlook Express next checks for mail, it will find the message and download it into the Inbox folder, for you to read and enjoy!

The Main Outlook Express Window

After the initial opening window, Outlook Express uses three other main windows, which we will refer to as: the Main window which opens next; the Read Message window for reading your mail; and the New Message window, to compose your outgoing mail messages.

The Main window consists of a Toolbar, a menu, and five panes with the default display shown in our example in Fig. 7.8. You can choose different pane layouts, and customise the Toolbar, with the **View**, **Layout** menu command, but we will let you try these for yourself.

The Folders List

The folders pane contains a list of your mail folders, your news servers and any newsgroups you have subscribed to. There are always at least five mail folders, as shown in Fig. 7.10. You can add your own with the **File**, **Folder**, **New** menu command from the Main window. You can delete added folders with the **File**, **Folder**, **Delete** command. These operations can also be carried out after right-clicking a folder in the list. You can drag messages from the Message list and drop them into any of the folders, to 'store' them there.

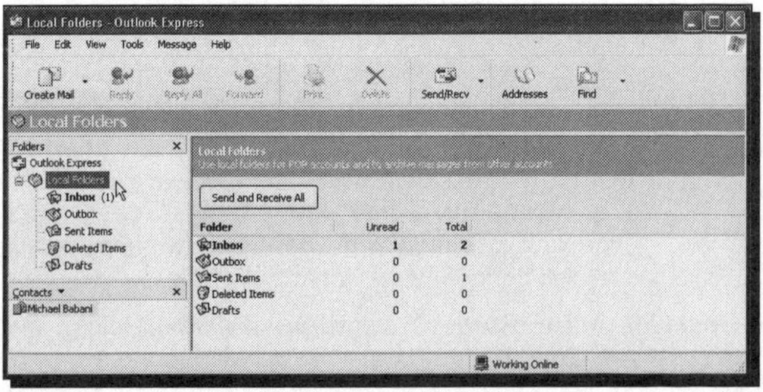

Fig. 7.10 The Local Folders Pane.

Note the icons shown above, any new folders you add will have the same icon as that of the first added folder.

The Contacts Pane

This pane simply lists the contacts held in your Address Book. Double-clicking on an entry in this list opens a New Message window with the message already addressed to that person.

The Message List

When you select a folder, by clicking it in the Folders list, the Message list shows the contents of that folder. Brief details of each message are displayed on one line, as shown in Fig. 7.11.

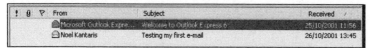

Fig. 7.11 Received Messages in Ascending Date Order.

The first column shows the message priority, if any, the second shows whether the message has an attachment, and the third shows whether the message has been 'flagged'. All of these are indicated by icons on the message line. The 'From' column shows the message status icon (listed on the next page) and the name of the sender, 'Subject' shows the title of each mail message, and 'Received' shows the date it reached you. You can control what columns display in this pane with the **View**, **Columns** menu command.

To sort a list of messages, you can click the mouse pointer in the title of the column you want the list sorted on, clicking it again will sort it in reverse order. The sorted column is shown with a triangle mark, as shown in Fig. 7.12 below.

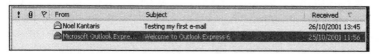

Fig. 7.12 Received Messages in Descending Date Order.

As seen on the screen dump above, the received messages have been sorted by date, with the most recently received message appearing at the top. This is our preferred method of display.

Message Status Icons

This icon	Indicates this
📎	The message has one or more files attached.
!	The message has been marked high priority by the sender.
↓	The message has been marked low priority by the sender.
📖	The message has been read. The message heading appears in light type.
✉	The message has not been read. The message heading appears in bold type.
📨	The message has been replied to.
📨	The message has been forwarded.
🗒	The message is in progress in the Drafts folder.
✉	The message is digitally signed and unopened.
✉	The message is encrypted and unopened.
✉	The message is digitally signed, encrypted and unopened.
📖	The message is digitally signed and has been opened.
📖	The message is encrypted and has been opened.
📖	The message is digitally signed and encrypted, and has been opened.
⊞	The message has responses that are collapsed. Click the icon to show all the responses (expand the conversation).
⊟	The message and all of its responses are expanded. Click the icon to hide all the responses (collapse the conversation).
▽	The unread message header is on an IMAP server.
🗑	The opened message is marked for deletion on an IMAP server.
⚑	The message is flagged.
ƒ	The IMAP message is marked to be downloaded.
⊞ƒ	The IMAP message and all conversations are marked to be downloaded.
⊟ƒ	The individual IMAP message (without conversations) is marked to be downloaded.

Fig. 7.13. Table of Message Status Icons.

The Preview Pane

When you select a message in the Message list, by clicking it once, it is displayed in the Preview pane, which takes up the rest of the window. This lets you read the first few lines to see if the message is worth bothering with. If so, double clicking the header, in the Message list, will open the message in the Read Message window, as shown later in the chapter.

You could use the Preview pane to read all your mail, especially if your messages are all on the short side, but it is easier to process them from the Read Message window.

The Main Window Toolbar

Selecting any one of the local folders displays the following buttons on Outlook's Toolbar.

 Opens the New Message window for creating a new mail message, with the To: field blank.

 Opens the New Message window for replying to the current mail message, with the To: field pre-addressed to the original sender. The original Subject field is prefixed with Re:.

Opens the New Message window for replying to the current mail message, with the To: field pre-addressed to all that received copies of the original message. The original Subject field is prefixed with Re:.

 Opens the New Message window for forwarding the current mail message. The To: field is blank. The original Subject field is prefixed with Fw:.

Prints the selected message.

 Deletes the currently selected message and places it in the Deleted Items folder.

 Connects to the mailbox server and downloads waiting messages, which it places in the Inbox folder. Sends any messages waiting in the Outbox folder.

 Opens the Address Book.

Finds a message or an e-mail address using Find People facilities of the Address Book.

The Read Message Window

If you double-click a message in the Message list of the Main window the Read Message window is opened, as shown below.

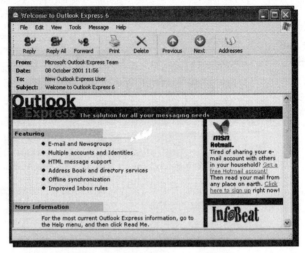

Fig. 7.14 The Read Message Window.

This is the best window to read your mail in. It has its own menu system and Toolbar, which lets you rapidly process and move between the messages in a folder.

The Read Message Toolbar

This window has its own Toolbar, but only two icons are different from those in the Main window.

Previous - Displays the previous mail message in the Read Message window. The button appears depressed if there are no previous messages.

Next - Displays the next mail message in the Read Message window. The button appears depressed if there are no more messages.

Creating New Messages

We briefly looked into the creation of a new message and the New Message window earlier in the chapter (Fig. 7.9). However, before we activate this window again and discuss it in detail, let us first create a signature to be appended to all outgoing messages.

Your Own Signature

You create a signature from the Main window using the **Tools**, **Options** command which opens the Options dialogue box shown below when its Signature tab is selected and the **New** button is clicked.

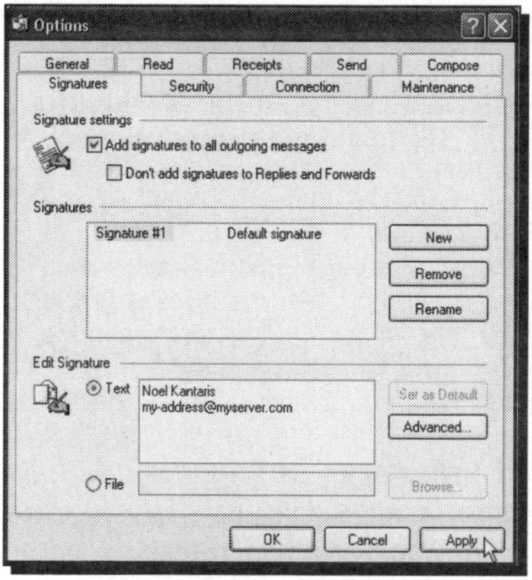

Fig. 7.15 The Options Dialogue Box.

You could also create a more fancy signature file in a text editor like Notepad, or WordPad, including the text and characters you want added to all your messages, and point to it in the **File** section of this box. You could choose to **Add signatures to all outgoing messages** which is preferable, or you could leave this option blank and use the **Insert**, *Signature* command from the New Message window menu system.

The New Message Window

This is the window, shown below, that you will use to create any messages you want to send electronically from Outlook Express. It is important to understand its features, so that you can get the most out of it.

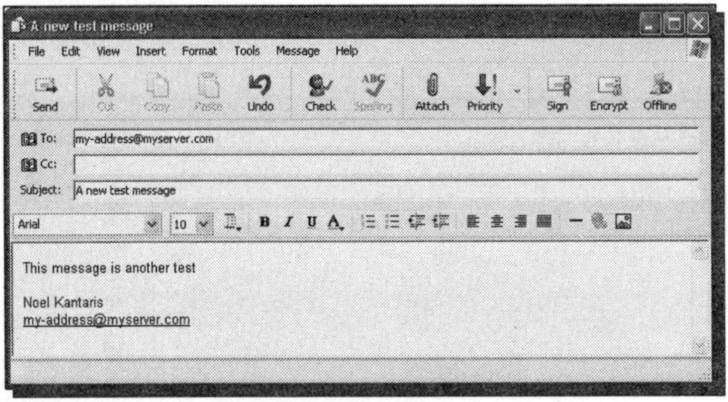

Fig. 7.16 The New Message Window.

As we saw, this window can be opened by using the **Create Mail** Toolbar icon from the Main window, as well as the **Message**, **New Message** menu command. From other windows you can also use the **Message**, **New Message** command, or the <Ctrl+N> keyboard shortcut. The newly opened window has its own menu system and Toolbar, which let you rapidly prepare and send your new e-mail messages.

Message Stationery

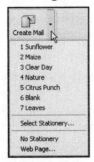

Fig. 7.17 Stationery.

Another Outlook Express feature is that it lets you send your messages on pre-formatted stationery for added effect.

To access these, click the down arrow next to the **Create Mail** button in the Main window and either select from the **1** to **7** list, as shown here, or use the **Select Stationery** command to open a box with many more stationery types on offer.

The New Message Toolbar

The icons on the New Message Toolbar window have the following functions:

 Send Message - Sends message, either to the recipient, or to the Outbox folder.

 Cut - Cuts selected text to the Windows clipboard.

 Copy - Copies selected text to the Windows clipboard.

Paste - Pastes the contents of the Windows clipboard into the current message.

Undo - Undoes the last editing action.

 Check Names - Checks that names match your entries in the address book, or are in correct e-mail address format.

 Spelling - Checks the spelling of the current message before it is sent, but is only available if you have Word, Excel, or PowerPoint.

 Attach File - Opens the Insert Attachment window for you to select a file to be attached to the current message.

Set Priority - Sets the message priority as high or low, to indicate its importance to the recipient.

 Digitally sign message - Adds a digital signature to the message to confirm to the recipient that it is from you.

Encrypt message - Encodes the message so that only the recipient can read it.

 Work Offline - Closes connection to the Internet so that you can process your mail offline. The button then changes to **Work Online.**

Message Formatting

Outlook Express provides quite sophisticated formatting options for an e-mail editor from both the **Format** menu and Toolbar. These only work if you prepare the message in HTML format, as used in Web documents. You can set this to be your default mail sending format using the Send tab in the **Tools**, **Options** box.

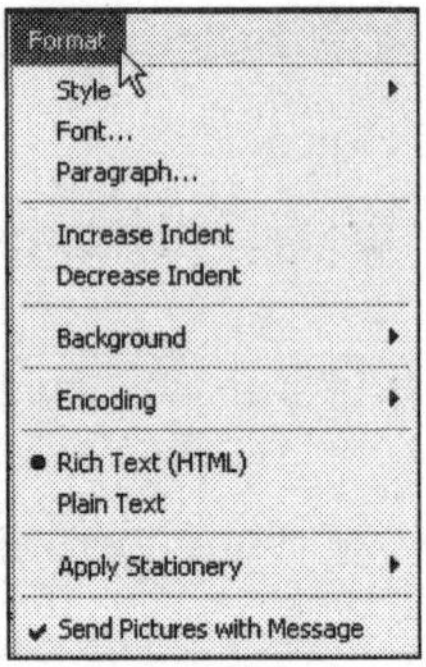

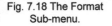

Fig. 7.18 The Format Sub-menu.

To use the format for the current message only, select **Rich Text (HTML)** from the **Format** menu, as we have done here. If **Plain Text** is selected, the black dot will be placed against this option on the menu, and the formatting features will not then be available.

The Format Toolbar shown below is added to the New Message window when you are in HTML mode and all the **Format** menu options are then made active.

Fig. 7.19 The Format Toolbar.

All of the formatting features are well covered elsewhere in the book so we will not repeat them now. Most of them are quite well demonstrated in Microsoft's opening message to you. You should be able to prepare some very easily readable e-mail messages with these features, but remember that not everyone will be able to read the work in the way that you spent hours creating. Only e-mail programs that support MIME (Multi-purpose Internet Mail Extensions) can read HTML formatting. When your recipient's e-mail program does not read HTML, and many people choose not to, the message appears as plain text with an HTML file attached.

Note: At the risk of being called boring we think it is usually better to stick to plain text without the selection of any message stationery; not only can everyone read it, but it is much quicker to transmit and deal with.

Using E-mail Attachments

If you want to include an attachment to your main e-mail message, you simply click the **Attach** Toolbar button in the New Message window, as shown in Fig. 7.20 below.

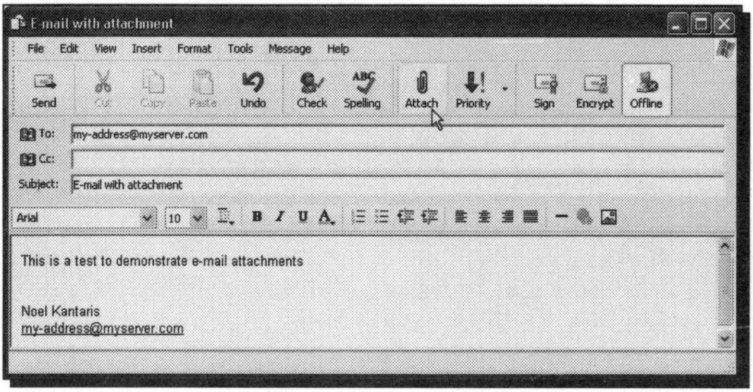

Fig. 7.20 Adding an Attachment to an E-mail.

This opens the Insert Attachment dialogue box (Fig. 7.21), for you to select the file, or files, you want to go with your message.

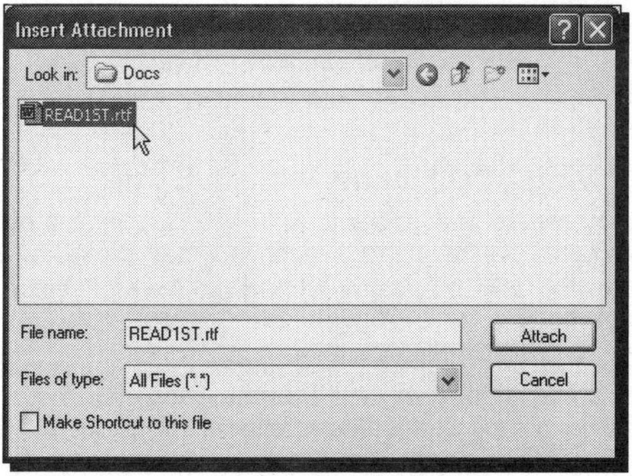

Fig. 7.21 The Insert Attachment Dialogue Box.

In Outlook Express the attached files are placed below the **Subject** text box. In Fig. 7.22 we show two attachments, each with a distinctive icon that tells the recipient what each file is; the first a graphics .jpg file, the second a text .rtf document. It is only polite to include in your e-mail a short description of what the attachments are, and which applications were used to create them; it will help the recipient to decipher them.

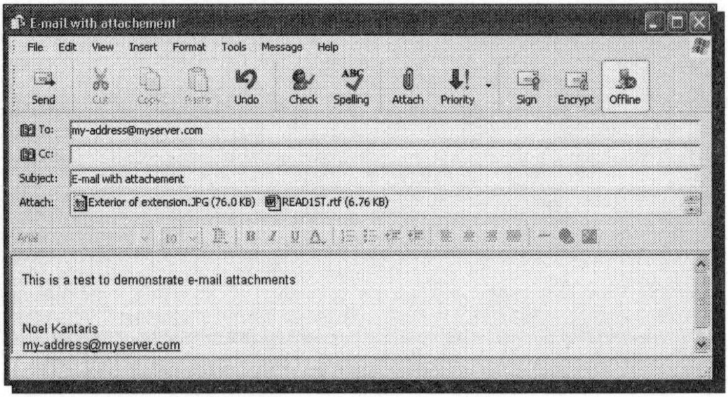

Fig. 7.22 Adding an Attachment to an E-mail.

Clicking the **Send** icon on the Toolbar, puts each e-mail (with its attachments, if any) in Outlook's **Outbox** folder. Next time you click the **Send/Recv** Toolbar icon, Outlook Express connects to your ISP and sends all the e-mails stored in it.

Receiving Attachments with an E-mail

To demonstrate what happens when you receive an e-mail with attachments, we have sent the above e-mail to our ISP, then a minute or so later we received it back, as shown in Fig. 7.23 on the next page.

Note that the received e-mail shows the graphics (.jpg) file open at the bottom of the Preview pane, but there is no indication of any other attachments. To find out how many attachments were included with the received e-mail, double-click the e-mail to open it in its own window and reveal all of them in the **Attach** box shown in Fig. 7.24 on the next page.

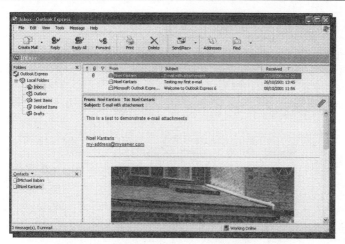

Fig. 7.23 A Received E-mail with Attachments.

Fig. 7.24 An E-mail Opened in its Own Window.

To view or save an attachment file, left-click its entry on the list. This opens the Warning box shown in Fig. 7.25.

Each attached file can be saved opened in situ or saved to disc by selecting **Open it** or **Save it to disk**.

Fig. 7.25 The Open Attachment Warning Window.

Replying to a Message

When you receive an e-mail message that you want to reply to, Outlook Express makes it very easy to do. The reply address and the new message subject fields are both added automatically for you. Also, by default, the original message is quoted in the reply window for you to edit as required.

With the message you want to reply to still open, click the

Reply

Reply to Sender Toolbar icon to open the New Message window and the message you are replying to will, by default, be placed under the insertion point.

With long messages, you should not leave all of the original text in your reply. This can be bad practice, which rapidly makes new messages very large and time consuming to download. You should usually edit the quoted text, so that it is obvious what you are referring to. A few lines may be enough.

Removing Deleted Messages

Whenever you delete a message it is actually moved to the Deleted Items folder. If ignored, this folder gets bigger and bigger over time, so you need to check it frequently and manually re-delete messages you are sure you will not need again.

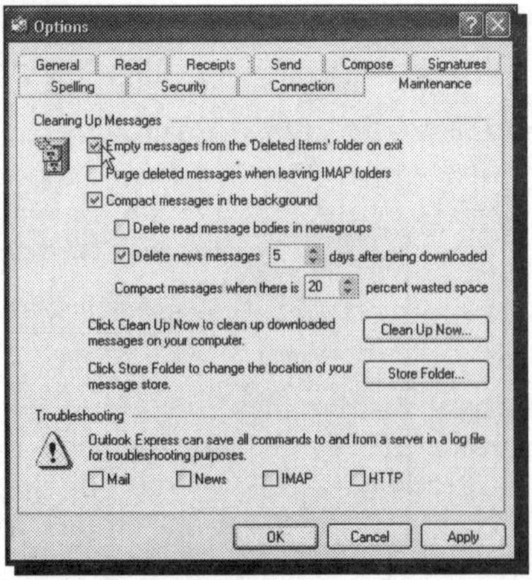

If you are confident that you will not need this safety net, you can opt to **Empty messages from the 'Deleted Items' folder on exit** in Maintenance tab settings of the **Tools**, **Options** box, opened from the Main window, as shown in Fig. 7.26.

Fig. 7.26 Cleaning up Messages.

Organising your Messages

Perhaps most of the e-mail messages you get will have no 'long term' value and will be simply deleted once you have dealt with them. Some however you may well need to keep for future reference. After a few weeks it can be surprising how many of these messages can accumulate. If you don't do something with them they seem to take over and slow the whole process down. That is the reason for the Folders List.

As we saw earlier you can open and close new folders in this area, and can move and copy messages from one folder into another.

Fig. 7.27 Moving a Message.

To move a message, you just select its header line in the Message List and with the left mouse button depressed 'drag' it to the folder in the Folders List, as shown in Fig. 7.27. When you release the mouse button, the message will be moved to that folder.

The copy procedure is very much the same, except you must also have the <Ctrl> key depressed when you release the mouse button. You can tell which operation is taking place by looking at the mouse pointer. It will show a '+' when copying, as on the right.

The System Folders

Outlook Express has five folders which it always keeps intact and will not let you delete. Some of these we have met already.

The *Inbox* holds all incoming messages; you should delete or move them from this folder as soon as you have read them.

The *Outbox* holds messages that have been prepared but not yet transmitted. As soon as the messages are sent they are automatically removed to the *Sent Items* folder. You can then decide whether to 'file' your copies of these messages, or whether to delete them. As we saw earlier, deleted messages are placed in the *Deleted Items* folder as a safety feature.

The *Drafts* folder is used to hold a message you closed down without sending it - the program will ask you whether to save such a message in this folder. We also use the Drafts folder to store our message pro-formas and unfinished messages that will need more work before they can be sent.

Spell Checking

Many of the e-mail messages we receive seem to be full of errors and spelling mistakes. Some people do not seem to read their work before clicking the 'Send' button. With Outlook Express this should be a thing of the past, as the program is linked to the spell checker that comes with other Microsoft programs. If you do not have any of these, the option will be greyed out, meaning that it is not available.

To try it out, prepare a message in the New Message window, but make an obvious spelling mistake, maybe like ours below. Pressing the Spelling Toolbar button, the **F7** function key, or using the **Tools, Spelling** menu command, reveals the drop-down sub-menu shown below in Fig. 7.28.

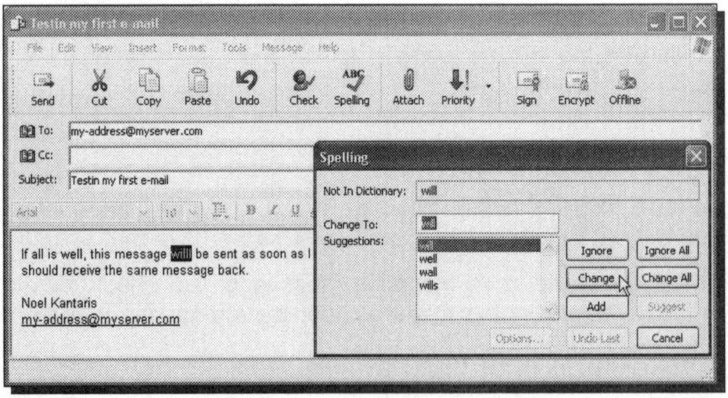

Fig. 7.28 Using the Spell Checker.

Any words not recognised by the checker will be flagged up as shown. If you are happy with the word just click one of the **Ignore** buttons, if not, you can type a correction in the **Change To:** field, or accept one of the **Suggestions:**, and then click the **Change** button. With us the **Options** button always seemed 'greyed out', but you can get some control over the spell checker on the settings sheet opened from the main Outlook Express menu with the **Tools**, **Options** command, and then clicking the Spelling tab.

The available options, as shown in Fig. 7.29, are self-explanatory so we will not dwell on them. If you want every message to be checked before it is sent, make sure you select the **Always check spelling before sending** option.

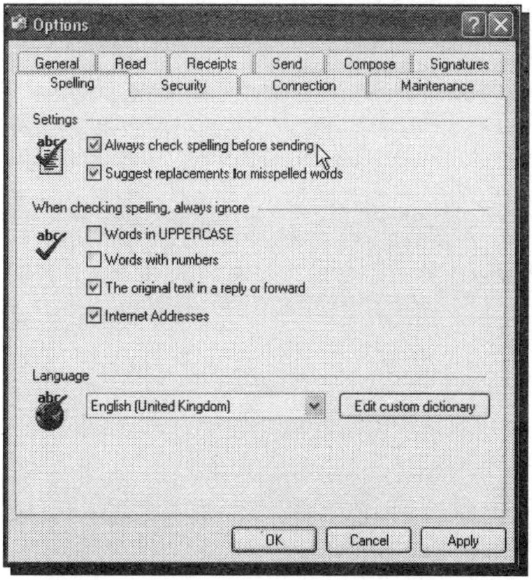

Fig. 7.29 The Options Spelling Dialogue Box.

In the above dialogue box, you could also choose to have the Spell Checker ignore **Words with numbers**, if you so wished, before clicking the **Apply** button.

Connection at Start-up

While you are looking at the program settings, open the **Tools**, **Options**, Connection tabbed sheet, shown in Fig. 7.30.

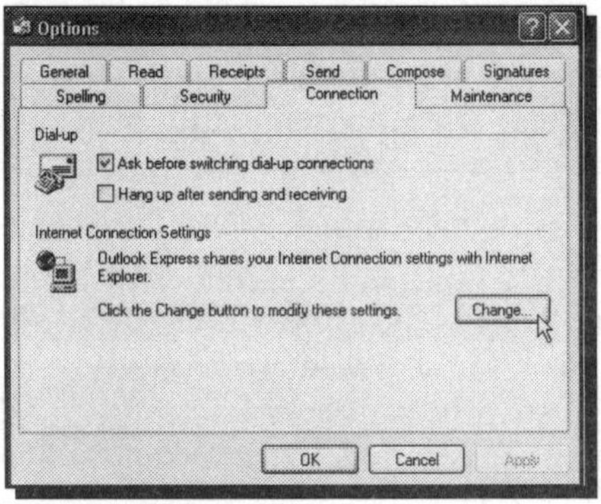

Fig. 7.30 The Options Connection
Dialogue Box.

This gives you some control of what happens when you open Outlook Express, depending on your connection settings for Internet Explorer. If you have a modem connection to the Internet, it can be annoying when a program goes into dial-up mode un-expectedly. To look at these settings, click the **Change** button which displays the dialogue box in Fig. 7.31.

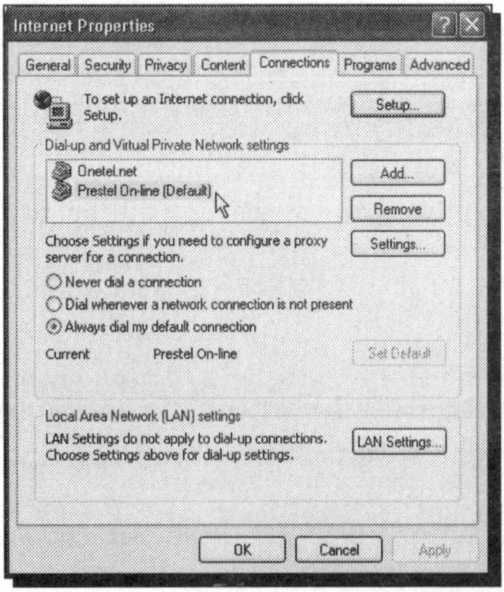

Fig. 7.31 The Internet Properties Dialogue Box.

Next, select the **Never dial a connection** option so that you only 'go on line' (as long as you have not chosen to **Work Offline** from the **File** menu option), when you click the Send/Recv toolbar icon shown here. If you have more than one Internet connection, the down arrow to the right of the icon lets you select which one to use.

If, on the other hand, you have a permanent Internet connection, you might like to deselect the **Never dial a connection** option.

Printing your Messages

It was originally thought by some, that computers would lead to the paperless office. That has certainly not proved to be correct. It seems that however good our electronic communication media becomes most people want to see the results printed on paper. As far as books are concerned, long may that last!

Outlook Express 5 lets you print e-mail messages to paper, but it does not give you any control over the page settings it uses. You can, however, alter the font size of your printed output as it depends on the font size you set for viewing your messages. As shown here, you have five 'relative' size options available from the **View**, **Text Size** menu command.

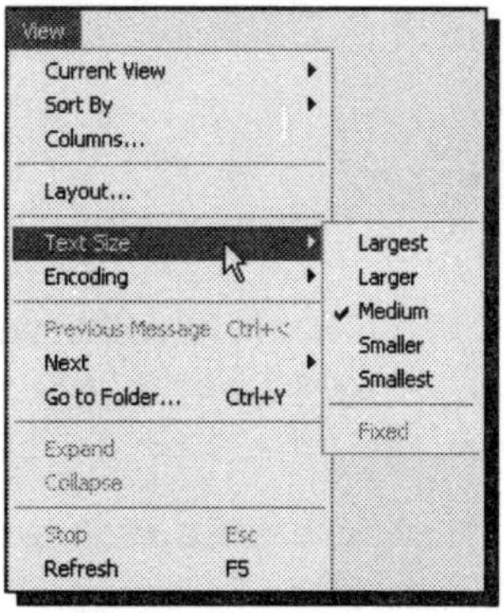

When you are ready to print a message in the Read Message window, use the <Ctrl+P> key combination, or the **File**, **Print** menu command, to open the Print dialogue box shown in Fig. 7.33 on the next page with its General tab selected.

Fig. 7.32 The View Menu.

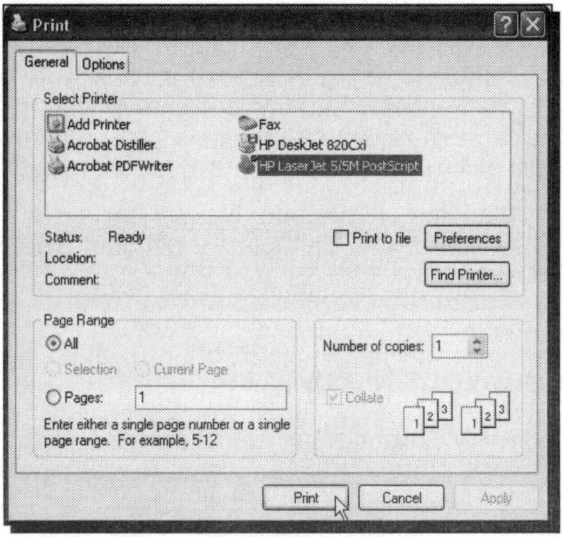

Fig. 7.33 The Print Dialogue Box.

Make sure the correct printer, **Page Range**, and **Number of copies** you want are selected, then click **Print**. You can also start the printing procedure by clicking the Print Toolbar icon shown here.

If the message has Web page links on it, there are two useful features in the Options tab of the Print dialogue box shown above. These are:

* The **Print all linked documents** option, which when checked not only prints the message, but also all the Web pages linked to it.

* The **Print table of links** option, which when checked, gives a hard copy listing of the URL addresses of all the links present in the page.

Outlook Express Help

Outlook Express has a built-in Help system, which is accessed
with the **Help**, **Contents and Index** menu command, or the **F1**
function key. These open a Windows type Help window, as
shown in Fig. 7.34 below.

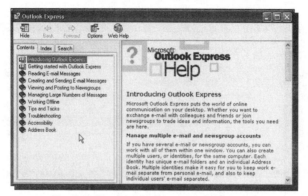

Fig. 7.34 The Outlook Express Help System.

We strongly recommend that you work your way through all the
items listed in the **Contents** tabbed section. Clicking on a
closed book icon will open it and display a listing of its contents.
Double-clicking on a list item will then open a window with a few
lines of Help information.

Another way of browsing the Help system is to click the
Index tab and work your way through the alphabetic listing. The
Search tab, on the other hand, opens a search facility you can
use by typing your query in the **Type in the keyword to find**
text field and clicking the **List Topics** button, then selecting one
of the topics found and clicking **Display** to open Help
information on it.

The Help provided by Microsoft with Outlook Express, is a
big improvement over some earlier versions of the program,
and it is well worth spending some time getting to grips with it. If
you are connected to the Internet, the Web Help icon accesses
the Support Online from Microsoft Technical Support, which
can give more specific help with the program.

The Address Book

E-mail addresses are often quite complicated and not at all easy to remember. With Outlook Express there is a very useful Address Book built in and accessed by clicking the menu icon with the same name. Below in Fig. 7.35, we show part of an example.

Address Book - Main Identity

File Edit View Tools Help

New   Properties   Delete   Find People   Print   Action

Shared Contacts
Main Identity's Contacts

Type name or select from list:

Name	E-Mail Address	Business Ph
Michael Babani	michael@babanibooks.com	0207 12312
Noel Kantaris	noel@kantaris.com	0129 12121
Phil Oliver	phil@philoliver.com	0129 32132

3 items

Fig. 7.35 The Address Book Screen.

Once in the Address Book, you can manually add a person's full details and e-mail address, in the Properties box that opens when you click the New Toolbar icon and select **New Contact**, as shown here. Selecting **New Group** from this drop-down menu lets you create a grouping of e-mail addresses, you can then send mail to everyone in the group with one operation.

To send a new message to anyone listed in your Address Book, open a New Message window and use the **Tools**, **Select Recipients** command, or click on any of the **To:** or **Cc:** icons shown here on the left.

In the Select Recipients box which is opened (Fig. 7.36), you can select a person's name and click either the **To:->** button to place it in the **To:** field of your message, the **Cc:->** button to place it in the **Cc:** field, or the **Bcc:->**button to place it in the **Bcc:** field.

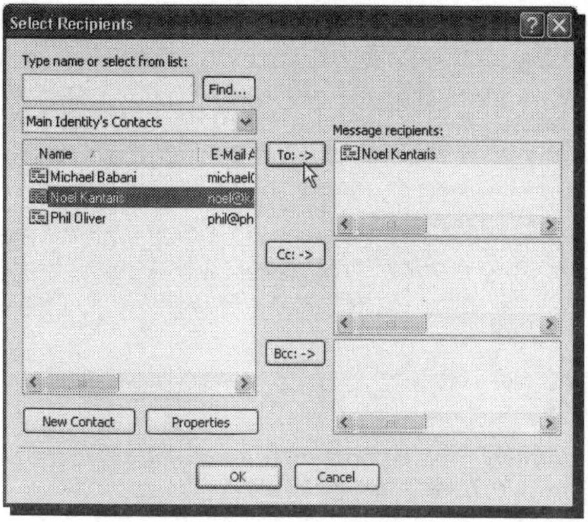

Fig. 7.36 The Select Recipients Screen.

The **New Contact** button lets you add details for a new person to the Address Book, and the **Properties** button lets you edit an existing entry, as shown in Fig. 7.37 below.

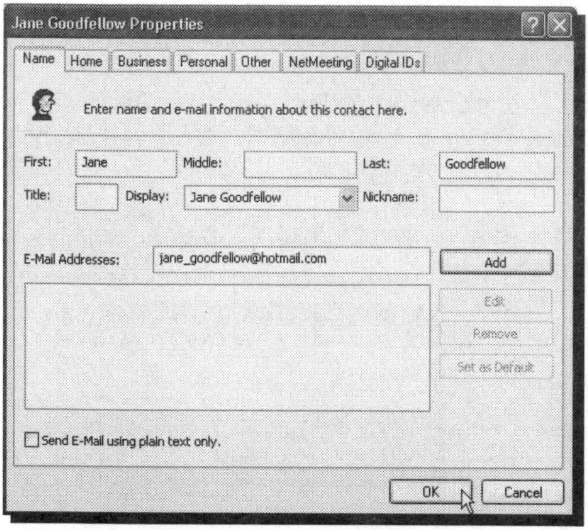

Fig. 7.37 A Recipient's Properties Screen.

Exporting and Importing an Address Book

Amongst the most valuable assets you might have on your old computer is your Address Book. After all, you have spent endless hours (over a period of time) compiling it and the last thing you want is to lose it, either because you are changing computer or because of some mishap.

Outlook Express has the facility to export your Address Book from your old computer, then import it into your new one. The same method can also be used to make a backup of your Address Book.

In your old computer, start Outlook Express, then in the Address Book:

- Use the **File**, **Export** command and click the **Address Book (WAB)** option.

- In the displayed Select Address Book File to Export to dialogue box, type a suitable name in the **File name** box and click the **Save** button.

In your new computer, start Outlook Express, then in the Address book:

- Use the **File**, **Import** command and click the **Address Book (WAB)** option.

- In the displayed Select Address Book File to Import from dialogue box, locate the drive and file holding your Address Book information and click the **Open** button.

A few seconds later, Outlook express displays the very welcome message:

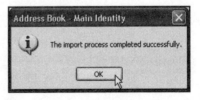

It takes less time to do than to read how to do it, and you can save yourself hours of work and frustration! Go on, do it.

Address Book Help

We will leave it to you to find your way round this very comprehensive facility. Don't forget that it has its own Help system that you can use with the **Help**, **Contents and Index** menu command. An example section is shown open in Fig. 7.38.

Fig. 7.38 The Address Book Help System.

In this chapter of the book, we have tried to cover sufficient information on Outlook Express, so that you can get on with the job of sending and receiving e-mail effectively, being one of the most used activities on the Internet. If, however, you want to know more about this subject, such as using News groups, or would like to learn how to use the Internet Explorer 6 (also supplied with Windows XP) to surf the Net, then may we suggest you have a look at our book *Internet Explorer 6 and Outlook Express 6 explained* (BP513), also published by Bernard Babani (publishing) Ltd.

8

Controlling Multimedia

Windows XP has a multitude of 'hidden' features built into it to improve the PC's multimedia performance, which is simply the ability to play sound and images (both still and moving) through a computer, usually from a CD-ROM or DVD disc. These new multimedia features lead to a big improvement in both video and audio speed, quality, and ease of use.

Whether all the features described in the next few pages work on your PC will depend on your system. Most of them require at least a CD-ROM player, a sound card and speakers, to be fitted and correctly set up. Other options require additional hardware. For example, to use the Web TV you need a TV tuner card, to use portable digital devices you need a CompactFlash or SmartMedia reader and media, while to use the Windows Movie Maker you need a fast modem, a good quality microphone and a video capture device.

The Windows Media Player 8

The Windows Media Player can be activated by either clicking 
its icon on the Quick Launch Toolbar, or selecting it from the **Start**, **Programs**, **Accessories**, **Entertainment** cascade menu, shown in Fig. 8.1.

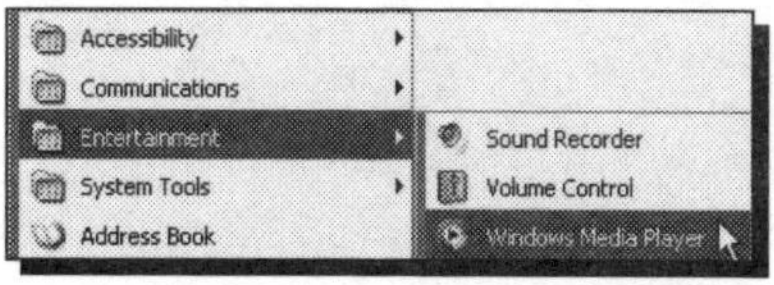

Fig. 8.1 The Entertainment Menu.

Either of these actions displays the screen shown in Fig. 8.2 on the next page, with the Media Player in Full Mode in its own window. The window can be maximised in the usual way.

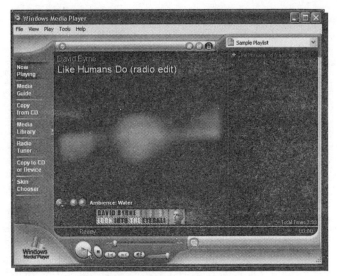

Fig. 8.2 The Windows Media Player.

Clicking the Play button (the one pointed to in Fig. 8.2) starts playing the music that came with the package. When playing starts, an additional button appears at point marked A on the bottom right of the screen, as shown in Fig. 8.3, which when clicked maximises the visual part of the player's display to fill up the screen. To return to Full Mode press <Esc>. On the same display we show a list of available visualisations. You can scroll through these visualisations using the two adjacent buttons.

Fig. 8.3 The List of Available Visualisations.

Clicking the button marked B in Fig. 8.3 on the previous page, displays the Media Player in Skin Mode as shown in Fig. 8.4 below.

Fig. 8.4 The Media Player Skin Mode.

You can return to Full Mode either by clicking the button pointed to in Fig. 8.4, or by clicking the large button at the bottom right of the screen to reveal a menu with several choices, as shown in Fig. 8.5. From here you can **Switch to full mode**, **Select a New Skin**, **Open** a folder on your computer or the network you

Fig. 8.5 Skin Mode Menu

might be connected to, so that you can load an appropriate media file, or use the **Open URL** option to search the Internet or intranet for a media file. You can even hide the large button by selecting **Hide Anchor Window**. To get it back, use the **Tools**, **options** menu command, click the Player tab and check the **Display anchor window when in skin mode** box.

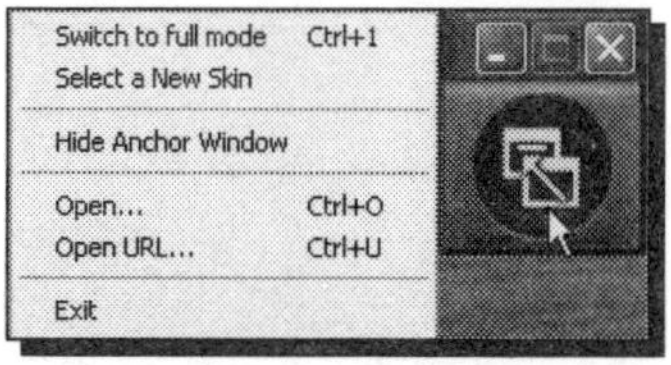

Now choose the **Select a New Skin** option from the Skin Mode menu (Fig. 8.5), to display the screen in Fig. 8.6 below.

Fig. 8.6 The Media Player's Skin Option List.

To see an example of another skin, select 'Compact', and click the **Apply Skin** button above the list to action it. The display now changes to the one in Fig. 8.7 in which we also display its hidden options. To reveal or hide details of a playing media file, click on the oval handles at the end of the extensions.

Fig. 8.7 The Media Player Playing an Audio File in Compact Mode.

To see the Media Player in action in Full Mode return to it and click the **Now Playing** button on the left of the screen.

The various options displayed on the left of the Media Player when in Full Mode (see Fig. 8.6) are shown below. What these options offer when you activate them are:

Watch a currently playing file. When playing music you can select an 'Ambience'.

Find the latest music, movie trailers, and news updates on the Internet.

Copy CD music to your computer's hard disc.

Create play lists and manage media.

Set radio station pre-sets.

Transfer files to a portable device.

Customise the player.

Watching a Currently Playing Media File

Figures 8.2 and 8.4 show what you see when the Media Player is playing an audio file. You can select a different audio file by using the **File, Open** command, to choose a file stored on your computer, or use the **File, Open URL** command (also shown to the left), to browse your network or access the Internet for an audio or video file which can then be added to your library.

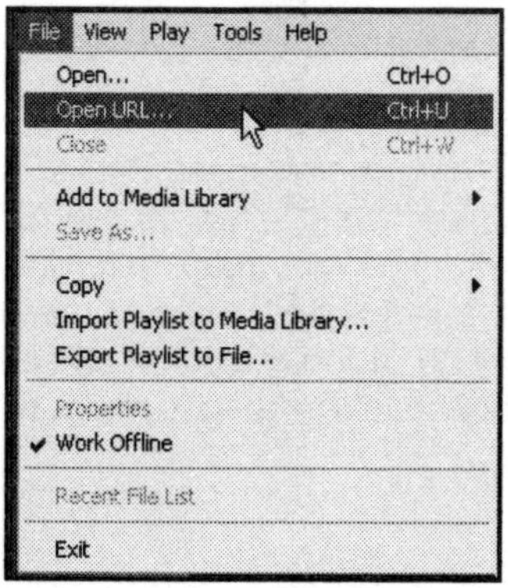

Fig. 8.8 The File Menu Options.

Using the Media Guide

This option requires you to be connected to the Internet before
you can use it. Having connected, click the option to display a
screen similar to the one in Fig. 8.9 below.

Fig. 8.9 Using the Media Guide.

From here you can find entertainment (both audio and video)
and information. We suggest you play a bit with this option to
find out what is available.

However, the results of trying to play music when connected
via a modem are not that good. The program attempts
buffering sections of music, but while you are listening to these
it stops while buffering the next section of the music. Perhaps
if you had a wide-band Internet connection the results might be
a lot different.

Using the CD Audio Option

Use this option to copy music from a CD to your computer's hard disc, or get information about the CD from the Internet (provided you are already connected to it before activating the option).

When you place a CD in your computer's CD-ROM drive, Windows automatically detects its contents and suggests loading the Media Player. Accepting the suggestion, it starts playing the music on the CD and displays the Now Playing screen (see Fig. 8.2). Selecting the **CD Audio** option displays a screen similar to the top half of the one shown in Fig 8.10.

At the top of the screen you will find three radio buttons, the first to **Copy Music**, the second to **Get Names**, and the third to give you **Album Details**. Of these, the second and third require you to be already connected to the Internet.

Fig. 8.10 The CD Audio Option Screen.

Clicking the **Get Names** button displays information about the Artist similar to the one at the bottom of the screen in Fig. 8.10; if not, a search facility is provided.

The Media Library

The first time you use this option, the Media Player searches your system for media files and then displays the screen in Fig. 8.11 below.

Fig. 8.11 The Media Library Screen with Audio Artist Selected.

As you can see, both Audio and Video files are searched for and a treelike structure is displayed in a separate pane. Selecting **Audio, Artist** displays an appropriate list on the right pane of the screen, as shown above. Double-clicking on one of these artists starts playing the chosen track. If the chosen file was a video, the Media Player reverts to the Now Playing screen before playing the video, as shown in Fig. 8.12, on the next page.

Obviously, it will be highly unlikely if what is available on our system is to be found on your PC, although one or two media files might be the same as they are installed by Windows XP. It is worth spending some time examining the Media Library structure because you can use it to manage and organise your music collection and video files and create custom play lists.

Fig. 8.12 Playing a Video Clip.

The radio buttons at the top of the Media Library screen (Fig. 8.11) and shown below magnified, can help you to organise your playlist. Most of these are self-explanatory, except for the last four which have the following functions.

Add to Library

Delete media from Library or Playlist

Move media up in the Playlist

Move media down in the Playlist.

Finally, note that you can change the brightness, contrast, hue, and saturation of the playing video.

Using the Radio Tuner

The Radio Tuner option has to be a winner. You can have immediate access to over 3,000 Internet-radio stations from all over the world that use the Microsoft Windows Media format. The screen in Fig. 8.13 displays information on the radio station we selected to try the Media Player. It actually works extremely well, so watch out; you could be amassing a sizeable telephone bill!

Fig. 8.13 Listening to a Radio Station.

To use the Radio Tuner, you must first connect to the Internet before you select the option. Having done so, two panels are displayed, as shown above. On the left panel, a list of preselected stations is displayed, while on the right panel and under the **Find More Stations** link is a small selection of certain types of music and under that a **Search Keyword** text box. With these you can either look for more stations or search for stations by language.

Clicking the **Find More Stations** button displays a further screen with an additional list of stations which are the Editor's Picks. Clicking the down arrow against this entry reveals the long list of options shown in Fig. 8.14. Selecting **World Music**, for example, will produce a long list of World stations.

Alternatively, you could type a language in the **Search Keyword** text box to list the stations available on the Internet in that language. For example, typing Greek in the text box, displays two entries for the same Lesvos station (at two different speeds) and one Canadian station which probably plays Greek music occasionally, as shown in Fig. 8.15.

Fig. 8.14 Type of Music.

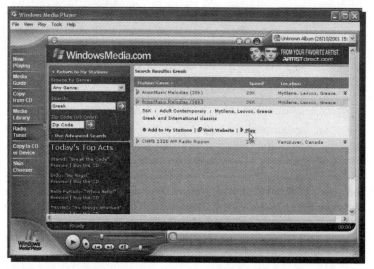

Fig. 8.15 A List of Stations Found by Using the Search Keyword Facility.

Transferring Files to a CD or Device

You can use the **Copy to CD or Device** option to transfer music from your PC to CD or other devices, such as palm-size PCs, Smart Media, Iomega Jaz and Zip drives, CompactFlash cards, or the next generation of portable music devices. If you are copying to a CD, place the CD in the CD-ROM drive first. Selecting this option, displays the screen shown in Fig. 8.16.

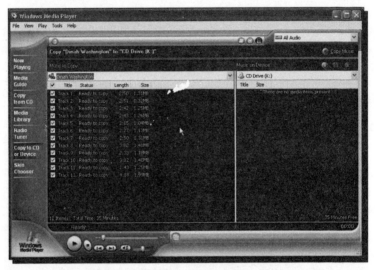

Fig. 8.16 Using the Portable Device Option.

Next, select in the left panel the music you want to copy to your portable device, then click the **C̲opy Music** radio button located at the top of the screen. That is all it takes, provided you have the right equipment for the operation. To choose a portable device select the **File**, **Copy**, **Copy to Portable Device** command.

Types of blank CDs - You can copy tracks either to a recordable CD (CD-R) or a rewritable CD (CD-RW). With CD-Rs, you can copy tracks only once. With CD-RWs, you can copy tracks many times, but if you want to copy tracks to a previously used CD-RW, you must use another program or My Computer to erase the disc before you can use the Player to copy tracks to the CD-RW again.

Customising the Media Player

You can customise the looks of your Media Player by selecting one of several predefined looks. What we have shown so far has been mainly the Default Media Player look. Clicking on the **Skin Chooser** button, displays a list of several choices. In the screen below (Fig. 8.17), we show what the Windows XP option looks like. As you select each option from the list on the left panel, a preview of that option appears on the right panel.

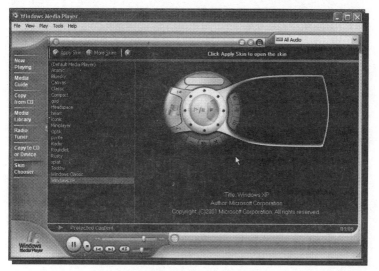

Fig. 8.17 A different Media Player Skin.

To select a different skin for your Media player, select it from the list, then click the **Apply Skin** radio button located at the top of the screen. You can use the other two radio buttons to either download more skins from the Internet, or delete a selected skin from the list.

Which skin you use for your Media Player is a matter of personal preference. However, we found that only the Default, Classic and Compact skins gave a sufficiently large display area for watching a video clip in comfort when in Skin Mode. With all the skins, when in Full Mode, you can use the **View, Full Screen** menu command for maximum screen size viewing (to return to normal size press the <Esc> key).

Media Player Help

The Windows Media Player has a comprehensive help facility which you should spend a bit of time investigating. Use the **Help**, **Help Topics** menu command to display the screen shown in Fig. 8.18 below.

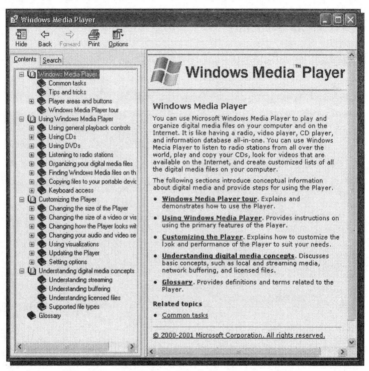

Fig. 8.18 The Windows Media Player Help System.

On the left panel we show all the main books of the Help System opened to emphasise how much information is included. In fact, when using the Media Player, we found that one had to guess one's response to using certain aspects of it. For example, when searching for a radio station you are not told that you should be searching by language, as was the case with the previous version of the Media Player. That's where the Help System is extremely useful; look up the first help topic in **Listening to radio stations** to see what we mean.

The Sound Recorder

To record a sound, use the Sound Recorder from the Entertainment group, but apart from a sound card and speakers you will also need a microphone connected to your computer. You can use the Sound Recorder not only to record, mix, play, and edit sounds, but also link sounds to or insert sounds into a document.

To start using the Sound Recorder to record audio, first make sure you have an audio input device, then activate the recorder using the **Start**, **All Programs**, **Accessories**, **Entertainment** command and click the **Sound** Recorder option. Next, use the **File, New** command and press the 'Record' button pointed to in Fig. 8.19. When you finish

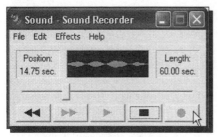

recording, click the Stop button (the one next to the Record button), rewind the recorded music on the Sound Recorder and use the **File, Save As** command to save your recording to a **.wav** file with an appropriate name.

Fig. 8.19 The Sound Recorder.

To play a recorder file, use the **File, Open** command, select a file and press the 'Play' button.

We have also found this accessory very useful for playing existing **.wav** sound files. The Wav sub-folder of Windows/ Help/Tours/WindowsMediaPlayer/Audio/wav folder contains several such files, but they cannot be edited. To edit your own sound file, use the **Effects** menu to 'play around' with the sound, and the **Edit** menu to insert and mix other sound files into the loaded one.

For more information on how to edit audio files, link sounds to, or insert sounds into a document, have a look at the extensive Help topics of the Sound Recorder. In the end, the only way to learn is to experiment, so good luck and have fun!

The Windows Movie Maker

The Movie Maker is new to Windows XP. You can now edit and rearrange your home-made video cam movies, make a shorter version of them, add a still picture and voice over, and either post them to your Web site for all to see, or send them as an attachment to an e-mail to your favourite people.

The Windows Movie Maker can be found in the **All Programs, Accessories** folder. Left-clicking its icon, shown here to the left, starts the program and displays a screen similar to the one in Fig. 8.20.

Fig. 8.20 The Windows Movie Maker Screen.

The displayed screen is divided into three panes, with the left pane showing the folder holding your video collection. Windows XP automatically created during installation a sub-folder within My Documents, named My Videos, and placed within this folder any video films that it might have found on your computer. In our case one of our collections is the My Family folder, shown open with three segments, called clips, of the video film showing in the middle pane.

Selecting each clip of the video displays that clip in the right pane of the Movie Maker screen, as shown in Fig. 8.20. Each selected segment can then be played by clicking the 'Play' button to be found below the display area.

At the top of the Movie Maker screen there is the usual selection of menu options and Toolbar icons, while at the bottom of the screen is the 'Workspace' area. It is here that you assemble your movie, which can be viewed either as a 'timeline' (focuses on timing) or 'storyboard' (focuses on sequencing) view. In the timeline view, you can synchronise video clips with audio clips or create fading transitions between clips with the help of a number of tools that appear at the far left of the Workspace area.

Recording your Film

You can use the Windows Movie Maker to record from a variety of sources, such as a camcorder, television, radio, or CD. As far as audio sound is concerned, most sound cards can be used as they support audio in. If, however, you are recording from a camcorder or the television, then you will require a video capture card or equivalent.

To record using the Movie Maker, use the **File**, **Record** menu command, which opens the dialogue box in Fig. 8.21.

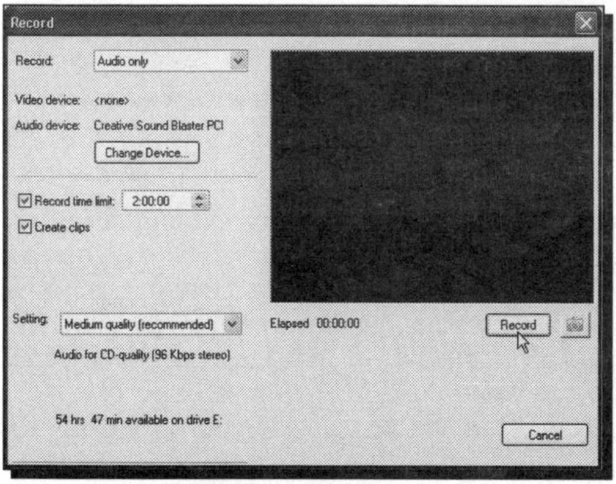

Fig. 8.21 The Record Screen of the Movie Maker.

On this dialogue box you can specify the maximum time of the recording, the device you will be recording from, and whether you will be recording video only, audio only, or both - if you are recording from a camera, don't forget to switch it to playback before starting to record. Next, when you are ready, click the **Record** button on the dialogue box of Fig. 8.21.

By default, your recording will be broken up into manageable chunks of clips. These are the ones shown in Fig. 8.20, and you can monitor what is being recorded, as shown in Fig. 8.22 below.

Fig. 8.22 Monitoring what you Record.

You can stop recording at any time by clicking the **Stop** button, or you can let it run through the specified time. When recording has finished, you will be asked for a filename under which to save your newly created Windows Media File. The file format for this type of media has a 300:1 compression ratio, which means you can store up to 23 hours of video on 1 GB of disc space. So now is the time to upgrade your hard disc!

Editing Video Clips

Video clips can be edited at will, and can be rearranged to produce the final film sequence. To rearrange the sequence of your creation, drag the clips in the sequence you want them to appear in your final film onto the Workspace area. You can even add a voice-over by selecting the **File**, **Record Narration** menu command.

A clip can be edited by trimming it, splitting it, or joining it. To trim a clip, start playing it, and when the point is reached where you want to trim it, use the **Clip, Set Start Trim Point** menu command. When you reach the end point of the trim, use the **Clip, Set End Trim Point** command. If you change your mind, use the **Clip, Clear Trim Points**. An alternative method is to use the trim handles in Timeline view and move them to where you want to cut the clip.

To split a clip, play the clip, and when you reach the desired point, use the **Clip, Split** command. The original clip is then split into two chunks that can be dragged independently onto the workspace area. To join clips together into one long one, select the first, press the <Shift> key down, then click on the last one and use the **Clip, Combine** command.

In Fig. 8.23, we display a selected film sequence together with an imported audio file while the movie is actually playing. The audio file was incorporated into our collection using the **File, Import** command, and choosing a file from My Music folder. You can also import a title clip that you created in Paint.

To save your creation on your hard disc, use the **File, Save Project** menu command. This allows you to return to it later for further editing, or additions. To save such edited work with another name, so that you can retain the original, use the **File, Save Project As** command.

Finally, you might like to include 'transitions' between clips so that you do not have abrupt changes from one clip to the other. To do this, switch to Timeline view, select the rightmost of the two clips you are creating a transition between, and drag it slightly so that it overlaps the left clip. The shaded area indicates the length of the overlap.

Fig. 8.23 The Final Movie Assembly while Playing.

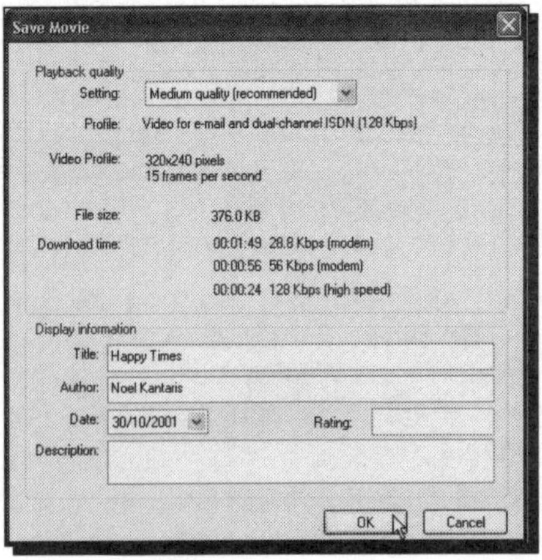

Finally, when you are satisfied that no more edits will be required, save the movie using the **File, Save Movie** menu command. This displays the dialogue box shown in Fig. 8.24, in which you can specify the quality settings which will affect its size on the disc.

Fig. 8.24 Saving a Movie.

Playing and Sending your Movie

Having created your movie, you can either play it, using the
Windows Media Player, as shown in Fig. 8.25 below, or send it
as an e-mail to a friend.

Fig. 8.25 Playing a Saved Movie in the Media Player.

Sending a Movie as an E-mail Attachment

Having saved a movie, you can send it to a friend as an
attachment to an e-mail. The easiest way of doing this is by first
selecting your movie file then using the **File, Send To, Mail
Recipient** command, as shown in Fig. 8.26 on the next page.

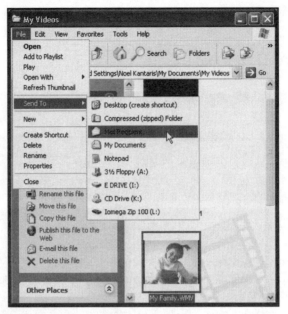

Fig. 8.26 Selecting the File, Send To, Recipient Menu Option.

Outlook Express now opens a new mail screen with the file already attached to it ready to be sent, as shown in Fig. 8.27.

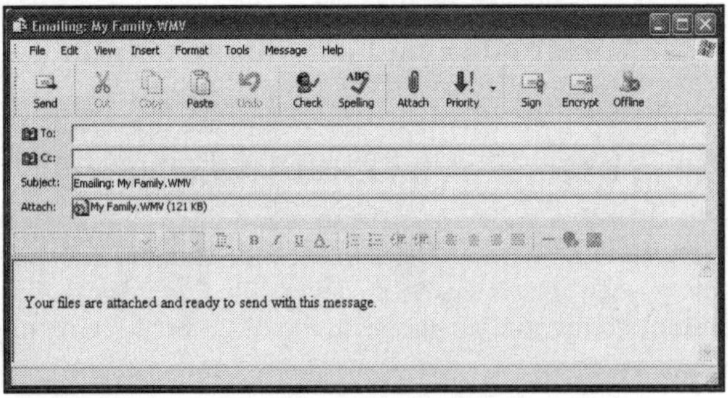

Fig. 8.27 The Attached Movie File Ready to be Sent.

All you have to do now is select an unfortunate recipient from your Address Book and write a few words of explanation!

9

Communications Utilities

The Fax Utility

You can use the Fax utility to fax a text document or graphic image as easily as clicking the Print icon on an open document in a Windows-based program. Fax supports scanned graphic images and will automatically convert graphics to the appropriate file format before you send them.

To send and receive faxes all you need is a fax device, such as a fax modem - it must support fax capabilities, not just data standards. As we saw in Chapter 3, installing a fax printer driver is easy. You will have to go through the described procedure as Windows XP does not install the fax printer driver during Windows Setup. Once this is done, you can send faxes from a local fax device attached to your computer, or with a remote fax device connected to fax resources located on a network.

If you have a fax device installed, click **Start**, then select **All Programs, Accessories, Communications, Fax** to display the available command options shown in Fig. 9.1.

Fig. 9.1 The Fax Menu Options.

Below we give a brief explanation of each fax command option.

Command	Action
Fax Console	Displays incoming and outgoing faxes and allows you to view and manage your faxes. Clicking this option displays the screen shown in Fig. 9.2 on the next page.

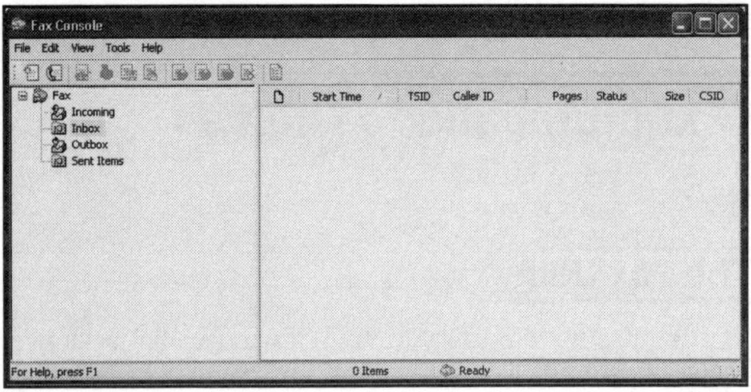

Fig. 9.2 The Fax Console Screen.

The **File** menu options allow you to send a fax (it starts the Send Fax Wizard asking you for the recipient's name and other details - you can use the information held in your Address Book, and specify multiple recipients for the one fax), receive a fax now, view, print, save and mail a fax. While a fax is being sent, you can pause or resume its transmission, restart or delete it. You can also import sent faxes or received faxes into the Fax Consult.

The **Edit** menu options allow you to select faxes in various ways for further operations.

The **View** menu options allow you to configure what you see and how you see it on the Fax Console.

The **Tools** menu options allow you to enter sender information, create, open, copy or delete personal cover pages, display the fax printer's status, start the Fax Configuration Wizard, or display the fax properties and monitor screens.

Fax Cover Page Editor Creates and edits cover pages used when sending faxes. The editor allows you to design a template (it also includes drawing facilities), to be used each time you send a fax, as shown in Fig. 9.3 on the next page.

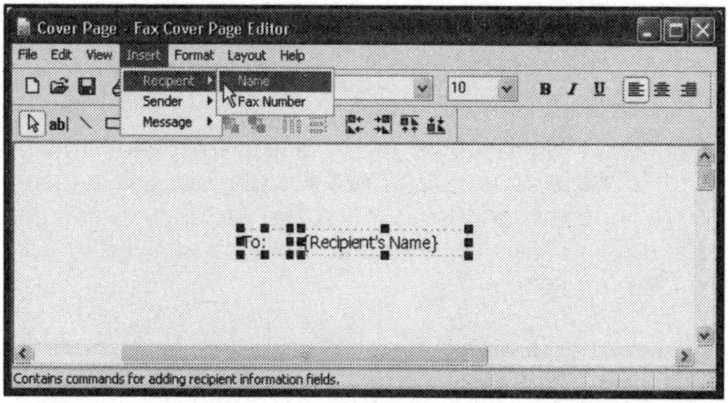

Fig. 9.3 The Fax Cover Page Editor.

As demonstrated above, you must use the **Insert** menu command to insert what you would like to appear on your fax template, such as recipient's name and fax number, sender's name, fax number, company, address and other details - the field **Note** is where you type the body of your fax. Inserted options can be moved to the desired position on the plate (use the <Ctrl> key to group together fields you want to move together) and formatted accordingly. A simple example is given in Fig. 9.4 below.

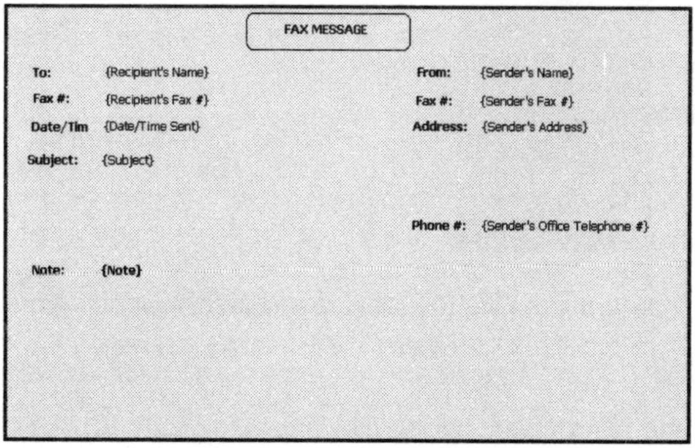

Fig. 9.4 The Designed Cover Page.

The designed template (we hope yours is more imaginative than ours) is saved in the **My Documents\Personal Coverpages** folder with the .cov extension.

Send a Fax   Sends a fax that consists only of a cover page. Clicking this menu option starts the Send Fax Wizard.

To illustrate the procedure of sending a fax, we will now step through a made-up example. We suggest you use a friend you can rely on to respond to your first fax, so that you can find out if your system is set up and functioning correctly. It might be a good idea to phone first!

To begin the process, start the Send Fax Wizard by clicking the **Start** button, then select **All Programs, Accessories, Communications, Fax** and click the **Send a Fax** option. On the **Welcome to the Send Fax Wizard** screen, shown in Fig. 9.5 you will read that if you want to fax a document you should use your word processor and print the document to the Fax printer. This facility is only for short, one page, messages.

Fig. 9.5 The First Send Fax Wizard Screen.

Click the **Next** button, which displays the second Wizard screen shown in Fig. 9.6 on the next page. On this screen, click the **Address Book** button - we assume here that you have by now several people in your Address Book (see the end of Chapter 7 where we cover this utility).

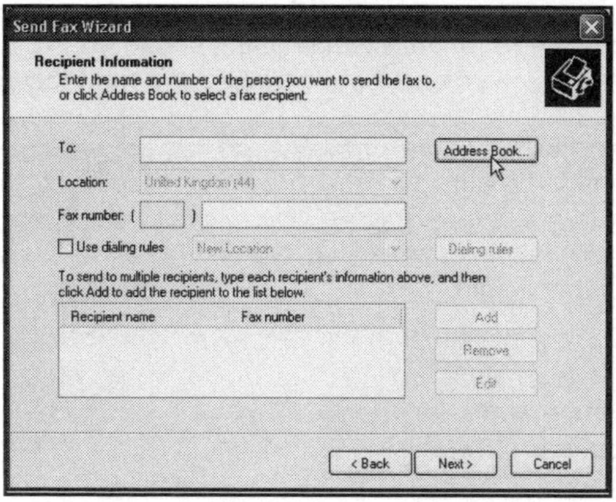

Fig. 9.6 The Second Send Fax Wizard Screen.

On the displayed screen, select the Main Identity's Contacts from the drop-down list, shown in Fig. 9.7, then choose the person you want to send a fax to, and click the **To** button so that the name is transferred in the **Message Recipients** box.

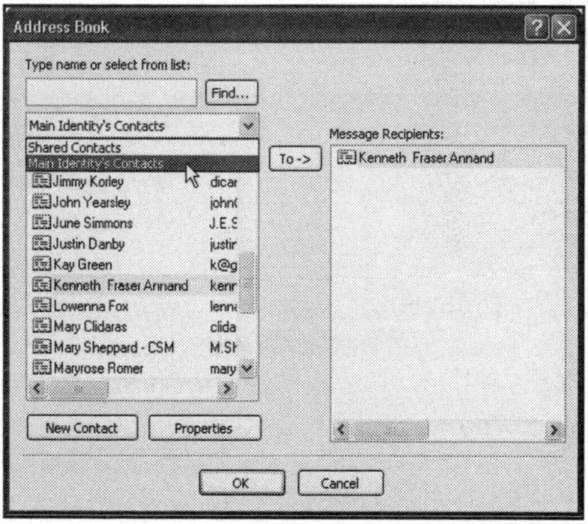

Fig. 9.7 The Third Send Fax Wizard Screen.

Pressing the **OK** button, displays the next Wizard screen, shown in Fig. 9.8. On this screen, you can add more recipients, or remove a selected one, before clicking the **Next** button.

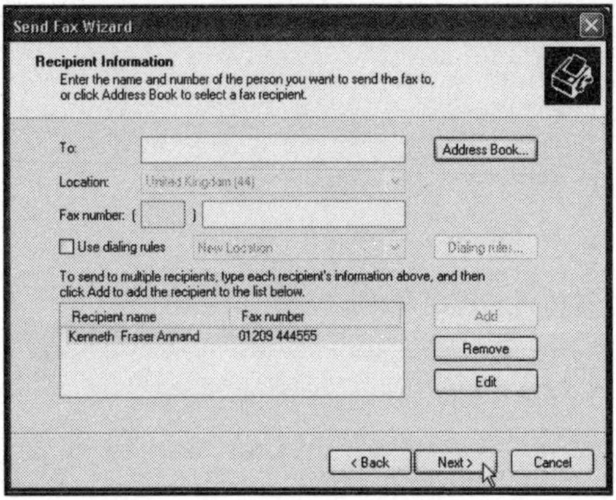

Fig. 9.8 The Fourth Send Fax Wizard Screen.

Next, select one cover page template from the drop-down list shown in Fig. 9.9, type a few words in the **Subject line** box, and your main message in the **Note** box.

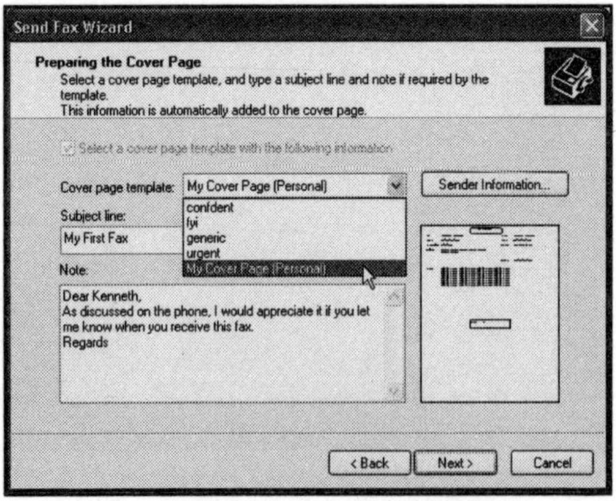

Fig. 9.9 The Fifth Send Fax Wizard Screen.

Pressing the **Next** button, displays the next Wizard screen in which you can select to send the fax now or later when it might be cheaper.

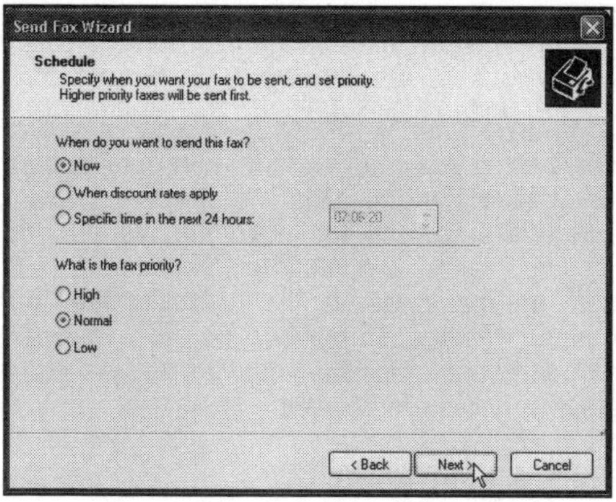

Fig. 9.10 The Sixth Send Fax Wizard Screen.

Clicking the **Next** button, completes the Send Fax Wizard by displaying the summary screen, as shown in Fig. 9.11 below.

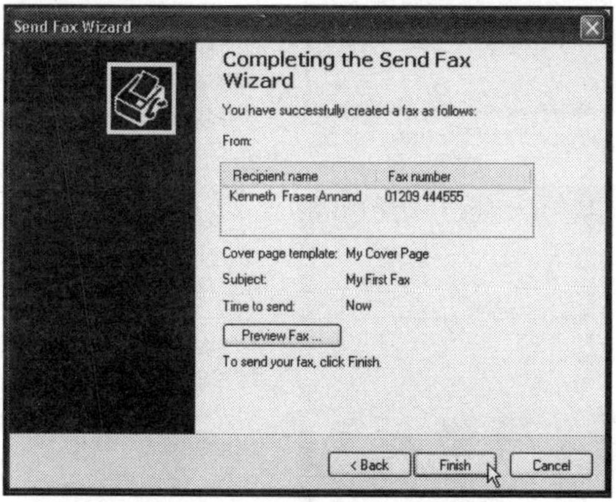

Fig. 9.11 The Last Send Fax Wizard Screen.

Finally, clicking the **Finish** button, activates the Fax modem, rings the specified number, and sends the fax.

HyperTerminal

The HyperTerminal utility also allows you to connect your computer to other computers in different locations via a modem, so that you can interchange information. You could, for example, search a library catalogue, or browse through the offerings of a bulletin board.

However, before you can connect to an outside service, you need to know their communications settings. For example, you need to know the settings for 'maximum speed', 'data bits', 'stop bits', and 'parity', though most of these can be safely assumed to be the same as the default values offered by HyperTerminal. Finally, before you can make the connection, you might need your credit card and to know a password or two, as these services are not free.

Starting HyperTerminal

To start HyperTerminal, click the **Start** button, and point to **All Programs**, **Accessories**, **Communications** and click the

Fig. 9.12 Default Telnet Program Box.

Fig. 9.13 The Connection Description Window.

HyperTerminal option. This displays a box (Fig. 9.12) in which you are asked whether you want to make Hyper Terminal the default Telnet program. Clicking **Yes** or **No** starts HyperTerminal itself. If you choose **No**, this box will be displayed again next time you activate the program.

Every time you access HyperTerminal, the window shown in Fig. 9.13 is opened to help you make a new connection. Every call connection can be named and saved with an icon, so that in future it is very easy to recall the same number.

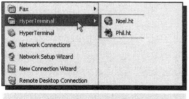

Fig. 9.14 The Connect To Window.

After typing in a connection name, click the **OK** button which opens the Connect To window, shown in Fig. 9.14. Enter the phone number of the site you want to connect to, then click the **OK** button to display the **Connect** window shown in Fig. 9.15. To use the default modem settings, just click the **Dial** button to attempt a connection.

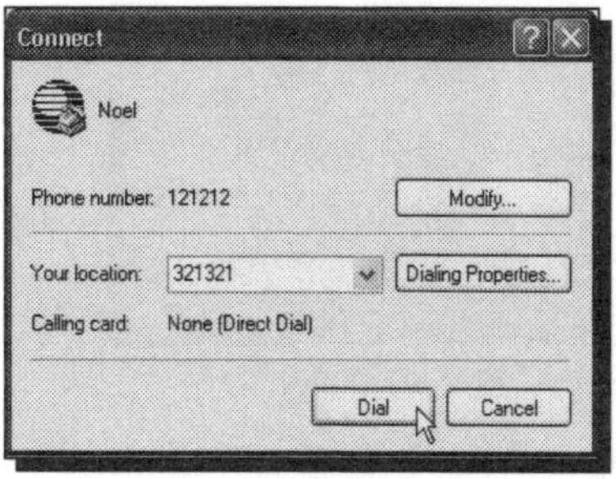

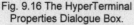

Fig. 9.15 The Connect Window.

To call the same number again in the future, use the new Hyper Terminal entry in the **Communications** sub-menu where all saved connections are to be found (Noel & Phil in our example in Fig. 9.16).

For more information about how to use HyperTerminal, click its Help menu and browse through the **Contents**, shown below in Fig. 9.17.

Fig. 9.16 The HyperTerminal
Properties Dialogue Box.

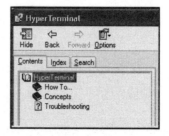

Fig. 9.17 The HyperTerminal
Help Contents.

Specifying Communications Settings

If you have trouble getting through, you may need to fine tune the settings. To do this, 'open' a call in the HyperTerminal window, as shown in Fig. 9.18, click on the **Cancel** button of the Connect To window, then use the **File**, **Properties** menu command to change call settings, or if necessary, to **Configure** the modem so that it speaks the same 'language' as the remote system.

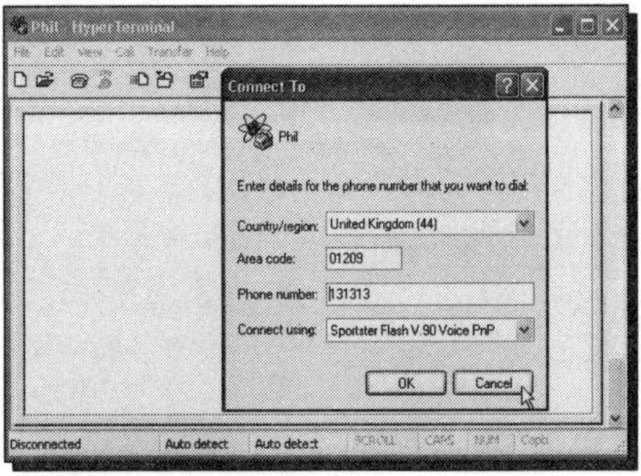

Fig. 9.18 Opening a HyperTerminal Connection.

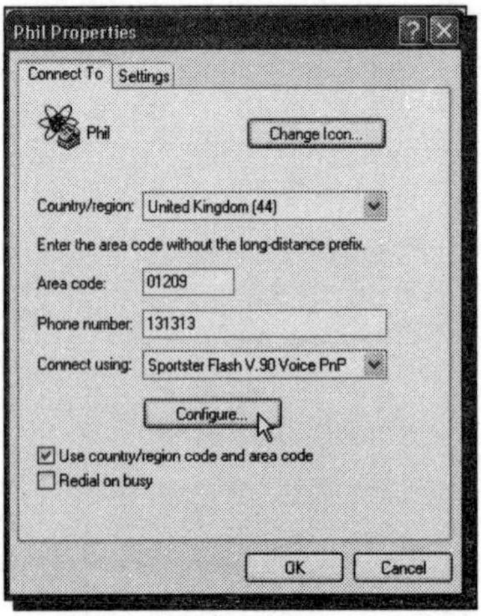

This opens the tabbed Properties dialogue box shown in Fig. 9.19. Normally, you will find that the default parameters in this are the ones you want to use. However, in case you need to change them, we list on the next page some alternatives and their usage.

Fig. 9.19 The HyperTerminal Properties Dialogue Box.

Option	*Result*
Port speed	Specifies the transmission, or baud, rate at which your PC communicates with your modem. Typically most serial modem connections support 115.2 Kbps, which is set during installation of the modem.
Data bits	Specifies the number of data bits (binary digits) that each data packet, sent or received, contains. Most online services use '8' data bits, although a few use '7'.
Parity	Allows you to specify how the receiving computer verifies the accuracy of the data you are sending. Typically this is 'None', as most connections these days use more sophisticated error checking techniques.
Stop bits	Specifies the time between transmitted characters. This is nearly always set to '1'.
Modulation	Allows you to specify what modulation HyperTerminal should use so as to be compatible with the modem signals of the computer you are trying to connect to. Most modems fall within the 'Standard' type, but if you have trouble connecting, try switching to a non-standard modulation type.

Setting Terminal Preferences

The terminal type used by the destination site will determine the terminal type which should be used for a connection. HyperTerminal supports several common types, but in most cases the **Auto detect** option will sort this out automatically.

To make a manual selection, click the Settings tab of the Properties sheet, as shown in Fig. 9.20 on the next page, with the **Emulation** list open. Select the correct terminal option and then click the **Terminal Setup** button to set its preferences.

File Transfer Protocols

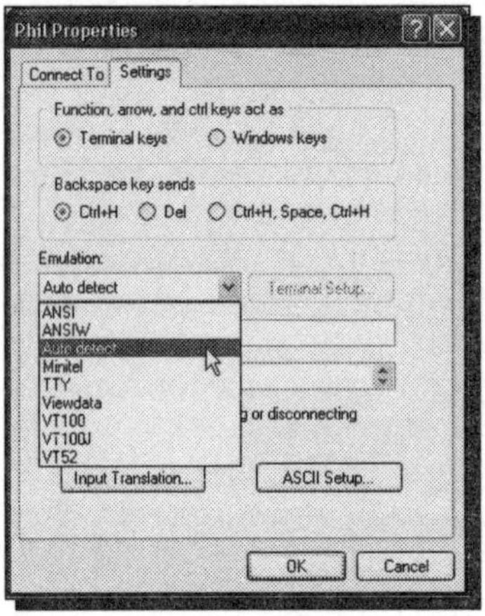

Fig. 9.20 The Properties Settings Emulation List.

Before you can send or receive files, use the HyperTerminal's **Transfer** command (Fig. 9.21) to specify the transfer protocol in either the **Send**, or **Receive** operation. The type of files you send or receive will be either binary or text files.

Text files: are normally prepared with a text editor, such as WordPad or Notepad, and saved in unformatted ASCII with only a few formatting codes such as carriage returns and linefeeds. Use the Settings tab on the Properties dialogue box and press the ASCII Setup button to display a sheet on which you can specify the transmission parameters for this type of file.

Binary files: are normally program or picture files which contain characters from both the ASCII and the extended ASCII

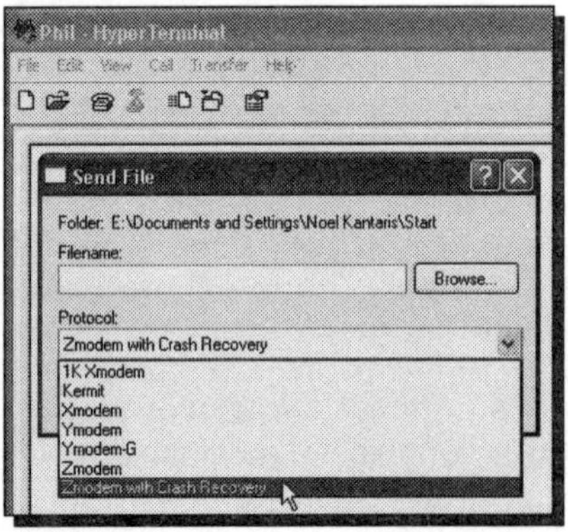

Fig. 9.21 Available Send File Protocols.

character sets.

HyperTerminal supports many of the most popular protocols; which one to use depends on the receiving site. Use Zmodem with Crash Recovery whenever possible as it gives the fastest transfer rates and remembers its place if your transmission is interrupted.

Home Networking

Windows XP allows you to easily connect two or more computers at home or in a small business, so that they can share files, printers, modems, and a single connection to the Internet. Even better, the Network Setup Wizard guides you through the procedure and makes the whole process of networking painless. However, before we activate the Home Networking Wizard, we need to discuss what hardware you require for making such connections.

Hardware Requirements for Networking

Apart from having two or more computers, the following additional hardware is essential:

- Network Adapters - otherwise known as Network cards which have to be plugged into one of the slots (PCI or ISA slot) inside your computer, or for more modern computers a USB connection at the back of your computer.

- Network Media - this includes the cables or other methods used to connect the computers together.

- Internet Connection - this is optional, but can provide access to the Internet for all the networked computers by sharing one Internet connection. The hardware for this could be an ordinary or wireless modem, a broadband cable modem, or an ISDN or DSL connection.

In addition to the above hardware, at least one computer should be running Windows XP, while the rest can be running under Windows 95/98 or Windows Me. After connecting your computers together, you must run the Network Setup Wizard first on the computer running Windows XP, then on all the others.

To start the Network Setup Wizard select it from the **Start**, **All Programs, Accessories, Communications** sub-menu. Alternatively, start My Computer and click the My Network Places link shown in Fig. 9.22.

Fig. 9.22 The My Networking Places Link in My Computer.

This opens the screen in Fig. 9.23 in which you click the Set up a home or small office network link.

Fig. 9.23 The My Networking Wizard Icon.

Either action will display the screen shown in Fig. 9.24 below.

Fig. 9.24 The Opening Screen of the Home Networking Wizard.

Assuming that your Network Adapters are installed and that the computers are appropriately connected, clicking **Next** displays the screen in Fig. 9.25. If, you have not installed or connected your Network Adapters, Windows XP asks you to do so before going on.

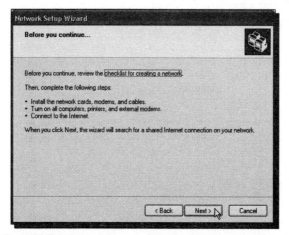

Fig. 9.25 The Second Screen of the Home Networking Wizard.

Clicking **Next**, displays the third Wizard screen shown in Fig. 9.26 below.

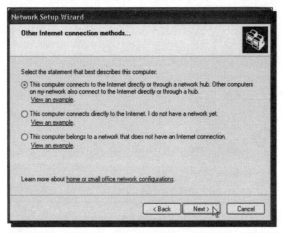

Fig. 9.26 The Third Screen of the Home Networking Wizard.

Before selecting which network configuration you want, have a look at the **View an example** link in each option. Finally specify the type of connection and click **Next** to display the next screen, shown in Fig. 9.27, where you are asked to select a connection to the Internet from a list.

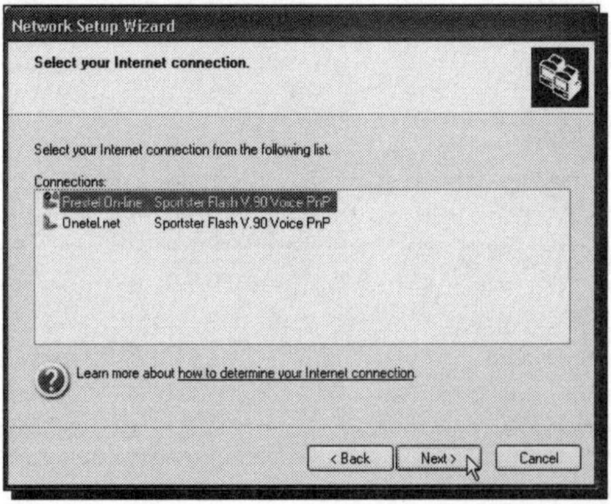

Fig. 9.27 The Fourth Screen of the Home Networking Wizard.

On the fifth Wizard screen you give your computer a unique name, while on the sixth you specify the group it belongs to. Finally, the seventh Wizard screen is displayed summarising the selected settings, as shown in Fig. 9.28. Clicking **Next**, applies these settings with rather colourful visualisation effects.

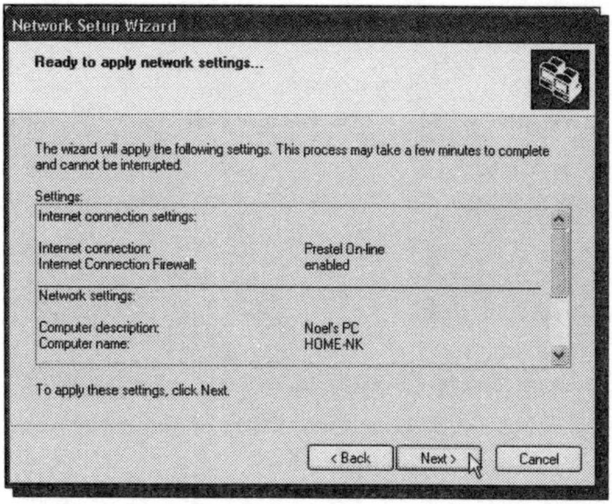

Fig. 9.28 The Seventh Screen of the Home Networking Wizard.

The next Wizard screen asks you whether you would like to create a Network Setup Disc which can then be used on the other computers on the network, particularly those running Windows 95/98 or Windows Me, so that you can run the Home Network Wizard on them. If you do have such computers on the network, follow the instruction on the screen to complete the installation.

If the other computers on the network are to use your Internet connection, then their versions of Internet Explorer will have to be reconfigured. From each such PC, run the New Connection Wizard from the **Control Panel** by double-clicking the **Internet Options** icon, selecting the Connections tab and clicking the **Setup** button. Then select the **Connect to the Internet** option, and on the next screen choose the **Set up my connection manually** option.

Finally, the last Wizard screen is displayed as shown in Fig. 9.29.

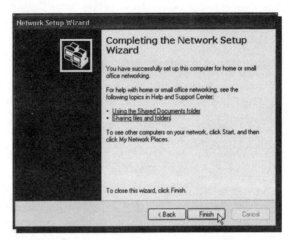

Fig. 9.29 The Last Screen of the Home Networking Wizard.

To share files and folders select them and drag them into the Shared Documents folder. For greater flexibility, you also have the choice of Password protecting selected folders. In addition, if a printer was connected to the computer you are working with, it would have been detected and you could share that one as well.

Activating the Firewall

If you are using a network, it is a good idea to activate the Internet Connection Firewall (ICF) provided by Windows XP. A firewall is a software security system that is used to set restrictions on what information is communicated from your home or small office network to and from the Internet. It protects your network from uninvited outside access - the ICF software sits between a network and the outside world.

 To activate the firewall, click **Start**, **Control Panel**, then double-click the **Network Connections** icon, shown here, to display the window in Fig. 9.30 on the next page.

Fig. 9.30 The Network Connections Window.

Next, select the **Dial-up** connection and click the **Change settings of this connection** entry under the **Network Tasks**. In the displayed Properties dialogue box click the Advanced tab and check the **Protect my computer and network by limiting or preventing access to this computer from the Internet** box shown in Fig. 9.31.

Clicking the **Settings** button, displays another window, shown in Fig. 9.32, in which you can select restrictions appropriate to your system set-up.

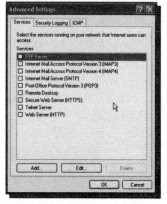

Fig. 9.31 The Properties Window.

Fig. 9.32 The Advanced Settings Window.

Use the Help System for a detailed explanation of these advanced settings.

Towards the Mobile Office

Several of Windows XP's features are geared to making life a little easier for those who use computers on the move.

Dial-Up Networking

With Dial-Up Networking, you can access shared information on another computer, even if your computer is not connected to the network. To do this you must dial directly to the network server, which controls the resources of the network. If you have a computer at home, you can dial in to your office network server and connect to your work computer. Obviously, both your computer at home and the network server at work must have modems installed.

The easiest way of starting Dial-Up Networking is to click **Start**, **Control Panel**, then double-click the **Network Connections** icon to display the window in Fig. 9.33 below.

Fig. 9.33 The Network Connections Window.

Now click the **Create a New Connection** option which starts the New Connection Wizard, the second screen of which is shown in Fig. 9.34 on the next page.

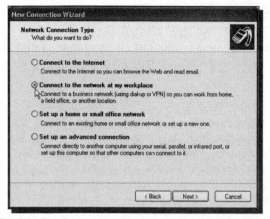

Fig. 9.34 The Second New Network Connection Wizard Screen.

Next click the **Connect to the network at my workplace** radio button followed by the **Next** button to display the third Wizard screen, as shown in Fig. 9.35.

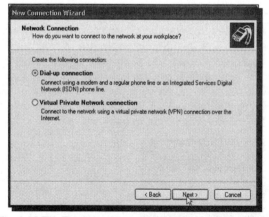

Fig. 9.35 The Third New Network Connection Wizard Screen.

Having selected **Dial-up connection**, click the **Next** button to proceed with the set-up, and eventually, you will be asked to give a name to your new connection. Next time you click **Start**, **Connect To**, you will find an extra service listed in the menu. To connect to this service, click its icon, enter a password and click the **Dial** button on the displayed Connect dialogue box.

Using Briefcase or Offline Files

In Windows XP you can choose to work with files that are stored on your main computer or files that are stored on a network. Which option you choose depends on your needs at the time.

- Use the Briefcase tool if you frequently transfer files between computers using a direct cable connection or a removable disc. With Briefcase, you can synchronise the files you modified on another computer with their counterparts on your main computer. Furthermore, you can keep your files organised by creating multiple briefcases.

- Use the Offline Files tool if you want to work with shared files on a network. Using Offline Files, you can make changes to shared files while disconnected from the network and then synchronise them the next time you are connected to the network.

Briefcase Files: You can use the Briefcase feature to keep your copies of files updated when you work on them away from your main PC. The two main uses are if you work with a portable computer, such as a laptop, when away from the office, or if you transport files home in the evening on removable discs to work on your own PC. Sooner or later, you end up with the situation that the two sets of files are different and you don't know which one to use.

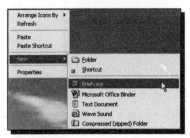

Fig. 9.36 Creating a New Briefcase.

Windows XP does not automatically place the Briefcase icon on your desktop. To activate the tool, right-click on an empty area of your desktop, then select **New, Briefcase** from the cascade menu shown in Fig. 9.36. This selection places the New

Briefcase icon on your desktop with its name highlighted ready for you to rename.

To use Briefcase with a portable computer, you connect the portable and desktop computers and drag the files from the folders on your main computer to the Briefcase folder icon on your portable. When you next return to the office, after working on the files, reconnect to your main computer, open the Briefcase and click **Update All** in the Briefcase menu to automatically update the files on your main computer with the modified ones in your Briefcase. Sounds a little complicated, but it's not really.

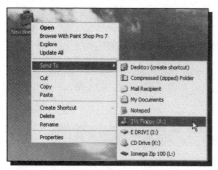

Fig. 9.37 Moving Briefcase to a Floppy.

To use a Briefcase with a floppy, you first copy the Briefcase icon onto the floppy disc (right-click it and select the **Send To** option, as shown in Fig. 9.37), then use My Computer to locate the folder (or file) you want to take home, click the **Copy this folder** (or **file**) option, then click the floppy in the displayed Copy Items dialogue box which then displays the Briefcase on the floppy, as shown in Fig. 9.38.

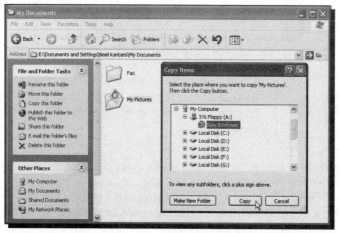

Fig. 9.38 Transferring Files to the Briefcase on the Floppy.

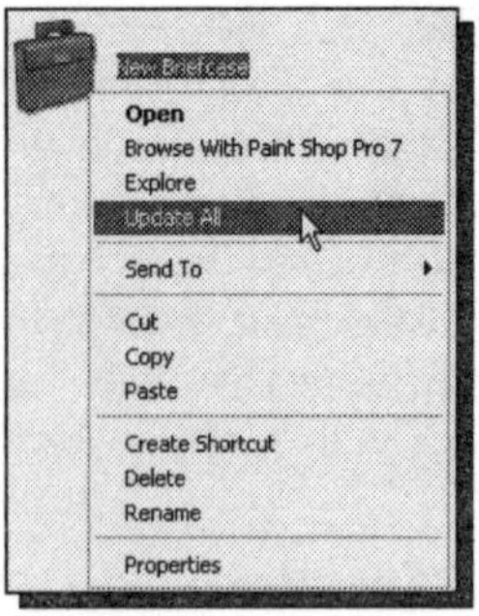

Fig. 9.39 Updating Files.

Next, take the floppy home and burn the midnight oil, using the files from the Briefcase. No need to copy them anywhere, but obviously make sure you save your work back to the Briefcase before packing it in.

When back in the office, open your floppy, right-click on the Briefcase icon and select Update All, as shown in Fig. 9.39. Now to the clever bit. The window in Fig. 9.40 will open, listing any files that have been amended.

In our case, there was only one file changed. If you are happy with the suggested course of action in this window, click the Update button.

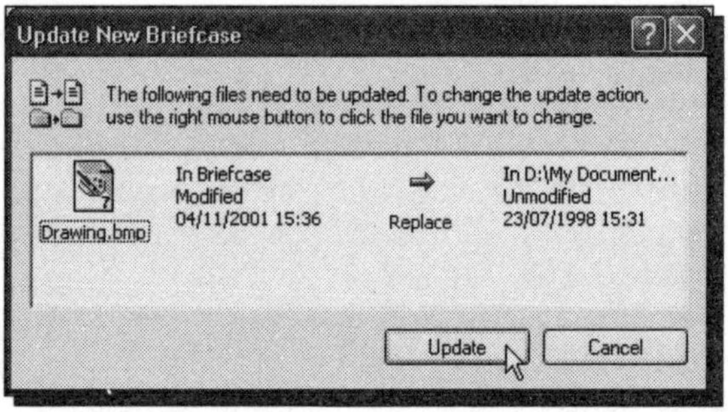

Fig. 9.40 The Update Briefcase Dialogue Box.

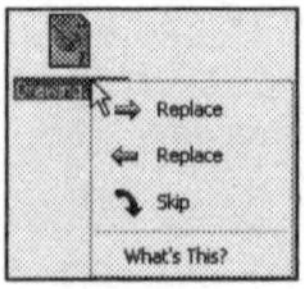

If not, you can right-click a file name and change the action, as shown to the left. The **What's This** option gives you some help, if you need it.

Note: It is essential that you close the Briefcase located on a removable disc, before you actually remove the disc from your PC. This is to ensure that the Briefcase database is updated, otherwise you will be in danger of losing data. If you are careless here, Windows tries to warn you with the message shown in Fig. 9.41 on the next page.

Fig. 9.41 The Save Briefcase Warning Message.

If you still ignore this, you do so at your peril - or rather your data's peril!

Offline Files: By using Offline Files, you can continue to work with network files and programs even when you are not connected to the network because, say, you have lost your connection to it or undocked your portable computer. In such a case, your view of shared network items that have been made available off-line remains just as it was when you were connected, and you can continue to work with them. With Offline Files, you have the same access permissions to those files and folders as you would have if you were connected to the network. When the status of your connection changes, an Offline Files icon appears in the status area, and an information balloon is displayed near it to notify you of the change.

When your network connection is restored or when you dock your portable computer, any changes that you made while working off-line are updated to the network. If more than one person makes changes to the same file, you are given the option of saving your version of the file to the network, keeping the other version, or saving both.

Your network system administrator can set up shared folders so that either every network file you open in that shared folder is automatically made available off-line, or only those network files you choose are made available off-line. However, unlike shortcuts to files, if a shortcut to a folder is made available off-line, the contents of that folder will not be made available off-line.

To set up your computer to use Offline Files, click **Start**, **My Computer**, then use the **Tools, Folder Options** menu command to display the Folder Options dialogue box shown in Fig. 9.42 on the next page.

On the Offline Files tab sheet, make sure that the **Enable Offline Files** check box is selected. Also, select **Synchronize all offline files before logging off** to get a full synchronisation or leave it unchecked for a quick synchronisation. A full synchronisation ensures that you have the most current versions of every network file that has been made available off-line, while a quick synchronisation ensures that you have complete versions of all your off-line files, though they may not necessarily be the most current versions.

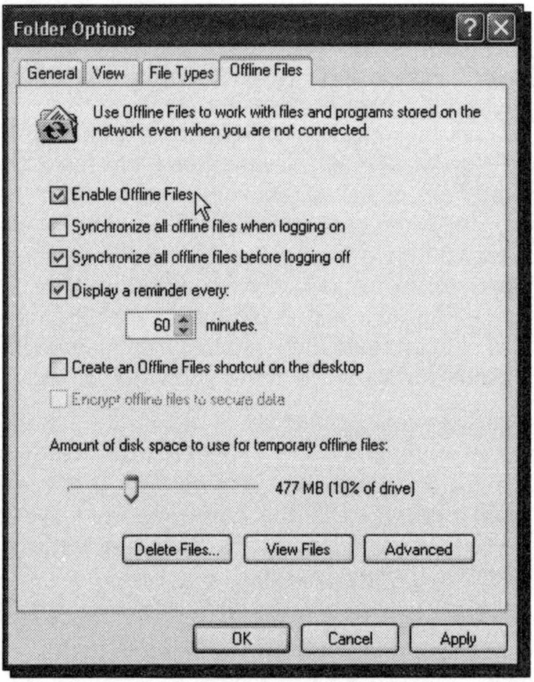

Fig. 9.42 The Folder Options Dialogue Box.

If you want to know more about the practicalities of Offline Files, may we suggest you approach your system administrator, as each such person will most certainly have a different idea on how such a system should work. Good luck!

10

System Tools

Windows XP, as you would expect, comes equipped with a full range of system utility programs so that you can maintain your PC's set-up as easily as possible. By default, access to all these tools is from the **Start** menu, using the **All Programs, Accessories, System Tools** route which opens the cascade menu options shown in Fig. 10.1 below.

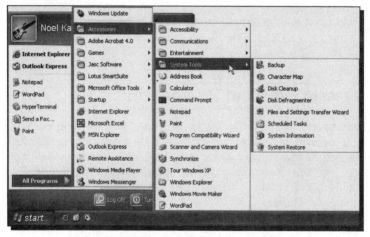

Fig. 10.1 The Cascade System Tools Menu.

We have already come across two of the **System Tools** sub-menu options; the **Character Map** and the **Files and Settings Transfer Wizard** were discussed in Chapter 6 (page 113 and 120). Of the remaining options, the **System Information** is the easiest to examine. This option offers a number of choices (Fig. 10.2), such as System Summary, Hardware Resources, etc., each one of which will be different for you from that of our system. Therefore, we leave it to you to examine the information of your own system.

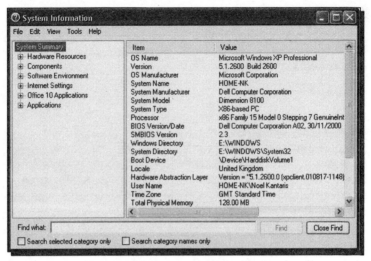

Fig. 10.2 The System Information Window.

System Problem Prevention

In versions of the OS prior to Windows Me, backing up both your system set-up and data files from hard disc to another storage medium, was essential. First with Windows Me and now with Windows XP, you have a threefold protection against System corruption. These are: System File Protection, Automatic Update, and System Restore, all of which will be discussed shortly. So now, all you have to look after is your data. After all, hard discs can 'crash' (though not as often these days as they used to) and your PC could be stolen, or lost in a fire, or flood. Any of these events would cause a serious data loss, unless you had a copy of it all, and stored it safely.

System File Protection

Windows applications sometimes can, and do, overwrite important System files which, in the past, could render your system unusable. Windows XP protects such System files by automatically restoring them to their original version, if any changes have been attempted by an application program.

Automatic Update

Windows XP can update automatically any System files, if these become available, from Microsoft's Web site. All you have to do is click **Start, All Programs**, and select the **Windows Update** menu option, as shown in Fig. 10.3.

After connecting to the Internet through your Internet Service Provider (ISP), you will be connected automatically to Microsoft's Web site, as shown in Fig. 10.4 below.

Fig. 10.3 The Windows Update Menu Option.

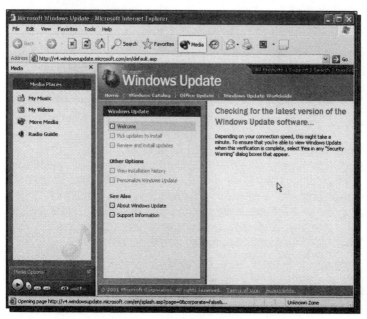

Fig. 10.4 Connecting to Microsoft's Update Home Page.

Next, click the Welcome link to get an appropriate list of updates for your system. However, in order to be able to download program patches to your system, the Windows Update program needs to have information relating to your system configuration, as shown in Fig. 10.5.

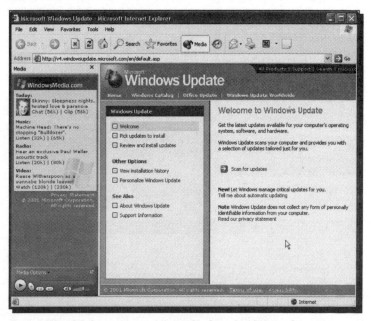

Fig. 10.5 Connecting to Microsoft's Scan for Updates Screen.

Once this is done, you can select which software to download, if any. Be careful you don't go overboard with your selection of downloads ... think of your telephone bill. On successful completion of program downloads, the Windows **Setup** program installs the new patches or programs to your system automatically, after which you can either go back to browse Microsoft's site, or you can disconnect from the Internet.

New to Windows XP is the ability of the program to manage critical updates automatically as you can see on the entry in the right panel of the updates screen. We suggest you spend some time finding out a bit more about this before you commit to it.

System Restore

If things go really wrong, System Restore can be used to return your PC to the last date it was working perfectly. Every time you start to install a new program, Windows XP takes a snapshot of your system prior to starting the new installation. Alternatively, you can force Windows to take a snapshot any time you choose.

 To examine the System Restore utility, use the **Start, All Programs, Accessories, System Tools** and click on its icon, shown here, which displays the screen in Fig. 10.6.

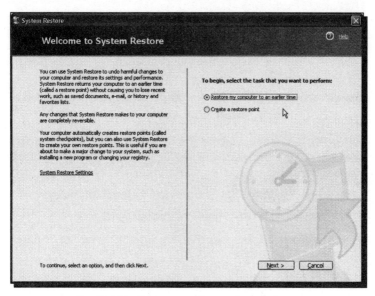

Fig. 10.6 The Welcome to System Restore Screen.

As you can see, from this screen you can select to Restore your computer to an earlier time, or create a Restore point. To demonstrate further what happens, we chose the **Restore my computer to an earlier time** option, then clicked the **Next** button. This displays a further screen, as shown in Fig. 10.7 on the next page.

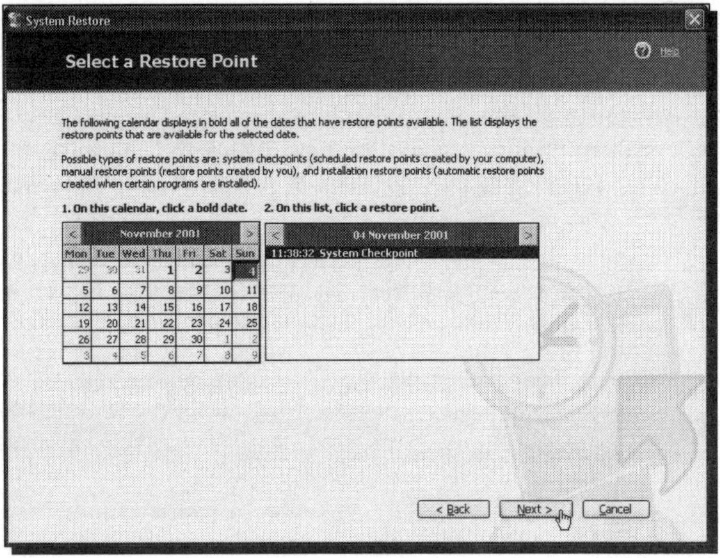

Fig. 10.7 Selecting a System Restore Point.

The dates shown in bold in the calendar are Restore points created by Windows XP. The three possible types of Restore points are:

- System Restore points created by your computer
- Manual Restore points created by you
- Restore points automatically created prior to installing certain programs.

If you select to create a Manual Restore point, Windows XP asks you to give a description of this Restore point so that you can identify it easily at a later stage, as shown in Fig. 10.8.

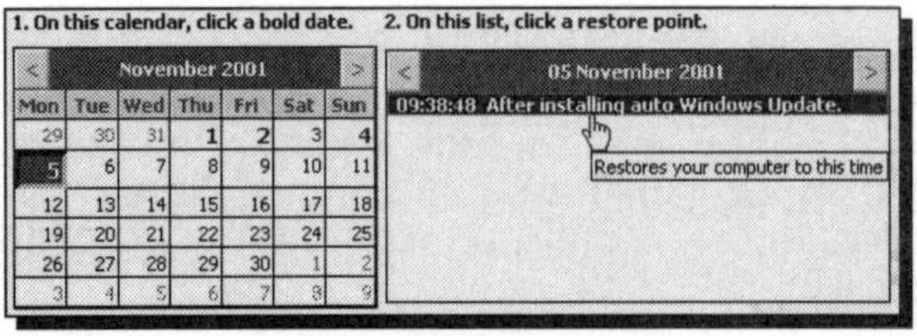

Fig. 10.8 A Manual Restore Point.

Disc Cleanup

You can run Disk Cleanup to help you free up space on your hard drive. The first thing that Disk Cleanup does after activation, is to ask you to select the drive you want to

clean up, as shown in Fig. 10.9. It then scans the specified drive, and then lists temporary files, Internet cache files, and un-necessary program files that you can safely delete, as shown in Fig. 10.10.

Fig. 10.9 Selecting a Drive.

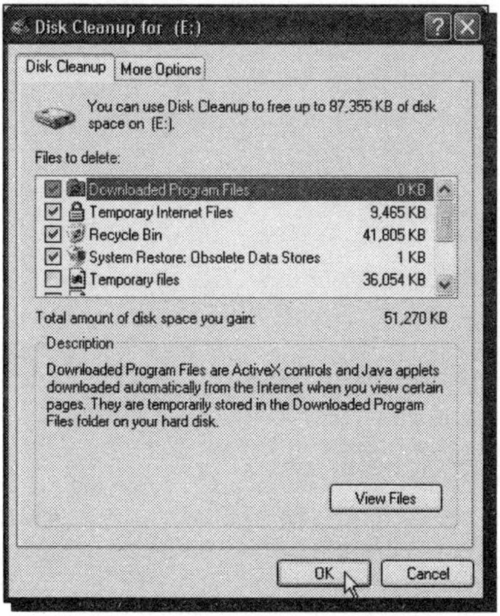

Fig. 10.10 Files Found by Cleanup.

As you can see, in our case, we could free 9,465 KB of disc space by simply deleting the Temporary Internet Files (Web pages stored on your hard disc for quick viewing), and 41,805 KB by deleting information in the Recycle Bin. The More Options tab allows you to remove Windows components and installed programs that you do not use any more.

Defragmenting your Hard Discs

 The Disk Defragmenter optimises a hard disc by rearranging the data on it to eliminate unused spaces, which speeds up access to the disc by Windows operations. You don't need to exit a running application before starting the Disk Defragmenter.

Choose which drive to defragment and you can defragment it in the background while working by minimising the utility onto the Task bar. On the other hand, you can watch the process of the operation.

For example, having selected a drive and clicking the **Analyze** button, you will be told whether defragmentation is needed or not. On the other hand, clicking the **Defragment** button, starts the process which is shown in Fig. 10.11 below.

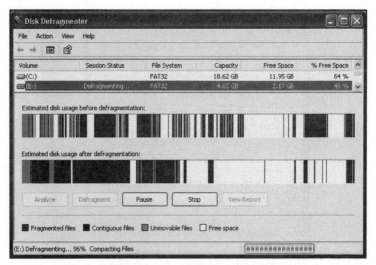

Fig. 10.11 Defragmentation in Progress.

On your screen you can see which files are fragmented (shown in red) and which files are not fragmented (shown in blue), while free space is shown in white. For large drives this process can take a long time, so make time for it!

Scheduled Tasks

The **Scheduled Tasks** option allows you to carry out several housekeeping tasks, such as disc cleanup, or defragmenting your data, at times convenient to you. Clicking its icon, opens the window shown in Fig. 10.12 below.

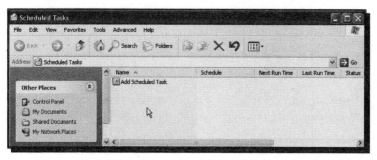

Fig. 10.12 The Scheduled Tasks Window.

On here, double-click the **Add Scheduled Task** icon to start the Wizard. Clicking **Next** on the first Wizard screen displays the second Wizard screen, shown in Fig. 10.13 below:

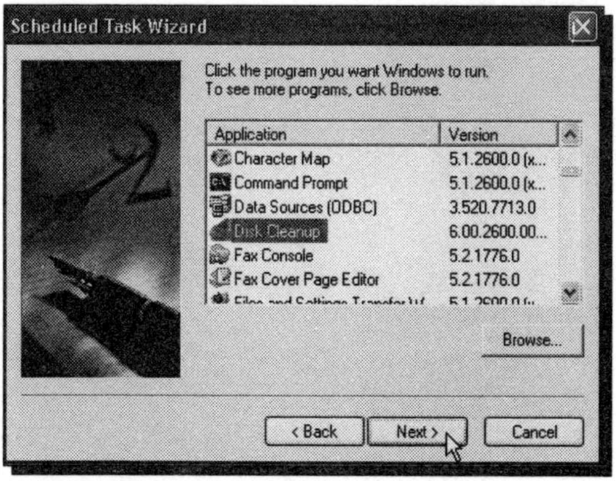

Fig. 10.13 The Second Scheduled Task Wizard.

On this screen (Fig. 10.13), select the task to be Scheduled then click the **Next** button to display:

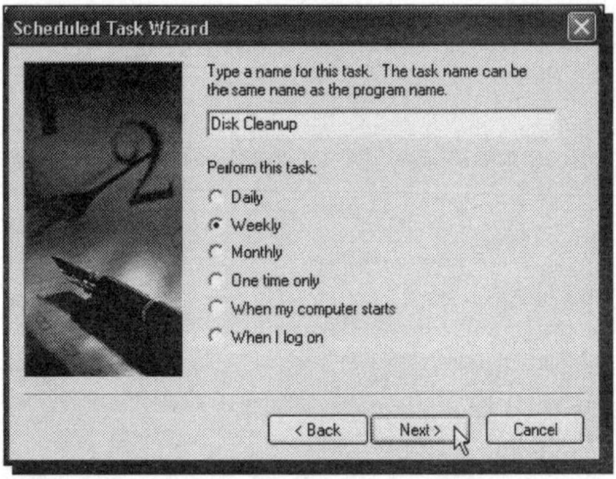

Fig. 10.14 The Third Scheduled Task Wizard Screen.

On this screen (Fig. 10.14) you are asked to specify the frequency at which you would like the selected task to be performed (we selected weekly in our example). Having done so, press the **Next** button to display the fourth Wizard screen, shown in Fig. 10.15 below.

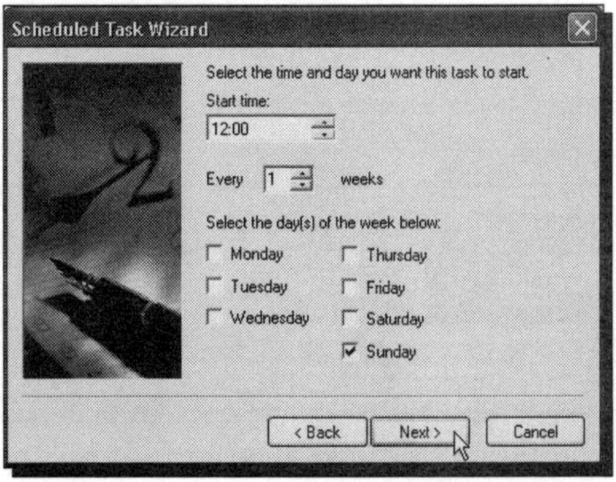

Fig. 10.15 The Fourth Scheduled Task Wizard Screen.

On this screen you are asked to specify when you want the selected task to be carried out. Obviously, your computer must be switched on in order to perform such scheduled tasks, so it's up to you to choose a convenient time. Having done so, press the **Next** button to display the fifth Wizard screen, shown in Fig. 10.16 below.

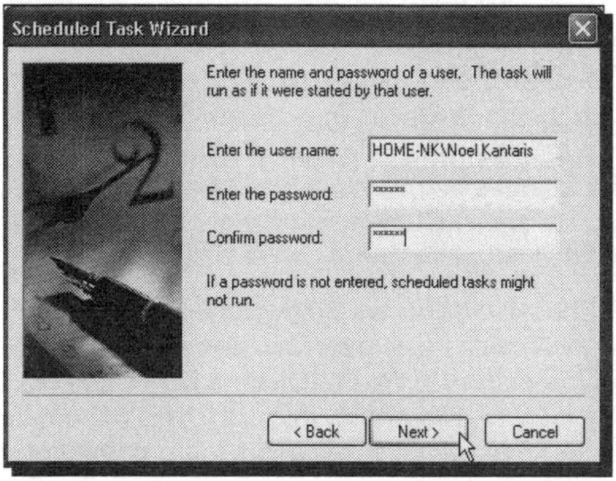

Fig. 10.16 The Fifth Scheduled Task Wizard Screen.

As you can see from the Wizard screen, you can enter the name of a user and a password. The task is then run as if it were started by the specified user. Clicking **Next**, displays the final Wizard screen and clicking the **Finish** button, performs the selected task at its chosen time.

It is a good idea to perform such tasks regularly, but make sure that

* your computer is switched on at the selected times, and

* you are not inconvenienced by your time selection.

It is, of course assumed that your PC's clock is showing the same time as your watch, otherwise you might get some unexpected surprises!

Power Saving Management

You can automatically put your computer into hibernation or standby, provided   you log on as an administrator, and your computer is set up by the manufacturer to support these options. If your computer is connected to a network, network policy settings may prevent you from completing these tasks.

Hibernation Mode

When your computer is put into hibernation mode, everything in the computer memory is saved on your hard disc, and your computer is switched off. When you turn the computer back on, all programs and documents that were open when you turned the computer off are restored on the desktop.

To initiate hibernation, activate the **Control Panel** and double-click the **Power Options** icon shown here. Then, in the displayed Power Options Properties dialogue box, click the Hibernate tab. If the Hibernate tab is unavailable, then this is because your computer does not support this feature. If it does, make sure the **Enable hibernation** box is checked, as shown in Fig. 10.17.

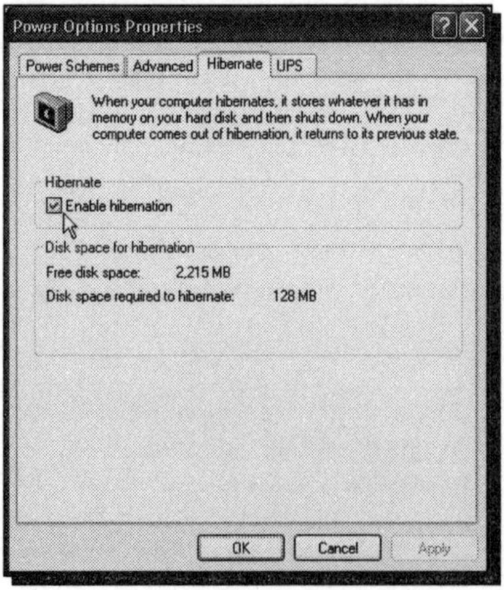

Fig. 10.17 The Power Options Properties Screen.

Next, click the Advance tab and select what you want under **Options**, then click the down-arrow button against the **When I press the power button on my computer** box and choose what you want to happen from the drop-down options list shown in Fig. 10.18.

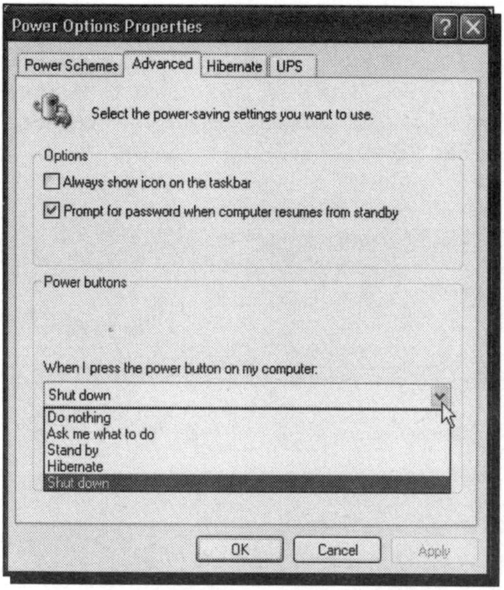

Fig. 10.18 The Power Button Options List.

Next, click the Power Schemes tab, and select a time in **System hibernates**. If you set this to, say, 'after 1 min', then you can sit back and see what happens. With our system, after one minute we were informed that it was safe to switch off the computer, which we did. When switching on the computer a few seconds later, Windows XP started up automatically (the dual boot option became unavailable) and loaded all the programs that happened to be loaded at the time of hibernation.

If you decide that you do not want your system to hibernate, just go through the procedure described above and uncheck the selected option in the Power Options Properties screen of Fig. 10.17. Finally, click the Power Schemes tab, and select 'never' for the time the **System hibernates**.

Standby Mode

When your computer is put into standby mode, information in computer memory is not saved to your hard disc. You must save all your work before putting your computer into standby mode, because if there is an interruption in power, all information in the computer's memory will be lost.

To initiate standby mode, activate the Control Panel and click on the Power Options icon. In the displayed Power Options Properties dialogue box, click the Power Schemes tab, as shown in Fig. 10.19.

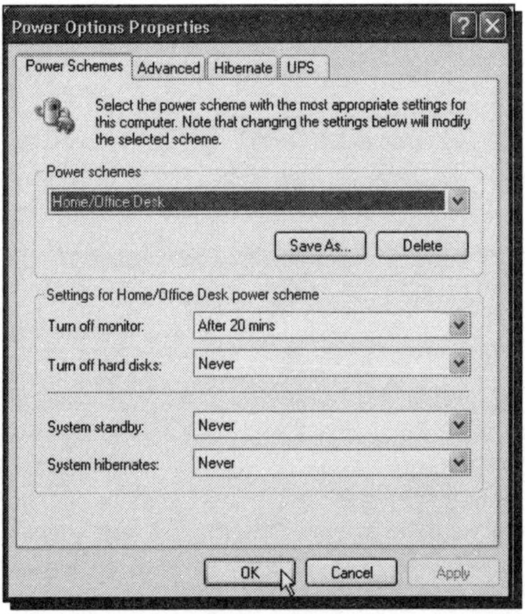

Fig. 10.19 The Power Options Power Scheme Screen.

If you are using a portable computer, you can specify one setting for battery power and a different setting for AC power. In fact, you can adjust any power management option that your computer's hardware configuration supports.

Drive Conversion to NTFS

If you did not choose to convert your Windows XP drive from the FAT file system to the NTFS file system during installation, you can do so at any time. However, before doing so, you must consider the various advantages and disadvantages associated with such a conversion. Although we have discussed this topic at the beginning of the book, we reiterate these again below.

* Do not convert your Windows XP drive to the NTFS file system if you intend to retain your Windows 95/98/Me installation, and you want to exchange document files between the two systems (in both directions).

* Convert to NTFS if you want to get better file security, including the Encrypting File System (EFS) which protects data on your hard drive by encrypting each file with a randomly generated key.

* Convert to NTFS if you want better disc compression and better support for large hard discs.

* Convert to NTFS if you have a large hard drive and don't want its performance to degrade as it does with the FAT or FAT32 system.

Finally, from an NTFS partition you can browse, read and write to files on the FAT or FAT32 partitions, but Windows 95/98/Me cannot detect the NTFS partition, so it cannot interfere with its settings. However, the conversion to NTFS is one-way, therefore, you will not be able to convert back to FAT or FAT32.

To convert your Windows XP FAT or FAT32 drive to NTFS, click on **Start** then select **All Programs, Accessories, Command Prompt** option, then type the following commands in two lines, pressing the <Enter> key at the end of each line, as shown in Fig. 10.20 below.

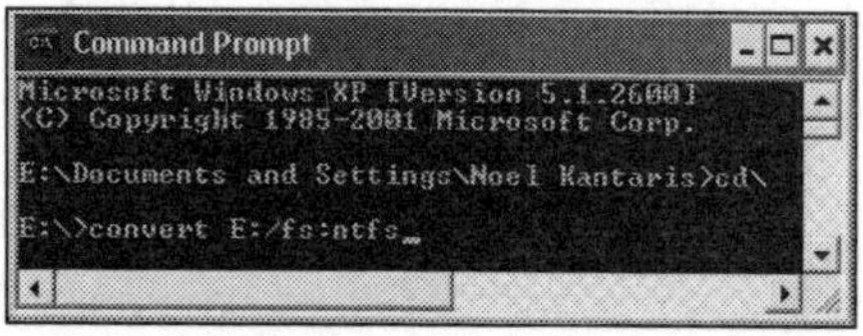

cd\
Convert E:/fs:ntfs

Fig. 10.20 Command Prompt.

Scanning a Hard Disc for Errors

Windows XP incorporates a utility that can check the integrity of your hard disc, and if it finds any errors, it can attempt to repair them. To start this utility, click My Computer then in the displayed screen right-click the drive you want to check, select **Properties** from the drop-down menu and click the **Tools** tab to display the screen in Fig. 10.21.

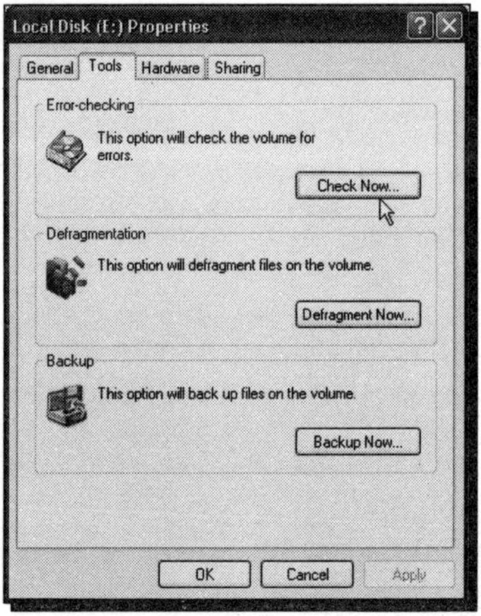

Fig. 10.21 The Disk Properties Screen.

As you can see, you have three choices; **Check Now** for disc errors, **Defragment Now**, or **Backup Now**. The last option is not available in the Windows XP Home edition.

Before you can start scanning your selected drive for errors, all running programs and applications on that drive must be closed. If you start this utility while a program on that drive is running, you will be informed of the fact in a warning box. If your disc or disc partition is formatted as NTFS, Windows automatically logs all file transactions, replaces bad clusters, and stores copies of key information for all files on the NTFS disc or disc partition.

The Backup Program

Because your system state data files are backed up by System Restore, Microsoft has only included the Backup program with the Windows XP Professional edition in which case the Backup program will be listed in the **System Tools**. The program should be used on a regular basis to back up both system set-up and data files from the hard disc to another, removable, storage medium, as hard discs can 'crash' (though not as often these days as they used to) and your PC could be stolen, or lost in a fire, or flood. Any of these events would cause a serious data loss, particularly to businesses, unless you had backed it all up, and stored it somewhere safely, preferably away from the vicinity of the PC.

Making a Back-up

We will step through the procedure of backing up, and then restoring, a selection of files. You should then be happy to carry on by yourself. Clicking the **Backup** icon in the **System Tools**, starts the Backup or Restore Wizard, as shown in Fig. 10.22.

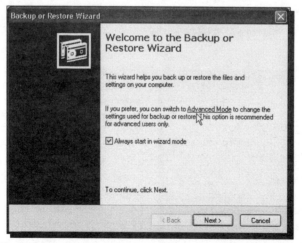

Fig. 10.22 The Windows XP Professional Backup Welcome Screen.

Note the **Advance Mode** link pointed to above. Activating this link allows you to schedule backups. We will look at this later.

The back-up procedure can be carried out on a tape, a floppy disc, or a removable disc. In our example, we first chose in the second Wizard screen to 'back up files and settings', then in the third Wizard screen we selected the 'Let me choose what to back up' option. In the fourth Wizard screen, shown in Fig. 10.23 below, we selected the My Documents folder by clicking the + sign to open its structure in the left-hand pane, then double-clicking the My Pictures folder to check it.

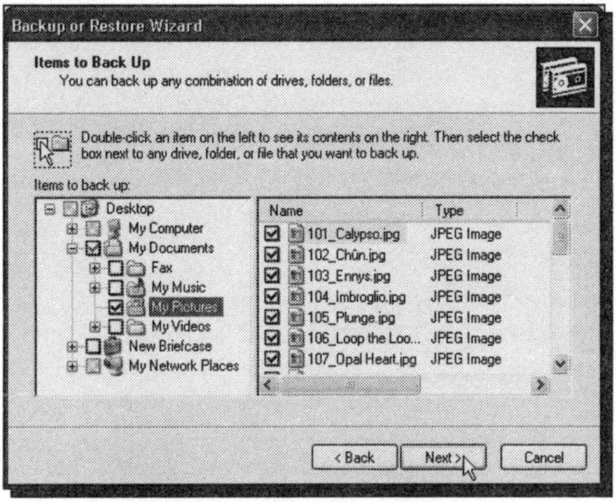

Fig. 10.23 Selecting items to Back Up.

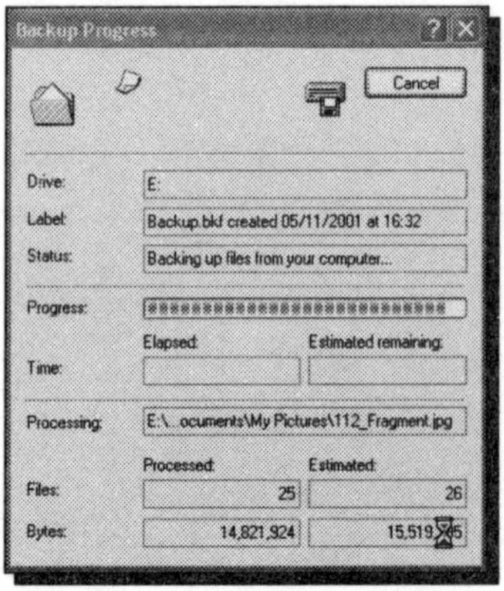

Fig. 10.24 Backing Up Process.

To select, or deselect, individual files, tick in their boxes in the right-hand pane, as shown above, and press the **Next** button. The Backup Wizard asks you to select what and where to back up, give a name to your back-up file that means something to you in the future, gives you a summary of what is intended, and lets you start the process. The window shown in Fig. 10.24, keeps you informed during the backing up process.

Backup Types

By default, during our demonstration, we have created a 'Normal' backup of the selected files. To see what other types of backup exist, first return to the opening screen of the Backup or Restore Wizard, then click the **Advance Mode** link to display the screen in Fig. 10.25.

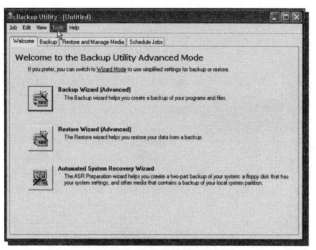

Fig. 10.25 The Advanced Backup Utility.

Next, use the **Tools, Options** command to open the Options

dialogue box shown in Fig. 10.26.

The Backup utility supports five methods of backing up data on your computer or network. These are listed on the next page.

Fig. 10.26 Selecting the Backup Type.

Normal Backup	Copies all selected files and marks them as having been backed up. With normal backups, you need only the most recent copy of the backup file or tape to restore all of the files. A normal backup is usually performed the first time you create a backup set.
Copy Backup	Copies all selected files but does not mark them as having been backed up. Copying is useful if you want to back up files between normal and incremental backups because it does not affect these other backup operations.
Differential Backup	Copies files created or changed since the last normal or incremental backup. It does not mark files as having been backed up. If you are performing a combination of normal and differential backups, restoring files and folders requires that you have the last normal as well as the last differential backup.
Incremental Backup	Backs up only those files created or changed since the last normal or incremental backup. It marks files as having been backed up. If you use a combination of normal and incremental backups, you will need to have the last normal backup set as well as all incremental backup sets in order to restore your data.
Daily Backup	Copies all selected files that have been modified the day the daily backup is performed. The backed-up files are not marked as having been backed up.

If the data files you are backing up are not very large in size, then using a normal backup is the easiest method. The backup set is stored on one disc or tape and restoring data from it is very easy.

If the amount of your storage space is limited, then back up your data using a combination of normal and incremental backups; it is the quickest method. However, recovering files can be time-consuming and difficult because the backup set can be stored on several discs or tapes.

Finally, backing up your data using a combination of normal and differential backups is more time-consuming, especially if your data changes frequently, but it is easier to restore the data because the backup set is usually stored on only a few discs or tapes.

Restoring your Files

To restore files that have been previously backed up, place the first disc of the set in the disc drive, activate the Backup or Restore Wizard and on the second Wizard screen click the Restore radio button followed by **Next**. Again, click the + sign to open the file structure in the left-hand pane of the Restore window, as shown in Fig. 10.27.

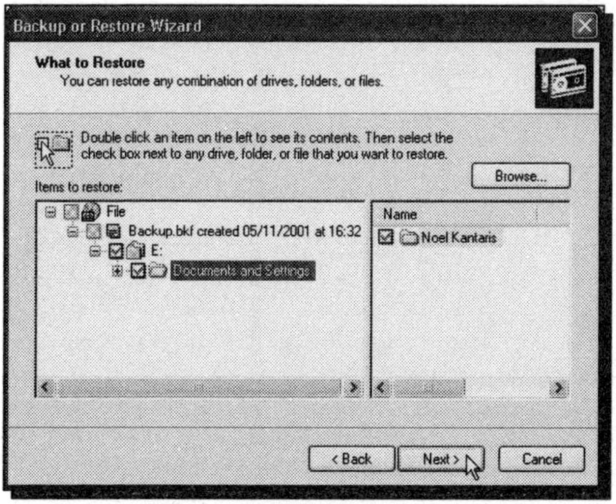

Fig. 10.27 Selecting the Backup Set to Restore.

Pressing the **Next** button, causes the program to display a Summary screen of the restore procedure. Clicking the **Advanced** button on this Summary screen, gives you a choice on where to restore the selected items, then what to do when restoring files that already exist, as shown in Fig. 10.28.

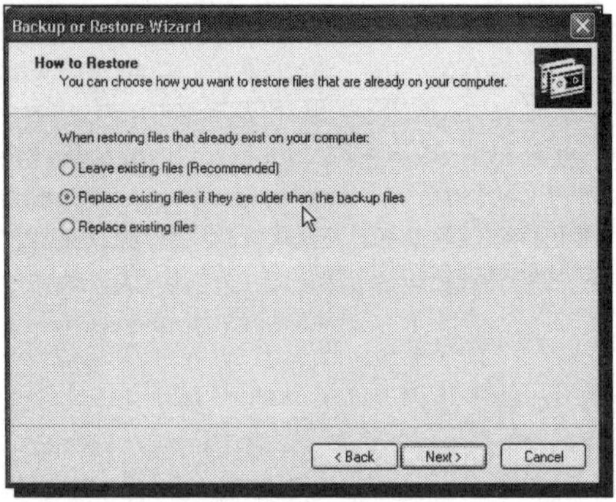

Fig. 10.28 Selecting How to Restore.

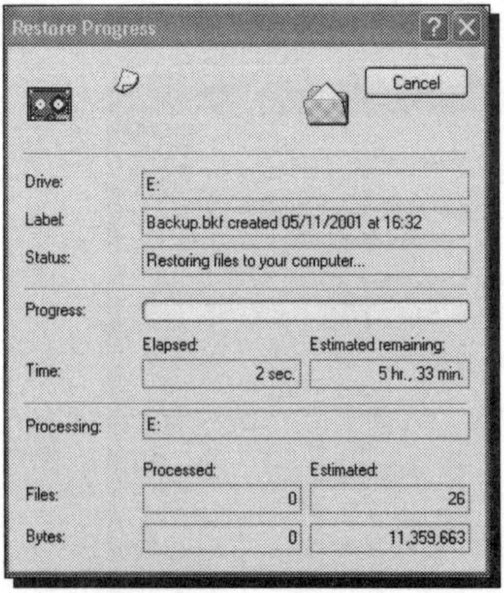

Fig. 10.29 The Restore Progress Screen.

A good choice would be to select the option to 'Replace the file on disk only if it is older than the backup copy'. After making an appropriate selection on file replacement and file security, pressing the **Finish** button causes the Wizard to start the restore process, as shown in Fig. 10.29.

Hopefully you should by now be completely sold on the Backup utility.

11

The Command Prompt

If you are an experienced PC user, you may well prefer to do much of your specialised work by entering instructions in the Command window. Windows XP, just like Windows NT/2000, still lets you do this.

To display the Command Prompt window, click **Start, All Programs, Accessories** and select the **Command Prompt** option from the cascade menu. This opens the window in Fig. 11.1 below.

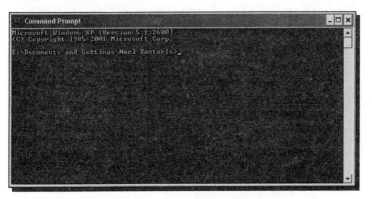

Fig. 11.1 The Command Prompt Window.

For this section of the book, you might find it more convenient to place a shortcut to the Command Prompt icon on your desktop. To do this, right-click its entry on the cascade menu, then select **Send To, Desktop** from the displayed drop-down menu.

If you are a Windows 95/98/Me user, you will notice the absence of the Toolbar from the above window. However, don't despair, as most of the commands provided by such a Toolbar can be carried out from the command menu.

To illustrate this, let us change the appearance of the Command Prompt screen so that you can display, say, black lettering on white background. To do this, click on the Command button (to be found at the upper left corner of the window) which displays the drop-down menu shown in Fig. 11.2 to the left. Next, select the **Properties** menu option which displays the dialogue box in Fig. 11.3.

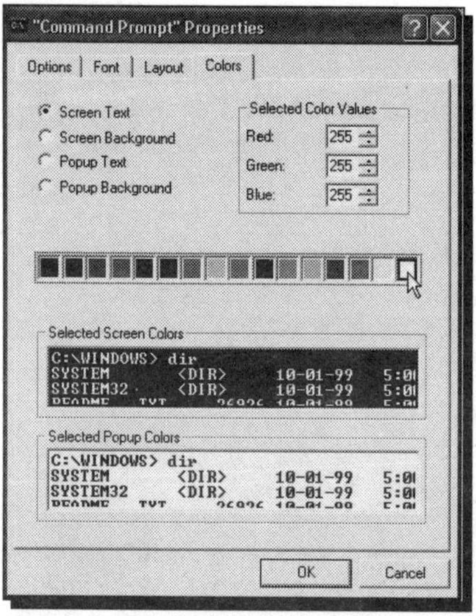

Fig. 11.2 The Command Shortcut Menu.

Here we show the Colors tab sheet in which we made the following selections:

Screen Text: Black
Screen Background: White
Popup Text: Blue
Popup Background: Grey.

In the Options tab sheet, you can select the Cursor Size, Display Options (window or full screen), Command History, and Edit Options. In the Font tab sheet you can select Font Size and Font Style. In the Layout tab sheet you

Fig. 11.3 The Properties Dialogue Box.

can select Screen Buffer Size, Window Size, and Window Position. Pressing the **OK** button, displays an additional dialogue box, asking you to select between 'Apply properties to current window only', or 'Modify shortcut that started this window'. Choosing the latter will make your selections default for all sessions of the Command Prompt.

In Windows XP, just like in Windows NT/2000, you use DOS commands in the Command Prompt window. To illustrate the point, type *dir* and press the <Enter> key. What is displayed is shown at the top half of the screen in Fig. 11.4.

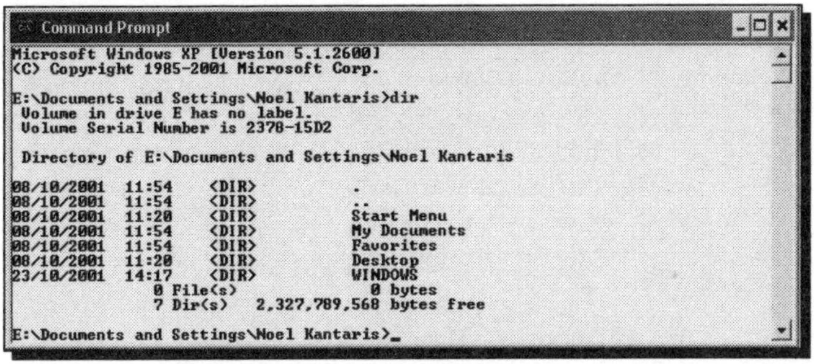

```
Command Prompt
Microsoft Windows XP [Version 5.1.2600]
(C) Copyright 1985-2001 Microsoft Corp.

E:\Documents and Settings\Noel Kantaris>dir
 Volume in drive E has no label.
 Volume Serial Number is 2378-15D2

 Directory of E:\Documents and Settings\Noel Kantaris

08/10/2001  11:54    <DIR>          .
08/10/2001  11:54    <DIR>          ..
08/10/2001  11:20    <DIR>          Start Menu
08/10/2001  11:54    <DIR>          My Documents
08/10/2001  11:54    <DIR>          Favorites
08/10/2001  11:20    <DIR>          Desktop
23/10/2001  14:17    <DIR>          WINDOWS
               0 File(s)              0 bytes
               7 Dir(s)   2,327,789,568 bytes free

E:\Documents and Settings\Noel Kantaris>_
```

Fig. 11.4 The Structure of the Disc Holding Windows XP.

This, of course, is a typical DOS screen. To prove the point, type ***dir /w*** and press the <Enter> key. In fact, with Windows XP, as with Windows NT/2000, the facility of using DOS commands in the Command Prompt window is mainly provided for backward compatibility and, therefore, if you want to adopt this method of working, we assume that you must be familiar with DOS commands, switches, filters, and batch files. Such files are most likely to be written by the System Administrator, to perhaps advertise to the network users, rules, events, or new packages.

All the available DOS commands are shown in Fig. 11.6, and can be displayed in the Command Prompt window by typing ***help*** followed by <Enter>. Information on individual commands can be displayed by either typing ***help command_name***, or typing ***command_name /?***. Either will produce an extensive list of command switches with explanation, as shown in Fig. 11.5.

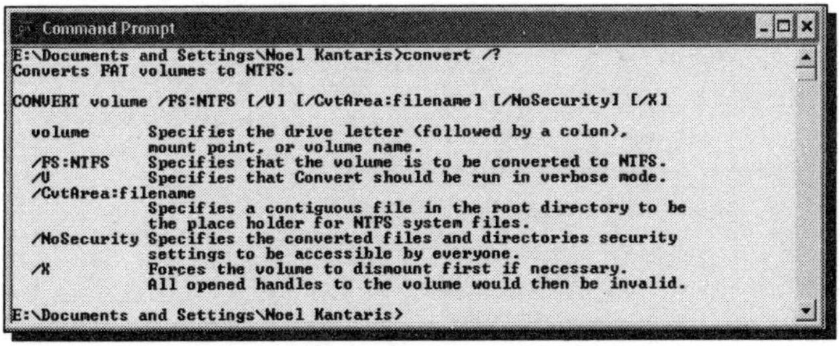

```
Command Prompt
E:\Documents and Settings\Noel Kantaris>convert /?
Converts FAT volumes to NTFS.

CONVERT volume /FS:NTFS [/V] [/CvtArea:filename] [/NoSecurity] [/X]

  volume      Specifies the drive letter (followed by a colon),
              mount point, or volume name.
  /FS:NTFS    Specifies that the volume is to be converted to NTFS.
  /V          Specifies that Convert should be run in verbose mode.
  /CvtArea:filename
              Specifies a contiguous file in the root directory to be
              the place holder for NTFS system files.
  /NoSecurity Specifies the converted files and directories security
              settings to be accessible by everyone.
  /X          Forces the volume to dismount first if necessary.
              All opened handles to the volume would then be invalid.

E:\Documents and Settings\Noel Kantaris>
```

Fig. 11.5 Getting Help with DOS Commands.

```
Command Prompt                                                     - □ ×

E:\Documents and Settings\Noel Kantaris>help
For more information on a specific command, type HELP command-name
ASSOC       Displays or modifies file extension associations.
AT          Schedules commands and programs to run on a computer.
ATTRIB      Displays or changes file attributes.
BREAK       Sets or clears extended CTRL+C checking.
CACLS       Displays or modifies access control lists (ACLs) of files.
CALL        Calls one batch program from another.
CD          Displays the name of or changes the current directory.
CHCP        Displays or sets the active code page number.
CHDIR       Displays the name of or changes the current directory.
CHKDSK      Checks a disk and displays a status report.
CHKNTFS     Displays or modifies the checking of disk at boot time.
CLS         Clears the screen.
CMD         Starts a new instance of the Windows command interpreter.
COLOR       Sets the default console foreground and background colors.
COMP        Compares the contents of two files or sets of files.
COMPACT     Displays or alters the compression of files on NTFS partitions.
CONVERT     Converts FAT volumes to NTFS.  You cannot convert the
            current drive.
COPY        Copies one or more files to another location.
DATE        Displays or sets the date.
DEL         Deletes one or more files.
DIR         Displays a list of files and subdirectories in a directory.
DISKCOMP    Compares the contents of two floppy disks.
DISKCOPY    Copies the contents of one floppy disk to another.
DOSKEY      Edits command lines, recalls Windows commands, and creates macros.
ECHO        Displays messages, or turns command echoing on or off.
ENDLOCAL    Ends localization of environment changes in a batch file.
ERASE       Deletes one or more files.
EXIT        Quits the CMD.EXE program (command interpreter).
FC          Compares two files or sets of files, and displays the differences
            between them.
FIND        Searches for a text string in a file or files.
FINDSTR     Searches for strings in files.
FOR         Runs a specified command for each file in a set of files.
FORMAT      Formats a disk for use with Windows.
FTYPE       Displays or modifies file types used in file extension associations.
GOTO        Directs the Windows command interpreter to a labeled line in a
            batch program.
GRAFTABL    Enables Windows to display an extended character set in graphics
            mode.
HELP        Provides Help information for Windows commands.
IF          Performs conditional processing in batch programs.
LABEL       Creates, changes, or deletes the volume label of a disk.
MD          Creates a directory.
MKDIR       Creates a directory.
MODE        Configures a system device.
MORE        Displays output one screen at a time.
MOVE        Moves one or more files from one directory to another directory.
PATH        Displays or sets a search path for executable files.
PAUSE       Suspends processing of a batch file and displays a message.
POPD        Restores the previous value of the current directory saved by PUSHD.
PRINT       Prints a text file.
PROMPT      Changes the Windows command prompt.
PUSHD       Saves the current directory then changes it.
RD          Removes a directory.
RECOVER     Recovers readable information from a bad or defective disk.
REM         Records comments (remarks) in batch files or CONFIG.SYS.
REN         Renames a file or files.
RENAME      Renames a file or files.
REPLACE     Replaces files.
RMDIR       Removes a directory.
SET         Displays, sets, or removes Windows environment variables.
SETLOCAL    Begins localization of environment changes in a batch file.
SHIFT       Shifts the position of replaceable parameters in batch files.
SORT        Sorts input.
START       Starts a separate window to run a specified program or command.
SUBST       Associates a path with a drive letter.
TIME        Displays or sets the system time.
TITLE       Sets the window title for a CMD.EXE session.
TREE        Graphically displays the directory structure of a drive or path.
TYPE        Displays the contents of a text file.
VER         Displays the Windows version.
VERIFY      Tells Windows whether to verify that your files are written
            correctly to a disk.
VOL         Displays a disk volume label and serial number.
XCOPY       Copies files and directory trees.

E:\Documents and Settings\Noel Kantaris>
```

Fig. 11.6 The Available DOS Commands.

Running DOS Programs

With Windows XP, just as in Windows 95/98/Me/NT/2000, the easiest way to issue a single DOS command that involves

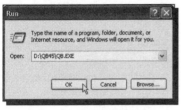

Fig. 11.7 The Run Window.

running a program, is in the **Run** window, shown in Fig. 11.7, opened from the **Start** menu. Its big advantage is that all previous commands are remembered. Clicking the down arrow, opens a small 'database' of your most used

commands, including path and file names, etc. The command itself is actioned in a 'one off' Command Prompt window, as shown in Fig. 11.8 below.

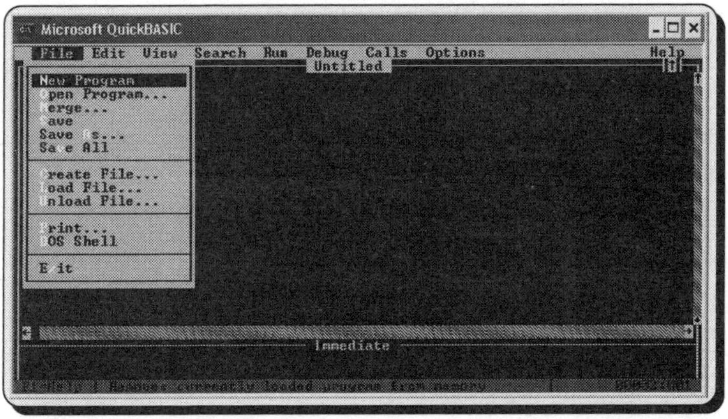

Fig. 11.8 Running a DOS Program in a Command Prompt Window.

To switch between full screen and a window, use the <Alt+Enter> key combination. When you have finished using this window you have to close it by clicking the **x** (close) button, in the top right-hand corner of the screen which displays the End Program warning box. To end the program, click the **End Now** button on the displayed box.

The MS-DOS Editor

Windows XP includes the **Edit** text editor, to be found in the \WINDOWS\system32 subdirectory, as shown in Fig. 11.9.

Users of MS-DOS will find the editor very familiar, as the version provided in Windows XP is identical to that provided with earlier Windows versions. Improvements over much earlier versions of the program are:

Fig. 11.9 Running the Windows Edit.

- You can open up to nine files at the same time, split the screen between two files, and easily copy and paste information between them.

- You can open files as large as 4MB.

- You can open filenames and navigate through the directory structure just as you can in the rest of Windows.

The editor is opened, as one would expect from its name, by typing **Edit** at the Command Prompt, as shown in Fig. 11.10.

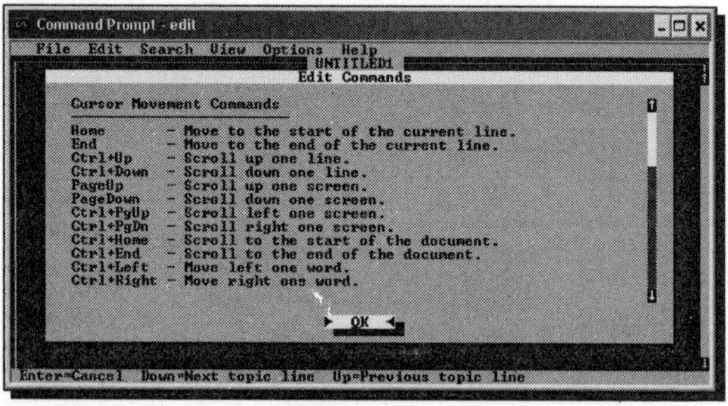

Fig. 11.10 The MS-DOS Text Editor.

The file opened in the editor's window above, is a **readme.txt** file in the background and a Cursor Movement Commands screen on the foreground, obtained by pressing the **F1** function key. To clear the screen, press the <Esc> key.

Copying Text from Old DOS Programs

You can copy text created in old DOS word processing programs and paste it in the latest and most favoured Windows application easily. To illustrate the process, we use below a letter we wrote more than five years ago, using our then loved Q&A word processor. You can follow the technique by using your own DOS word processed document.

First use the **Run** command to locate and load the DOS program, then open a document. Ours is shown in Fig. 11.11.

Fig. 11.11 Marking Text in a DOS Word Processing Program.

Next, click the Command button to open the drop-down menu and select the **Mark** option. This allows you to mark part or the whole of the document then use the **Edit, Copy** command to copy it onto the Windows clipboard, as shown in Fig. 11.12.

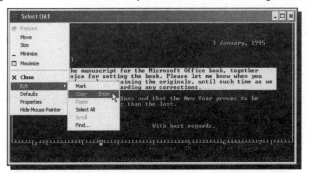

Fig. 11.12 Copying Text from a DOS Word Processing Program.

Finally, open your favourite Windows word processor and use its **Edit, Paste** command, to paste the contents of the clipboard into your new document. We used the WordPad application, as shown in Fig. 11.13 below.

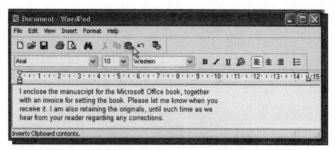

Fig. 11.13 Transferring Text into WordPad.

It is as easy as that. Perhaps this will prove the most useful and time saving capability of the Command Prompt for most users.

12

Glossary of Terms

Access control	A security mechanism that determines which operations a user is authorised to perform on a PC, a file, a printer, etc.
Active	Describes the folder, window or icon that you are currently using or that is currently selected.
Active partition	A partition from which an x86-based computer starts up. The active partition must be a primary partition on a basic disc.
ActiveX	A set of technologies that allows software components to interact with one another in a networked environment, regardless of the language in which the components were created.
Add-in	A mini-program which runs in conjunction with another and enhances its functionality.
Address	A unique number or name that identifies a specific computer or user on a network.
Administrator	For Windows XP Professional, a person responsible for setting up and managing local computers, their user and group accounts, and assigning passwords and permissions.

Anonymous FTP	Anonymous FTP allows you to connect to a remote computer and transfer public files back to your local computer without the need to have a user ID and password.
Applet	A program that can be downloaded over a network and launched on the user's computer.
Application	Software (program) designed to carry out a certain activity, such as word processing, or data management.
Archie	Archie is an Internet service that allows you to locate files that can be downloaded via FTP.
ASCII	A binary code representation of a character set. The name stands for 'American Standard Code for Information Interchange'.
ASP	Active Server Page. File format used for dynamic Web pages that get their data from a server based database.
Association	An identification of a filename extension to a program. This lets Windows open the program when its files are selected.
Audio input device	A device that records music and voice input into your computer, such as a microphone or a CD-ROM player.
Authentication	The process for verifying that an entity or object is who or what it claims to be.
Authoring	The process of creating web documents or software.
AVI	Audio Video Interleaved. A Windows multimedia file format for sound and moving pictures.

Backbone	The main transmission lines of the Internet, running at over 45 Mbps.
Background	The screen background image used on a graphical user interface such as Windows.
Backup	To make a back-up copy of a file or a disc for safekeeping.
Bandwidth	The range of transmission frequencies a network can use. The greater the bandwidth the more information that can be transferred over a network.
Banner	An advertising graphic shown on a Web page.
BASIC	Beginner's All-purpose Symbolic Instruction Code - a high-level programming language.
Basic volume	A primary partition or logical drive that resides on a basic disc.
Batch file	A file that contains commands which are automatically executed when the file is run.
Baud rate	The speed at which a modem communicates.
BBS	Bulletin Board System, a computer equipped with software and telecoms links that acts as an information host for remote computer systems.
Beta test	A test of software that is still under development, by people actually using the software.
Binary	A base-2 number system in which values are expressed as combinations of two digits, 0 and 1.

BIOS

On x86-based computers, the set of software routines that test hardware at startup, start the operating system, and support the transfer of data among hardware devices.

Bit

The smallest unit of information handled by a computer.

Bitmap

A technique for managing the image displayed on a computer screen.

Bookmark

A marker inserted at a specific point in a document to which the user may wish to return for later reference.

Boot partition

The partition on a hard disc that contains the operating system and its support files.

Boot up

To start your computer by switching it on, which initiates a self test of its Random Access Memory (RAM), then loads the necessary system files.

Broadband

A communications systems in which the medium of transmission (such as a wire or fibre-optic cable) carries multiple messages at a time.

Broadcast

An address that is destined for all hosts on a particular network segment.

Browse

A button in some Windows dialogue boxes that lets you view a list of files and folders before you make a selection.

Browser

A program, like the Internet Explorer, that lets you view Web pages.

Bug

An error in coding or logic that causes a program to malfunction.

Bus	A communication line used for data transfer among the components of a computer system.
Button	A graphic element in a dialogue box or toolbar that performs a specified function.
Bytes	A unit of data that holds a single character, such as a letter, a digit.
Cable modem	A device that enables a broadband connection to the Internet by using cable television infrastructure.
Cache	An area of memory, or disc space, reserved for data, which speeds up downloading.
Card	A removable printed-circuit board that is plugged into a computer expansion slot.
CD-R	Recordable compact disc.
CD-ROM	Read Only Memory compact disc. Data can be read but not written.
CD-RW	Rewritable compact disc. Data can be copied to the CD on more than one occasion and can be erased.
CGI	Common Gateway Interface - a convention for servers to communicate with local applications and allow users to provide information to scripts attached to web pages, usually through forms.
Cgi-bin	The most common name of a directory on a web server in which CGI programs are stored.
Chart	A graphical view of data that is used to visually display trends, patterns, and comparisons.

Click	To press and release a mouse button once without moving the mouse.
Client	A computer that has access to services over a computer network. The computer providing the services is a server.
Client application	A Windows application that can accept linked, or embedded, objects.
Clipboard	A temporary storage area of memory, where text and graphics are stored with the Windows cut and copy actions.
Cluster	In data storage, the smallest amount of disc space that can be allocated to hold a file.
Code page	A means of providing support for character sets and keyboard layouts for different countries or regions.
Command	An instruction given to a computer to carry out a particular action.
Command prompt	A window used to interface with the MS-DOS operating system.
Compressed file	One that is compacted to save server space and reduce transfer times. Typical file extensions for compressed files include .zip (DOS/Windows) and .tar (UNIX).
Configuration	A general purpose term referring to the way you have your computer set up.
Controls	Objects on a form, report, or data access page that display data, perform actions, or are used for decoration.
Cookies	Files stored on your hard drive by your Web browser that hold information for it to use.

CPU

The Central Processing Unit; the main chip that executes all instructions entered into a computer.

Cyberspace

Originated by William Gibson in his novel 'Neuromancer', now used to describe the Internet and the other computer networks.

Data access page

A Web page, created by Access, that has a connection to a database; you can view, add, edit, and manipulate the data in this page.

Data packet

A unit of information transmitted as a whole from one device to another on a network.

Database

A collection of data related to a particular topic or purpose.

DBMS

Database management system - A software interface between the database and the user.

Default

The command, device or option automatically chosen.

Defragmentation

The process of rewriting parts of a file to contiguous sectors on a hard disc to increase the speed of access and retrieval.

Desktop

The Windows screen working background, on which you place icons, folders, etc.

Device driver

A special file that must be loaded into memory for Windows to be able to address a specific procedure or hardware device.

Device name	A logical name used by DOS to identify a device, such as LPT1 or COM1 for the parallel or serial printer.
Dial-up connection	The connection to a network via a device that uses the telephone network. This includes modems with a standard phone line, ISDN cards with high-speed ISDN lines, or X.25 networks.
Dialogue box	A window displayed on the screen to allow the user to enter information.
Digital signature	A means for originators of a message, file, or other digitally encoded information to bind their identity to the information.
Direct Connection	A permanent connection between your computer system and the Internet.
Directory	An area on disc where information relating to a group of files is kept. Also known as a folder.
Disconnect	To detach a drive, port or computer from a shared device, or to break an Internet connection.
Display adapter	An expansion board that plugs into a PC to give it display capabilities.
DLL	Dynamic Link Library; An OS feature that allows files with the .dll extensions to be loaded only when needed by the program.
Document	A file produced by an application program. When used in reference to the Web, a document is any file containing text, media or hyperlinks that can be transferred from an HTTP server to a browser.

Domain	A group of devices, servers and computers on a network.
Domain Name	The name of an Internet site, for example www.microsoft.com, which allows you to reference Internet sites without knowing their true numerical address.
DOS	Disc Operating System. A collection of small specialised programs that allow interaction between user and computer.
Double-click	To quickly press and release a mouse button twice.
Download	To transfer to your computer a file, or data, from another computer.
DPI	Dots Per Inch - a resolution standard for laser printers.
Drag	To move an object on the screen by pressing and holding down the left mouse button while moving the mouse.
Drive name	The letter followed by a colon which identifies a floppy or hard disc drive.
DSL	Digital Subscriber Line - a broad-band connection to the Internet through existing copper telephone wires.
Dual boot	A PC configuration that can start two different operating systems.
DVD	Digital Video Disc; a type of optical disc technology. It looks like a CD but can store greater amounts of data.
EISA	Extended Industry Standard Architecture, for construction of PCs with the Intel 32-bit microprocessor.

E-mail	Electronic Mail - A system that allows computer users to send and receive messages electronically.
Embedded object	Information in a document that is 'copied' from its source application. Selecting the object opens the creating application from within the document.
Encrypted password	A password that is scrambled.
Engine	Software used by search services.
Ethernet	A very common method of networking computers in a LAN.
Expansion slot	A socket in a computer, designed to hold expansion boards and connect them to the system bus.
Extract a file	Create an uncompressed copy of the file in a folder you specify.
FAQ	Frequently Asked Questions - A common feature on the Internet, FAQs are files of answers to commonly asked questions.
FAT	The File Allocation Table. An area on disc where information is kept on which part of the disc a file is located.
File extension	The suffix following the period in a filename. Windows uses this to identify the source application program. For example .mdb indicates an Access file.
Filename	The name given to a file. In Windows 95 and above this can be up to 256 characters long.
Filter	A set of criteria that is applied to data to show a subset of the data.

Firewall	Security measures designed to protect a networked system from unauthorised access.
Floppy disc	A removable disc on which information can be stored magnetically.
Folder	An area used to store a group of files, usually with a common link.
Font	A graphic design representing a set of characters, numbers and symbols.
Format	The structure of a file that defines the way it is stored and laid out on the screen or in print.
Fragmentation	The scattering of parts of the same file over different areas of the disc.
Free space	Available disc space that can be used to create logical drives within an extended partition.
Freeware	Software that is available for downloading and unlimited use without charge.
FTP	File Transfer Protocol. The procedure for connecting to a remote computer and transferring files.
Function key	One of the series of 10 or 12 keys marked with the letter F and a numeral, used for specific operations.
Gateway	A computer system that allows otherwise incompatible networks to communicate with each other.
GIF	Graphics Interchange Format, a common standard for images on the Web.
Gigabyte	(GB); 1,024 megabytes. Usually thought of as one billion bytes.

Graphic	A picture or illustration, also called an image. Formats include GIF, JPEG, BMP, PCX, and TIFF.
Graphics card	A device that controls the display on the monitor and other allied functions.
Group	A collection of users, computers, contacts, and other groups.
GUI	A Graphic User Interface, such as Windows, the software front-end meant to provide an attractive and easy to use interface.
Handshaking	A series of signals acknowledging that communication can take place between computers or other devices.
Hard copy	Output on paper.
Hard disc	A device built into the computer for holding programs and data.
Hardware	The equipment that makes up a computer system, excluding the programs or software.
Help	A Windows system that gives you instructions and additional information on using a program.
Helper application	A program allowing you to view multimedia files that your web browser cannot handle internally.
Hibernation	A state in which your computer shuts down after saving everything in memory on your hard disc.
Hit	A single request from a web browser for a single item from a web server.
Home page	The document displayed when you first open your Web browser, or the first document you come to at a Web site.

Host	Computer connected directly to the Internet that provides services to other local and/or remote computers.
Hotlist	A list of frequently used Web locations and URL addresses.
HTML	HyperText Markup Language, the format used in documents on the Web.
HTML editor	Authoring tool which assists with the creation of HTML pages.
HTTP	HyperText Transport Protocol, the system used to link and transfer hypertext documents on the Web.
Hub	A common connection point for devices in a network.
Hyperlink	A segment of text, or an image, that refers to another document on the Web, an intranet or your PC.
Hypermedia	Hypertext extended to include linked multimedia.
Hypertext	A system that allows documents to be cross-linked so that the reader can explore related links, or documents, by clicking on a highlighted symbol.
Icon	A small graphic image that represents a function or object. Clicking on an icon produces an action.
ICS	Internet Connection Sharing.
Image	See graphic.
Insertion point	A flashing bar that shows where typed text will be entered into a document.
Interface	A device that allows you to connect a computer to its peripherals.

Internet	The global system of computer networks.
Intranet	A private network inside an organisation using the same kind of software as the Internet.
IP	Internet Protocol - The rules that provide basic Internet functions.
IP Address	Internet Protocol Address - every computer on the Internet has a unique identifying number.
ISA	Industry Standard Architecture; a standard for internal PC connections.
ISDN	Integrated Services Digital Network; a telecom standard using digital transmission technology to support voice, video and data communications applications over regular telephone lines.
ISP	Internet Service Provider - A company that offers access to the Internet.
Java	An object-oriented programming language created by Sun Microsystems for developing applications and applets that are capable of running on any computer, regardless of the operating system.
JPEG / JPG	Joint Photographic Experts Group, a popular cross-platform format for image files. JPEG is best suited for true colour original images.
Kernel	The core of layered architecture that manages the most basic operations of the operating system and the computer's processor.

Kilobyte	(KB); 1024 bytes of information or storage space.
LAN	Local Area Network - High-speed, privately-owned network covering a limited geographical area, such as an office or a building.
Laptop	A portable computer small enough to sit on your lap.
LCD	Liquid Crystal Display.
Linked object	An object that is inserted into a document but still exists in the source file. Changing the original object automatically updates it within the linked document.
Links	The hypertext connections between Web pages.
Linux	A version of the UNIX operating system for PCs which incorporates a Graphical User Interface (GUI) similar to that of Microsoft Windows.
Local	A resource that is located on your computer, not linked to it over a network.
Location	An Internet address.
Log on	To gain access to a network.
MBR	The first sector on a hard disc, which starts the process of booting the computer.
MCI	Media Control Interface - a standard for files and multimedia devices.
Megabyte	(MB); 1024 kilobytes of information or storage space.

Megahertz	(MHz); Speed of processor in millions of cycles per second.
Memory	Part of computer consisting of storage elements organised into addressable locations that can hold data and instructions.
Menu	A list of available options in an application.
Menu bar	The horizontal bar that lists the names of menus.
MIDI	Musical Instrument Digital Interface - enables devices to transmit and receive sound and music messages.
MIME	Multipurpose Internet Mail Extensions, a messaging standard that allows Internet users to exchange e-mail messages enhanced with graphics, video and voice.
MIPS	Million Instructions Per Second; measures speed of a system.
Modem	Short for Modulator-demodulator. An electronic device that lets computers communicate electronically.
Monitor	The display device connected to your PC, also called a screen.
Mouse	A device used to manipulate a pointer around your display and activate processes by pressing buttons.
MPEG	Motion Picture Experts Group - a video file format offering excellent quality in a relatively small file.
MS-DOS	Microsoft's implementation of the Disc Operating System for PCs.

Multimedia	The use of photographs, music and sound and movie images in a presentation.
Multitasking	Performing more than one operation at the same time.
My Documents	A folder that provides a convenient place to store documents, graphics, or other files you want to access quickly.
Network	Two or more computers connected together to share resources.
Network adapter	A device that connects your computer to a network.
Network server	Central computer which stores files for several linked computers.
Node	Any single computer connected to a network.
NTFS file system	An advanced file system that provides performance, security, reliability, and advanced features that are not found in any version of FAT.
ODBC	Open DataBase Connectivity - A standard protocol for accessing information in a SQL database server.
OLE	Object Linking and Embedding - A technology for transferring and sharing information among software applications.
Online	Having access to the Internet.
On-line Service	Services such as America On-line and CompuServe that provide content to subscribers and usually connections to the Internet.
Operating system	Software that runs a computer.

Page	An HTML document, or Web site.
Parallel port	The input/output connector for a parallel interface device. Printers are generally plugged into a parallel port.
Partition	A portion of a physical disc that functions as though it were a physically separate disc.
Password	A unique character string used to gain access to a network, program, or mailbox.
PATH	The location of a file in the directory tree.
PCI	Peripheral Component Interconnect - a type of slot in your computer which accepts similar type peripheral cards.
Peripheral	Any device attached to a PC.
Perl	A popular language for programming CGI applications.
PIF file	Program information file - gives information to Windows about an MS-DOS application.
Pixel	A picture element on screen; the smallest element that can be independently assigned colour and intensity.
Plug-and-play	Hardware which can be plugged into a PC and be used immediately without configuration.
POP	Post Office Protocol - a method of storing and returning e-mail.
Port	The place where information goes into or out of a computer, e.g. a modem might be connected to the serial port.

Posix	The specification for a look-alike UNIX operating system drawn up by the American National Standards Institute (ANSI). Linux is an independent Posix implementation.
PostScript	A page-description language (PDL), developed by Adobe Systems for printing on laser printers.
PPP	Point-to-Point Protocol - One of two methods (see SLIP) for using special software to establish a temporary direct connection to the Internet over regular phone lines.
Print queue	A list of print jobs waiting to be sent to a printer.
Program	A set of instructions which cause a computer to perform tasks.
Protocol	A set of rules or standards that define how computers communicate with each other.
Query	The set of keywords and operators sent by a user to a search engine, or a database search request.
Queue	A list of e-mail messages waiting to be sent over the Internet.
RAM	Random Access Memory. The computer's volatile memory. Data held in it is lost when power is switched off.
Real mode	MS-DOS mode, typically used to run programs, such as MS-DOS games, that will not run under Windows.
Refresh	To update displayed information with current data.

Registered file type	File types that are tracked by the system registry and are recognised by the programs you have installed on your computer.
Registry	A database where information about a computer's configuration is deposited. The registry contains information that Windows continually references during its operation.
Remote computer	A computer that you can access only by using a communications line or a communications device, such as a network card or a modem.
Resource	A directory, or printer, that can be shared over a network.
Robot	A Web agent that visits sites, by requesting documents from them, for the purposes of indexing for search engines. Also known as Wanderers, Crawlers, or Spiders.
ROM	Read Only Memory. A PC's non-volatile memory. Data is written into this memory at manufacture and is not affected by power loss.
Root	The highest or uppermost level in a hierarchically organised disc directory.
Screen saver	A moving picture or pattern that appears on your screen when you have not used the mouse or keyboard for a specified period of time.
Script	A type of program consisting of a set of instructions to an application or tool program.
Scroll bar	A bar that appears at the right side or bottom edge of a window.

Search	Submit a query to a search engine.
Search engine	A program that helps users find information across the Internet.
Serial interface	An interface that transfers data as individual bits.
Server	A computer system that manages and delivers information for client computers.
Shared resource	Any device, program or file that is available to network users.
Shareware	Software that is available on public networks and bulletin boards. Users are expected to pay a nominal amount to the software developer.
Shortcut	A link to any item accessible on your computer or on a network, such as a program, file, folder, disc drive, Web page, printer, or another computer.
Signature file	An ASCII text file, maintained within e-mail programs, that contains text for your signature.
Site	A place on the Internet. Every Web page has a location where it resides which is called its site.
SLIP	Serial Line Internet Protocol, a method of Internet connection that enables computers to use phone lines and a modem to connect to the Internet without having to connect to a host.
SMTP	Simple Mail Transfer Protocol - a protocol dictating how e-mail messages are exchanged over the Internet.
Socket	An endpoint for sending and receiving data between computers.

Software	The programs and instructions that control your PC.
Spamming	Sending the same message to a large number of mailing lists or newsgroups. Also to overload a Web page with excessive keywords in an attempt to get a better search ranking.
Spider	See robot.
Spooler	Software which handles transfer of information to a store to be used by a peripheral device.
SQL	Structured Query Language, used with relational databases.
SSL	Secure Sockets Layer, the standard transmission security protocol developed by Netscape, which has been put into the public domain.
Standby	A state in which your computer consumes less power when it is idle, but remains available for immediate use.
Subscribe	To become a member of.
Surfing	The process of looking around the Internet.
SVGA	Super Video Graphics Array; it has all the VGA modes but with 256, or more, colours.
Swap file	An area of your hard disc used to store temporary operating files, also known as virtual memory.
Sysop	System Operator - A person responsible for the physical operations of a computer system or network resource.
System disc	A disc containing files to enable a PC to start up.

System files	Files used by Windows to load, configure, and run the operating system.
Task Manager	A utility that provides information about programs and processes running on the computer. Using Task Manager, you can end or run programs and end processes, and display a dynamic overview of your computer's performance.
TCP/IP	Transmission Control Protocol/ Internet Protocol, combined protocols that perform the transfer of data between two computers. TCP monitors and ensures the correct transfer of data. IP receives the data, breaks it up into packets, and sends it to a network within the Internet.
Telnet	A program which allows people to remotely use computers across networks.
Text file	An unformatted file of text characters saved in ASCII format.
Thread	An ongoing message-based conversation on a single subject.
TIFF	Tag Image File Format - a popular graphic image file format.
Toggle	To turn an action on and off with the same switch.
Tool	Software program used to support Web site creation and management.
Toolbar	A bar containing icons giving quick access to commands.
TrueType fonts	Fonts that can be scaled to any size and print as they show on the screen.

Uninstall	When referring to software, the act of removing program files and folders from your hard disc and removing related data from your registry so the software is no longer available.
UNIX	Multitasking, multi-user computer operating system that is run by many computer servers on networks.
Upload/Download	The process of transferring files between computers. Files are uploaded from your computer to another and downloaded from another computer to your own.
URL	Uniform Resource Locator, the addressing system used on the Web, containing information about the method of access, the server to be accessed and the path of the file to be accessed.
USB	Universal Serial Bus - an external bus standard that enables data transfer rates of 12 Mbps.
Usenet	Informal network of computers that allow the posting and reading of messages in newsgroups that focus on specific topics.
User ID	The unique identifier, usually used in conjunction with a password, which identifies you on a computer.
Virtual Reality	Simulations of real or imaginary worlds, rendered on a flat two-dimensional screen but appearing three-dimensional.
Virus	A malicious program, downloaded from a web site or disc, designed to wipe out information on your computer.

Volume	An area of storage on a hard disc. A volume is formatted by using a file system, such as FAT or NTFS, and has a drive letter assigned to it.
W3C	The World Wide Web Consortium that is steering standards development for the Web.
WAIS	Wide Area Information Server, a Net-wide system for looking up specific information in Internet databases.
WAN	A communications network connecting geographically separated computers, printers, and other devices.
WAV	Waveform Audio (.wav) - a common audio file format for DOS/Windows computers.
Web	A network of hypertext-based multimedia information servers. Browsers are used to view any information on the Web.
Web Page	An HTML document that is accessible on the Web.
Web server	A computer that is maintained by a system administrator or Internet service provider (ISP) and that responds to requests from a user's browser.
Webmaster	One whose job it is to manage a web site.
WINSOCK	A Microsoft Windows file that provides the interface to TCP/IP services.
Wizard	A Microsoft tool that asks you questions and then creates an object depending on your answers.

Index

Companion Discs

COMPANION DISCS are available for most computer books written by the same author(s) and published by BERNARD BABANI (publishing) LTD, as listed at the front of this book (except for those marked with an asterisk). These books contain many pages of file/program listings.

There is no Companion Disc for this book.

To obtain companion discs for other books, fill in the order form below, or a copy of it, enclose a cheque (payable to **P.R.M. Oliver**) or a postal order, and send it to the address given below. **Make sure you fill in your name and address** and specify the book number and title in your order.

Book No.	Book Name	Unit Price	Total Price
BP		£3.50	
BP		£3.50	
BP		£3.50	
Name .... Address		Sub-total	£.............
		P & P (@ 45p/disc)	£.............
		Total Due	£.............
Send to: P.R.M. Oliver, West Trevarth House, West Trevarth, Nr Redruth, Cornwall, TR16 5TJ			

PLEASE NOTE

The author(s) are fully responsible for providing this Companion Disc service. The publishers of this book accept no responsibility for the supply, quality, or magnetic contents of the disc, or in respect of any damage, or injury that might be suffered or caused by its use.